The Early History of
Lincoln Castle

GW00597445

Occasional Papers in Lincolnshire
History and Archaeology, 12

The Early History
of Lincoln Castle

Edited by
Phillip Lindley

General Editor: Mark Bennet

The Society for Lincolnshire History and Archaeology,
Jews' Court, Steep Hill, Lincoln LN2 1LS

Published by the Society for Lincolnshire History and Archaeology with the aid of a grant from
Lincolnshire County Council

First published 2004

ISBN 0 903582 21 X

Printed in Great Britain by Technical Print Services Ltd.,
Brentcliffe Avenue, Carlton Road, Nottingham, NG3 7AG
Telephone 0115 987 3771 Fax 0115 987 3905

The Early History of Lincoln Castle

Contents

FOREWORD

The origins of this book reach back nearly a decade. Jenny Vernon, then the manager of the castle, asked me to convene a conference on the castle's early history in 1995: we had worked together a few years earlier on a conference on Gainsborough Old Hall, which had resulted in a book published by the SLHA in 1991. However, Jenny's illness and her premature retirement, as well as her subsequent decision to become a Buddhist nun, meant that the conference relied heavily on the support of Rachel Harrison, David Lanes and Peter Allen to go ahead successfully. Then our publication plans were set back by the sad death of Christopher Sturman, who had been characteristically supportive. That the book has come to fruition at all is due to the work of Pearl Wheatley and, above all, to Mark Bennet, whose meticulous copy-editing, design and support have been inspirational.

What was abundantly clear at the conference, and what has become even more evident subsequently, is that the early history and architectural development of Lincoln castle are highly controversial. I was particularly delighted that David Stocker was able to accept my invitation to add his paper to those already submitted: David's work now provides a critical commentary and introduction to the other essays (which have not been systematically revised in the light of research since 1995, though the references have been updated). David Stocker espouses a radical new view of the nature and extent of the castle founded by the Conqueror in 1068, viewing it as a reoccupation of the entire Roman Upper City, with a rebuilding of the Roman gateways and the construction of a large motte below what is now known as the Lucy Tower. Michael Thompson – whose own view of the early castle is no less startling – and others here disagree with part or most of David's thesis. The chief areas of debate are: the extent of the castle founded in 1068, the function and chronological sequence of the two mottes for which this castle is so famous, and the dates and functions of the two stone towers which stand on the mottes (the 'Lucy' and 'Observatory' towers). Indeed, the date of almost all the early stone buildings of the castle is contentious. The contextualising essays by David Parsons and Pamela Marshall, however, provide helpful new material and new analyses as do the archaeological excavations summarised by Lisa Donel and Michael Jones. An historical context is admirably established by Paul Dalton, and Derek Renn writes with remarkable clarity about Cobb Hall Tower, a strengthening of the castle's defences in the early thirteenth century. Even if this book may seem at first sight to be a case study of how a group of eminent archaeologists and architectural historians can come to profoundly different views based on essentially the same visual and documentary evidence, the valuable new information it contains will enable thoughtful readers to come to their own conclusions.

Phillip Lindley
December 2004

The Two Early Castles of Lincoln

David Stocker

Introduction

Like the Royal castles in so many of our cathedral cities, Lincoln Castle is usually viewed as the city's second monument. No guidebooks start their account of the city's treasures with a visit, and no histories promote it as the city's principal sight. The Minster is always seen as Lincoln's premier building, as it has been since at least the twelfth century. The cathedral, after all, is the city's protector, Our Lady of Lincoln; the castle is merely the symbol of a remote external authority. It was the symbol of an external, Royal, authority when it was founded in 1068, and, indeed, it continues to belong to the County Council and to the Lord Chancellor.

But although it has never been viewed as the premier ancient site of the city, Lincoln Castle is a famous monument and it has been the object of many antiquarian studies. Since the eighteenth century its date and function have been discussed and celebrated. A number of early views were made by the Buck brothers during their visit in 1723-24,[1] and thenceforward the castle has been the subject of an unbroken stream of studies, plans, drawings and papers.[2] Perhaps the most important of all the works undertaken on the castle in the past 250 years was by the remarkable Lincoln antiquary, Edward Willson, who, in his role as Surveyor to the County between 1835 and 1845, had responsibility for the fabric whilst it underwent a massive restoration and conversion into a closed prison.[3] Willson used his position to undertake research into the fabric history, both by clearing areas of debris and undertaking excavations (inside the West Gate for example) and by making detailed records of many parts of the standing fabric. Because its appearance was changed so radically by this conversion, to this day it is not possible to make much of the structural history of Lincoln Castle without consulting the enormous archive of notes and drawings which Willson amassed during his career.[4]

By the start of the twenty-first century, then, a huge body of research had accumulated on which we can draw to help understand the castle's history and archaeology.[5] This book seeks to capitalise on that great body of material and provide some commentary on the many theories and opinions which have gone before. It cannot be conclusive, of course; in particular the post-excavation work on the large-scale excavations inside and outside the West Gate (between 1983 and 1989) has still to be published. A report is now in preparation and, as this is much the largest scientific excavation which has ever taken place here, the results will be crucial for our understanding of the whole site. The dating of pottery from these excavations has already provided one unexpected result – one which affects, radically, our understanding of the castle's sequence of development discussed in its place below – and we await further surprises as work proceeds. Furthermore the many minor excavations and watching briefs which have gone hand-in-hand with the programme of repair works over the past twenty years have also accumulated an important series of insights into the sequence of walls and banks, and some of these have been collected together in the paper below by Lisa Donel and Michael Jones.[6] This book, then, presents a series of studies of various aspects of the buildings and earthworks which form the castle at Lincoln. In this introductory paper, I intend to group the castle structures together and to explain them, not so much as individual buildings but as a succession of integrated complexes; by doing so Lincoln Castle can be related more easily, in the other papers in this volume, both to castles elsewhere and to the history of the city more broadly.

Lincoln's First Castle.

The *Anglo-Saxon Chronicle* records the foundation of the castle at Lincoln in 1068 as part of the campaign by William the Conqueror aimed at strengthening his hold on the East Midlands after moving against the rebellion in Yorkshire.[7] Eighteen years later, *Domesday Book* recorded how large William's castle was; it covered property equivalent to 166 houses.[8] By this measurement, Lincoln Castle was much the largest of all of the early castles whose area is mentioned in *Domesday*.[9] It has long been recognised that this measurement is not likely to represent actual houses, but rather an estimate of the taxable ground area covered by the newly founded castle; because of the foundation of the royal castle, it is argued, 166 taxable units had been lost to the crown.[10] It is only more recently, however, that we have been able to calculate the percentage of the occupied city taken up by these 166 units, and the results have been quite revolutionary as far as our understanding of the Norman topography of Lincoln is concerned. The Urban Archaeology Database (UAD), which was compiled between 1994-99 by Alan Vince and his colleagues at the City of Lincoln Archaeology Unit, has enabled us to map the total extent of occupation of Lincoln in 1086.[11] We can then take that area as equivalent to the 970 taxable units, which we can deduce constituted the whole city at the time of *Domesday Book*. Then, using the UAD, we are able to see that the 166 units of the castle constituted about 17% of the total inhabited area of the city in 1086. The present castle enclosure, however, constitutes only 4% of the area inhabited in 1086 and, consequently, this enclosure cannot be the castle referred to in *Domesday*.

Furthermore, since at least 1984, the suggestion has been abroad that the early castle at Lincoln included not only the area of the present castle, but also the whole of the Upper Roman enclosure (Fig.1).[12] The suggestion that the castle founded in 1068 was, in fact, the Roman Upper City (and not the present enclosure) seemed to be proved conclusively when Dr Vince made the calculation, using the UAD data, that the area within the old Roman walls constituted about 16% of the total occupied area of the city in 1086 – within 1% of the proportion of the whole city which the taxation assessment in *Domesday Book* implied was occupied by the castle.[13] The conclusion that the Castle founded in 1068 was in fact a re-occupation of the former Roman walled enclosure and not the present earthwork and masonry enclosure now seems inescapable.

Acceptance of this argument clearly necessitates a radical reassessment of the dating of the present castle enclosure, which has always been taken to be that founded in 1068 – (a version of that view of the development of the castle is presented by Dr Thompson below). Following Dr Vince's work, however, the present castle enclosure will have to be viewed as a secondary structure, constructed at some date after the initial foundation, and within one corner of the original castle enclosure of 1068. Contemporaneously with the UAD, work on the pottery finds from the West Gate

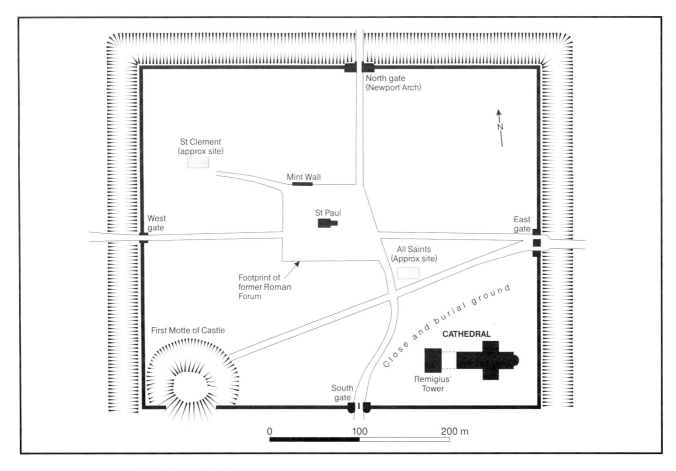

Fig.1. Reconstruction of the plan of the former Roman enclosure of the Upper City at Lincoln c.1090 (Drawn by Dave Watt based on plans by Alan Vince, copyright English Heritage).

excavations of 1983-89 by Jane Young and her team has provided archaeological corroboration for this later dating of the present castle enclosure.[14] Although they have yet to be studied in detail, and the results have yet to be published, Ms Young's preliminary analysis suggests that the characteristic late eleventh-century pottery types (called SNLS and TORK), ubiquitous in layers of this date throughout the remainder of the city, were absent from the construction levels of the West Gate. Instead, these levels are dominated by wares that have been closely dated elsewhere in the city, and which we believe were only introduced after *c*.1100.[15] These results strongly suggest that the West Gate was not constructed until the early decades of the twelfth century. The architecture of the gate tower itself is comfortably placed in the early twelfth century and its architectural form is described and discussed in the paper below by Pam Marshall (p.58).

An analysis of other aspects of the present castle enclosure also seems to confirm that it dates from a later period than has previously been thought. The wall to the north of the West Gate, for example, appears to have been later in construction than the West Gate itself. It had previously been dated to the eleventh century by reference to its employment of 'herringbone' masonry, even though the value of this feature as an absolute dating mechanism for any period is debatable and masonry of this type has been recorded in a number of early twelfth-century buildings locally.[16] The wall to the north of the West Gate appears continuous with the wall extending along the north side of the enclosure, which also uses 'herringbone' masonry in its construction, although the fabric of the east curtain wall is more complex. The north bank and wall is at an offset alignment, relative to the Upper City walls and to the Roman street grid; running north-west to south-east (Fig.7 below). This alignment may also be respected,

however, by the extrapolated line of an early lane or path which seems to have linked the churches of St Mary of Lincoln, All Saints-in-the-Bail, St Paul-in-the-Bail and St Clement-in-the-Bail. Although the date of this lane is not known, it has been suggested that it predates the modern line of Eastgate, and although not in itself evidence for the date of the northern castle bank and curtain wall, it is presumably of an earlier date than the present bailey.[17] It is also conceivable that the north wall was planned to avoid the south-west corner of the former Roman forum (see Figs.1 and 6 below). The mound at the southern end of the east curtain wall, on which the Observatory Tower now sits, has also been dated to the mid twelfth century through ceramic finds.[18] The length of east curtain wall between the Observatory Tower and the East Gate is apparently integral with the tower itself, and presumably, therefore, is also of twelfth-century date. It retains a loop window which, although not precisely datable, probably belongs to this century. It is true that the Observatory Tower motte and the length of curtain wall to the north of it were built on a different alignment from the northern part of the eastern curtain, and this suggests that they are somewhat later in date than the earthwork and curtain to the north and west. But this is consistent with the observation that the twelfth-century pottery from the Observatory Tower motte is somewhat later in date than that from the West Gate.[19] At the western end of the circuit of walls of the present enclosure (i.e. the West Gate), therefore, we have ceramic evidence that the earthworks date from the early twelfth century and at the south-eastern corner (at the Observatory Tower) a second phase of construction can be dated by ceramics to the mid twelfth century. In neither excavation does the pottery give any support for an eleventh-century date for the construction of the earthworks or the walls that crown them.

It now seems clear therefore, that the castle of 1068 bore no resemblance to the enclosure we know today; rather it was a much larger enclosure, bounded by the earthworks and walls which surrounded the Roman Upper City. Centrally placed in each of the walls were the four cardinal Roman gates,[20] three of which – the north ('Newport Arch'), the east and the south gates – survived in their altered form long enough to be drawn by topographical artists. The fourth gate, the West Gate, appeared briefly in excavation in 1836 to the north of the present castle West Gate, but it was not recorded in sufficient detail, prior to its collapse, for us to judge whether or not it had been altered in the Norman period.[21] If the proposed sequence of events laid out above is correct, however, we would expect it to have been repaired and to have remained in use from 1068 until the start of the twelfth century, when it was buried by the earthworks of the present castle enclosure and replaced by the standing gate to its south. In the early drawings of the other three gates, however, we can see signs of considerable alteration and improvement in the Norman period, and although we cannot accurately determine when most of these alterations were carried out, we can now propose that they belonged to this early phase of Norman occupation, following the establishment of the castle in 1068, when they formed part of its defences. In fact it would be a surprise if these works to the Upper City gates were carried out as part of a programme of town defences; early Norman town defences newly constructed in stone are unusual[22] and, consequently, this thoroughgoing scheme to re-edify the Lincoln gates is actually more satisfactorily explained as a defensive measure for the new castle built by the Crown.

From two known surviving topographical drawings[23] we can suggest that the East Gate of the Roman fortress was substantially remodelled in the Norman period (Fig.2), although the excavations here between 1959 and 1966 seemed to show that this remodelling was mostly confined to its upper stories.[24] In this case both of the two original Roman archways were replaced with a pair of new archways, considerably above the Roman street level. The new gate-tower was offset slightly to the south relative to its Roman predecessor, such that the northern Roman arch head must have been removed and its remains buried beneath the new northern medieval carriageway. The southern of the two Roman archways was blocked and incorporated within the fabric of the wall between the two new Norman arches (Fig.3). Although the survival of the upper parts of this arch must indicate that some upper parts of the Roman gatehouse survived in the lower walls of its Norman replacement, the East Gate was evidently greatly altered in the Norman period, with perhaps only a small part of the original Roman gate surviving. To the north a substantial foundation which may have been the north-eastern corner of the north tower of the medieval gate was recovered set inside the foundations of the Roman north gate tower. To the south the southern tower of the Norman gate seems to have extended further south and east than the Roman one and may account for the 'jacketing' of the east face of the Roman tower reported from the 1959 excavation.[25] The dates of these alterations were not established during the excavations, but the character of the masonry shown in both surviving views indicates an early Norman date.[26] The reconstruction of the gate tower must have been completed by c.1130 when the bishop moved his hall and lodgings from his former palace into the chambers above this gateway.[27] We have argued elsewhere that it was this alteration in the function of the gatehouse which necessitated the blocking of the northern Norman arch[28] and, if this is correct, we can suggest that the original Norman reconstruction took place prior to c.1130 – most likely c.1070.

In its developed third-century form, Newport Arch, the northern Roman gatehouse, was originally a single carriageway, with flanking pedestrian passages and two bastions with bowed frontages facing north.[29] An extensive series of topographical views show, however, that the side

Fig.2. View of the East Gate of the Upper City from west c.1730 by Nathan Drake (Usher Art Gallery, Lincoln).

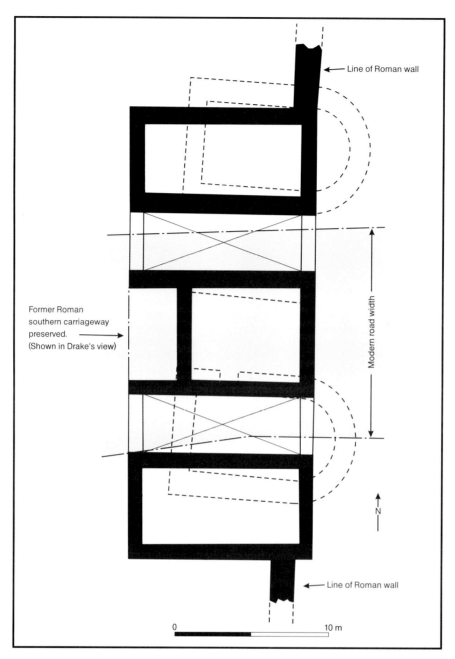

Fig.3. *Plan of East Gate of Upper City showing suggested relationship of Norman and Roman gatehouses. Based on Thompson and Whitwell 1973, Fig.8, with additional interpretation drawn from Fig.2 (above) and as described in the text (Drawn by Dave Watt, copyright David Stocker).*

passages were blocked when the upper parts of the Roman structure were re-designed as a substantial tower in the Norman period (Figs 4 and 5).[30] It seems that the outer (northern) arch of the Roman structure was replaced with a Norman arch some distance to the north of the original Roman position and, as at the East Gate, it was at a higher level than the Roman street. At Newport Arch, however, the street level had not risen so greatly as at the East Gate, and the original interior (south-facing) arch of the Roman structure still had sufficient clearance above the eleventh-century roadway for it to be incorporated into the south wall of the Norman structure, to act as the southern archway of the new gatehouse. The Roman arch has since outlasted the Norman structure into which it was incorporated. The 1954 excavations showed that, in the medieval reconstruction, the sub-semi-circular north fronts of the bastions were cased in a thick new wall that blocked the Roman pedestrian passages, presumably converting them into interior vaulted chambers. There is no reason to think that the solid chambers within the Roman

bastions did not survive to be assimilated into the new structure. Presumably here, as at the East Gate, there was a large chamber (or chambers) over the gate. Although the Norman re-edification of the North Gate cannot be dated precisely, an early Norman date was proposed by the excavators, and seems appropriate for the structure seen in the many antiquarian views.[31]

Nothing is known of any Norman alterations to the Roman South Gate, but it is a reasonable supposition that similar alterations were also made here. The original Roman gatehouse had at least two archways, although whether or not all were carriageways (as opposed to pedestrian archways) may still be open to some doubt.[32] The eastern gate passage, however, was already blocked by the late thirteenth century, by which time houses were built on the street to the north, reducing the width of the original street by half and restricting traffic to the single, western arch.[33] Although the earliest documentary reference to this restriction first occurs in 1270,[34] no evidence is available for the date of the original closure of

Fig.4. View of North Gate of Upper City from north. Drawing by R. D. Poilicy made prior to 1784 engraved by B. Howlett.

the eastern arch. Could this closure also have been undertaken as part of the original programme of conversion of the gates c.1070?

The reconstructed East Gate, with its two new arches, was an unusual structure for an early Norman gatehouse and the design may well have been governed by the Crown's intention to replicate the former Roman gatehouse in this position, which also had two carriageways. Similarly, the retention of Roman elements in the early Norman rebuilding of the North Gate may also represent a deliberate attempt to replicate the more ancient structure on the site. If this is so, the careful incorporation of the Roman masonry into both gates can be compared with the equally careful incorporation of the ruins of the Temple of Claudius into the new great tower at Colchester Castle during the same years.[35] Purely functionalist interpretations of such re-adoptions of Roman monuments are losing their appeal and recent scholarship has been inclined to see important symbolic meanings in the re-adoption of the ruins of earlier, particularly Roman monuments at later periods. In the cases of the great tower at Colchester and the East Gate of the first Lincoln Castle, the message is surely clear; the newly arrived Norman conquerors are presenting themselves as the inheritors of the Roman military tradition.[36] William's new regime wished to be seen as the new Rome. Although a similar symbolic message was probably intended in the incorporation of the Roman archway, the reconstructed North Gate was a much more typical Norman gatehouse design, with a single carriageway and a chamber above. The first gatehouse at Richmond Castle, built in the 1080s or 1090s, was probably a contemporary parallel.[37] The first West Gate,

similarly, could be seen as representing the same type of gatehouse, although here it may have retained a larger proportion of Roman fabric.

Of the wall which surrounded the first castle we know very little. Despite considerable study[38] very little evidence has been produced to suggest that the Roman walls were greatly altered during the medieval period, although they evidently stood as a complete circuit – probably with additions and alterations to their upper parts, as at London Wall for example. The excavations at Newport Arch, however, demonstrated that the re-edified gatehouse was accompanied by lengths of a new masonry wall, on a completely different alignment from their Roman predecessor.[39] Furthermore, excavations south-east of the Minster in 1984 revealed not only the Roman wall but also what was originally interpreted as an added tower, whose stratigraphic position requires that it is earlier in date than c.1190, even though this could have been a late Roman rather than a Norman addition.[40] It has recently been suggested that this was the sector of the Roman defences, at the southern end of the eastern wall, in which a new gateway was licensed between 1101 and 1115 to allow the Bishop access to his *domum*.[41] This gateway has been the subject of much discussion since the writ was first published by Canon Foster in 1931, and the conventional interpretation is discussed by Dr Thompson in his paper below. However the new re-interpretation of the layout of the Upper City at the start of the twelfth century allows us to argue that the castle wall through which the Bishop's gate was to be cut was, in fact, the former Roman wall and not the present castle circuit. It could, therefore, have been cut anywhere in the Roman

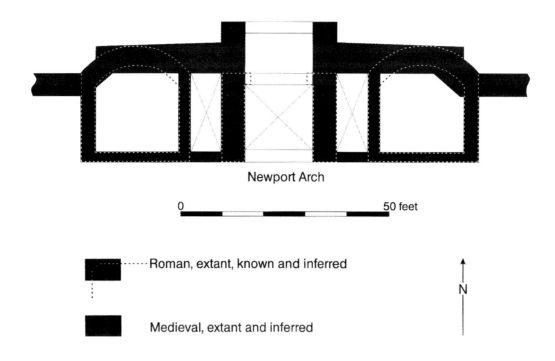

Newport Arch

0   50 feet

■----- Roman, extant, known and inferred

■ Medieval, extant and inferred

N

Fig.5. Plan of North Gate of Upper City showing relationship of Norman and Roman gatehouses. (Based on Thompson and Whitwell 1973, Fig.22) (Drawn by Dave Watt, copyright David Stocker).

enclosure, although there are compelling topographical reasons why a location in the south east corner is likely.[42] The replacement of the Roman wall along the eastern part of the southern side with a less substantial wall some 20m further north is presumed, however, to belong to the period of construction of the Bishop's Palace during the 1150s.[43]

Inside the huge enclosure of the early castle there were four church sites, three of which are known, or have been presumed, to have had their origins in the Anglo-Saxon period; All Saints-in-the-Bail, St Paul-in-the-Bail and St Mary of Lincoln (Fig.1). A study of the distribution of pottery types, has shown, however, that there was little burgage occupation within the enclosure until the twelfth century,[44] whilst the excavations at St Paul-in-the-Bail recovered a sunken-featured building constructed on the edge of the churchyard facing east, which was probably part of a larger complex.[45] Even so, the larger part of the enclosure that became the Castle in 1068 seems to have been quite sparsely populated. In one quarter of the first castle, however, there was a scene of great activity. Shortly after the foundation of the castle a great building site developed around the important Anglo-Saxon Minster of St Mary, in the south-eastern quarter of the enclosure. This church had been selected as the cathedral for the newly created bishopric of Lincoln, which was moved from Dorchester-on-Thames in 1072 or 1073.[46] It remains a controversial interpretation, but an expanding band of scholars now accept the view first put forward by Richard Gem in 1986 that the great western tower of the first cathedral, built in the last quarter of the eleventh century, is in fact a type of fortification.[47] This idea has been taken further recently with the suggestion that it may have been planned primarily as a great tower within our newly identified first castle, containing the major halls like those at Colchester Castle and the Tower of London, which would, presumably, have belonged to the Bishop. Its function as an entrance to the new cathedral, it is argued, may have been a secondary consideration.[48]

The only other structure which can still be argued to have formed a part of the first castle, founded in 1068, is the motte below the Lucy Tower (although not the Lucy Tower itself – which is clearly a mid twelfth-century building – see below). Famously, Lincoln Castle has two mottes and although debate has swung back and forth, most modern opinion has favoured the Lucy Tower motte as the original. The course of the debate is charted in Pam Marshall's and Dr Dalton's papers below.[49] Certainly the Lucy Tower motte looks the more significant of the two mounds; it is much the larger and it is placed on the cliff edge, dominating both the Roman enclosure to the north and the city and landscape to the south. It can be argued that the original line of the street now known as Eastgate was originally a direct route way between the East Gate of the Upper City and the motte and this, also, would suggest that this motte belongs to the earliest phase of the Castle's development.[50] Certainly, compared with the motte below the Observatory Tower, it is a major earthwork structure, apparently built in stratified bands of differing material, in the manner shown in the Bayeux Tapestry,[51] and we should presume that it was originally intended to have a major timber tower on top. The Observatory Tower motte, by contrast, is an irregularly shaped structure, which seems to have thrown up around the basement of a masonry tower, the construction of which is associated with mid twelfth-century pottery.[52]

Although the work of patching up, extending and re-edifying the Roman gates would have required considerable labour and even greater skill, our new understanding of the castle of 1068 makes it seem a much less labour-intensive structure than its successor – even though it covered a very large area. This should be expected perhaps, given the emergency circumstances in which it was founded in 1068. William's need to establish secure bases for quartering troops, and to implement an emergency regional government in the face of rebellion, may well have left little time for anything more than the adoption of a former Roman enclosure and the

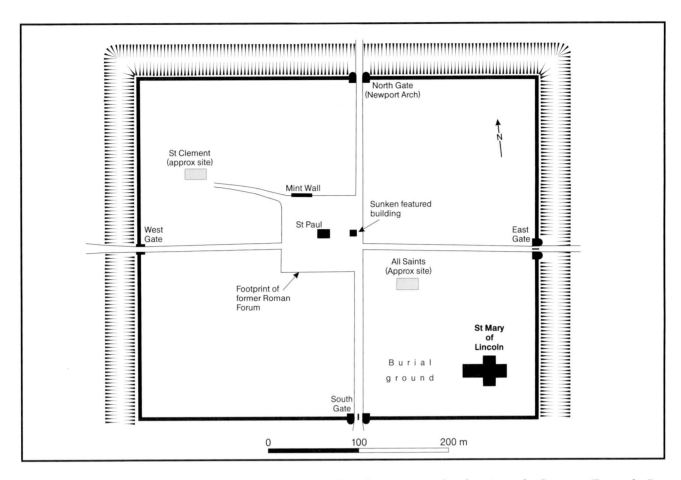

Fig.6. The former Roman enclosure of the Upper City at Lincoln in the years immediately prior to the Conquest (Drawn by Dave Watt based on plans by Alan Vince, copyright English Heritage).

construction of a motte to mark it out as the seat of local authority.

These developments in our understanding of the first castle at Lincoln should also lead us, perhaps, to reconsider some of the other early castles of the Conquest, and Dr Parsons considers both the national evidence for the earliest urban castles, and for the *burhs* which frequently preceded them, in his paper below.[53] At Cambridge, as Dr Parsons notes, the early castle (also founded in 1068) seems to have consisted of a dominant motte (perhaps with a contemporary bailey) established towards one corner of a pre-existing Roman enclosure, and the new motte at Cardiff (founded 1081) is similarly placed, although here there is no intermediate bailey.[54] But it was probably not the fact that these earlier enclosures were Roman which weighed most with the Conqueror – it may have been of greater significance that the enclosure was still in use as a defensive circuit. At places such as Buckingham, Northampton, and Wallingford, for example, the earliest castles seem to have taken the form of a motte established in the corner of an earthwork enclosure of post-Roman date.[55] In some cases these were new *burhs* established by Edward the Elder which dated from the so-called 're-conquest' of the Danelaw in the previous century, but in others (Northampton for example) the enclosures are more likely to have been somewhat earlier fortifications constructed by the 'defending' Anglo-Scandinavian levies.

This pattern of the establishment of castle mottes by William the Conqueror in the corners of these existing military enclosures inevitably raises the question whether the upper Roman enclosure in Lincoln was in fact the defensive *burh* established by the Vikings in the late ninth century. Unfortunately, although the parallels prompt this question with urgency, we still have no certain information on the point.

Dr Parsons notes the area enclosed by the Upper Roman city walls at Lincoln is very comparable with similar Anglo-Scandinavian *burhs*; it is, for example, almost exactly the same as the area presumed to have been occupied by the Viking *burh* at Nottingham (also about 13.7 ha), although it may be considerably smaller than the *burh* at Leicester (if that really was the whole of the Roman enceinte) and it is considerably larger than the presumed area of the north borough at Stamford (about 6 ha).

We are less than certain what character of activity we should expect within such defensive enclosures.[56] Such evidence as we have suggests that, in Lincoln, the Upper Roman enclosure was not intensively occupied. However, it may be that we should not expect intensive occupation within all such enclosures – the view that *burhs* were in effect commercial towns which happened to have been provided with civic defences by a beneficent lord is clearly an anachronism derived from studies of later medieval towns, mediated through concepts of nineteenth-century civic politics.[57] The truly successful commercial locations in pre-Conquest England were not necessarily contained within defences at all (see Torksey, for example, a few miles to the west of Lincoln)[58] and Dr Vince's analysis of the topography of Anglo-Scandinavian Lincoln, based on excavation results, shows that much of the commercial activity in late tenth- and eleventh-century Lincoln was along the riverside, both within and outside the former Lower Roman enclosure.[59] At such places, although the *burh* enclosure might be close at hand as a refuge for the proto-urban population during times of trouble, the locations of the serious businesses of trade and manufacture (and therefore the dwellings of the great majority) would have been dictated by pragmatic factors, such as how close they were to the market place or the river. In some early towns the *burh* enclosure might have been well placed with

15

respect to such mercantile considerations, but at some it evidently was not. Obviously we should ask whether or not the large area defined by the walls of the Lower Roman City was also within the *burh*, but unfortunately we have little direct evidence to bring to bear on the problem.[60] The results of excavations along the river suggest that the former walls of the Lower Roman City, which ran through the Anglo-Scandinavian settlement here, were not a dominant factor in its development. Along the waterfront the Roman walls may have functioned as property boundaries, but they do not seem to have formed any sort of military barrier in the tenth century, whilst the evidence for the viability of the walls along the west side of the Lower City at this period, where there has been considerable modern excavation, is inconclusive to say the best of it. Only along the eastern side of the circuit, where the former city ditch – the *werkdyke* – presumably remained a major barrier in the Anglo-Scandinavian period (possibly because it remained water-filled from springs in the hill-side), is there any evidence for the viability of the Roman defences prior to the thirteenth century. There is no reason to think, therefore, that the Lower Roman City was included within the Anglo-Scandinavian *burh*, although the point remains unproven. In 1066, then, the Upper City at Lincoln may have been a quiet enclosure standing within its repaired walls, above and apart from the City's main population centres, and occupied by a group of churches and with a few high-status halls and their associated buildings scattered within.

One indicator that the Upper City of Lincoln was a 'reserved' enclosure, distinct from the remainder of the city, is the fact that the area of land given by William I to Remigius for the foundation of the new cathedral was already 'toll-free'; i.e. it was not considered to be a part of the toll-paying city.[61] Another indicator that the late Anglo-Scandinavian upper enclosure in Lincoln may have been a relatively empty enclosure with a scatter of high status secular building complexes (perhaps including the sunken-featured building excavated on the eastern edge of St Paul's churchyard) interspersed with churches, might be the location here of the Lincoln house of the last Anglo-Saxon Earl of Northumbria, Morcar. At *Domesday* Earl Morcar's Lincoln house was held by Ernuin the priest and this same Ernuin also claimed ownership of the church of All Saints-in-the-Bail.[62] Although Earl Morcar's house was not necessarily near All Saints, the fact that Ernuin claimed ownership of both in 1086 might indicate that the two were connected. It might be the case, for example, that All Saints was part of a complex within the enclosure that contained not only important churches, but also the Earl's house. All Saints is given the distinctive title *monasterium* (i.e. Minster) in a royal document of 1114, and although it is not certain exactly what type of church is implied, this may indicate that the church was unusual. There was a similar connection between the churches in the Bail and the post-Conquest lords of Castle in the case of St Paul-in-the-Bail, which Countess Lucy or her family had owned and donated to Trentham Priory, Staffordshire.[63] Lucy was a descendant of Thorold, the first Norman Sheriff, and Thorold, of course, was in many ways the Norman successor of Morcar as vice-regent in Lincolnshire. Similar foundations of churches within the *haga* of great pre-Conquest aristocrats, such as those which might be inferred at All Saints and St Paul at Lincoln are met with in other early towns, for example in London at St Michael Bassishaw and St Mary Staining and in Chichester.[64] Not only do we have this evidence, no matter how insubstantial, that the Sheriffs had held seigneurial interests in the wider Roman Upper City before the present castle was created, but it is also possible that the second great aristocratic dynasty established within the first castle at Lincoln, the hereditary constables, may also have held parallel interests. In the later Middle Ages the baronial court of the De la Haye family, the hereditary Constables of Lincoln Castle, was held within *Bardolfhalle,* and, although the precise location of *Bardolfhalle* is unknown, it was within the Roman Upper City in the parish of St Clement – outside the present castle enclosure.[65]

The examples cited and discussed by Dr Parsons, of early castles formed by converting existing enclosures, are of Royal castles, or castles which played an important role in secular administration, but a closer parallel with the Lincoln case may be provided by the foundation of the castle at Peterborough, reportedly by another Thorold, the first Norman Abbot of Peterborough, probably in 1070.[66] Here, as at Lincoln, a motte was raised in the corner of the large *burh* enclosure, whose north and east boundaries have been discovered through excavation. As seems to have been the case at Lincoln, the interior of the enclosure at Peterborough was occupied, not by a town, but rather by an ecclesiastical community including several churches.[67] The Abbot of Peterborough and the Bishop of Lincoln were also alike in that they were both holders of senior baronies directly from William (each providing sixty knights). At Peterborough, therefore, as at Lincoln, the resulting castle is best seen as the manifestation of this secular power by these newly installed Norman clerics, and at both places the churchman, in right of his secular land-holdings, provided the Castle Guard at the new Castle, which now enclosed his church within its wall. The castle at Peterborough, of course, was constructed as a component in the tactical war against Hereward's rebellion in the Fens in 1069-71, and, given that we are now proposing that it has physical similarities with the new castle at Lincoln, we must ask whether the Lincoln Castle was not also built as much in response to the Fenland rebellion as it was to the rebellion in the North. It is usually said that Lincoln Castle was founded on William's return journey from York, by which time the northern rebellion had been temporarily quelled, but the Fenland rebellion of the following year must have broken out whilst it was under construction.[68] The possibility that the two physically similar castles were linked in this way is increased by the fact that, although the knights of the Abbot of Peterborough played the principal role in the suppression of Hereward's rebellion, they were joined in this campaign by the knights of Ivo Taillebois, who held Lincolnshire estates and would have owed service at Lincoln Castle in right of them[69] – indeed Taillebois probably became Sheriff of Lincolnshire not long afterwards. The subsequent development of the castles at Lincoln and Peterborough in the twelfth century, however, was quite different. At Lincoln, the role of the castle as the centre of County administration ensured that the Bishop would not retain personal dominance within it, and, as we shall see, he withdrew from the Castle in the 1130s. By contrast, at Peterborough, without such external administrative burdens, the Castle simply developed into the walled Abbey precinct, within which the Abbot's dominance was undisputed, and the motte – the seat of secular judgement – soon fell out of use.[70]

Finally, our observation that certain of these early castles may have consisted merely of the erection of a motte in one corner of an existing enclosure must have some bearing on the debate over the nature and function of royal castles during the first few decades following the Conquest. It seems that many of these pre-existing enclosures required merely the addition of a motte to make them serviceable for their new purpose and the reason for this is worth a moment's consideration. One could take a purely military view, that the motte (and presumably a timber tower on top of it) would provide a strong point for the final defence of the nobility, in which case we are making an important observation about the social distinctions between pre-Conquest and post-Conquest society – as such exclusive retreats were apparently not considered necessary before the Conquest.[71] But the motte is also a symbolic structure, emblematising the seat of lordly judgement, and an equally important impulse in their construction must have been the perceived need to make a very visible statement that a new judicial power was abroad in the land.[72] Sitting within the earlier defensive enclosure, then, the motte marked the take-over of the ancient seat of power by the new regime for the people of the county to see. The motte itself was the visible expression of the new lord's installation. Thinking of the motte is this way, of course, takes us back to debates held in the 1960s over the question whether the motte might itself be a structure arising first in the particular circumstances of political revolution following the Conquest in England.[73] If the motte is primarily a symbol of personal lordship, then its deployment in late eleventh-century England may have been thought by contemporaries to symbolise the newly imposed political system of personalised lordship in the Conqueror's regime. It is the case, however, that the motte seems to have been used in this way, as a symbol of lordship, in Normandy and elsewhere in the first half of the century.[74] In the later eleventh century, of course, Lincoln Castle had at least two lords – the Bishop and the Crown's representative – and, as one might expect in such circumstances, in our newly identified early Castle, both lordships have their symbolic structures. Thanks to our reassessment of the archaeological information from the Upper City we can now argue that the Crown's secular representative held the motte below the Lucy Tower, whilst the Bishop held the new stone great tower now rising adjacent to his Cathedral.

The twelfth-century castle

Our revised interpretation of the eleventh-century castle implies that the castle we see today is largely a monument of the twelfth century, and we have seen that, with the exception of the motte on which Lucy Tower stands, the surviving structures – earthwork and masonry – can be shown to be, or are likely to be, of that date (Fig.7). Such a date is consistent with their architectural parallels, some of which are discussed by Pamela Marshall in her paper below. The reasons for the conversion of the huge castle of 1068 into the smaller

enclosure we have today were no doubt complicated at the time, but even so we may be able to identify some of the more important factors. The unreasonably large size of the original enclosure may well have been an important consideration – defending such a length of wall would have posed serious man-power problems. Furthermore, the new Cathedral church would have been seriously inconvenienced by being placed within a castle, as it was at Old Sarum.[75] It may be, however, that a major factor in the reduction in the size of the castle was the desire of the Bishop of Lincoln to alter his own responsibilities for secular government. Originally the Bishop had been the most senior of the three lords who were dominant in county government and the Castle (providing twenty knights), the other lords being the Constable and the Sheriff.[76] Between 1123 and 1133, however, Bishop Alexander was granted permission to withdraw his knights from Lincoln Castle so that they could serve instead at the Bishop's private castle at Newark, where he would be in sole command of them.[77] Furthermore, at the same time he removed his episcopal hall to a new location outside Lincoln Castle.[78] We have no conclusive evidence as to where the early Bishop's hall was but, as we have noted, the only structural evidence still surviving may suggest that it was within the fortified west end of the cathedral itself.[79] Wherever the Bishop's hall was within the former Roman enclosure, it was removed, first in 1130-33 into the chambers over the East gate, and then, in 1137, the King granted the Bishop the land to the south, outside both the old Castle and the new Castle, for the construction of the Bishop's palace; on which land it still stands.[80]

These decisive moves on the part of the Bishop to withdraw from his feudal responsibilities in the shire castle seem to be contemporary with the major construction works on the present castle enclosure, and the coincidence of timing cannot be ignored. The withdrawal of the Bishop from the Castle

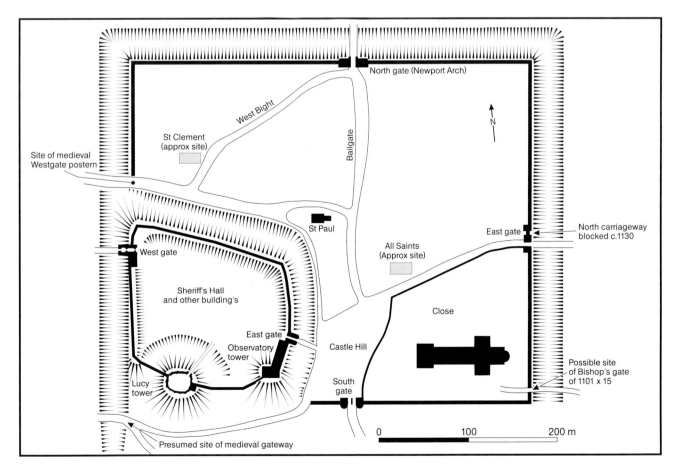

Fig.7. Development of the Second Castle of Lincoln, Bail and Close by c.1150 (Drawn by Dave Watt, copyright English Heritage).

was clearly not an issue when the writ granting consent for the creation of the gate through the wall was issued (c.1101-15), but was presumably contemplated when the Bishop removed his knights from service here (1123-33), and the process was physically underway when the Bishop moved his hall to the East Gate (1130-33). This spread of dates strongly suggests that the perpetrator of this radical re-organisation of the topography of the Upper City and the redefinition of the Bishop's role within the government of the city and county was Bishop Alexander 'the Magnificent' who held the see from 1123 to 1148.[81] Alexander was a member of that closely-knit generation of Henry I's clerics which also included Henry of Blois, Bishop of Winchester and Roger, Bishop of Salisbury (who was Alexander's uncle).[82] Although we are accustomed to thinking of these men as worldly politicians and extravagant patrons of the arts, rather than men of religious principle, the politics of the first three decades of the twelfth century in England were dominated by a single issue which had its origins in a serious theological debate – did the bishops' authority derive from their investiture with lands by the King or from their investiture by the Pope, via the Archbishop? To quote a recent study 'The root cause of the trouble was the dual role of bishops and great abbots who were both prelates with spiritual duties and the lords of temporal baronies'.[83] In this highly political contest the propriety of bishops holding important secular baronies from the King, like Alexander's twenty knights at the royal castle of Lincoln, came constantly into question.[84] Such questions would not arise if the Bishop withdrew from his secular Lincoln barony and caused his knights to serve at his own 'private' castle at Newark. Perhaps we can suggest, therefore, that Alexander's various steps to extract himself from his barony at the royal castle at Lincoln, which must have had the effect of creating a purely secular barony in his place within the reduced castle enclosure and, also, the creation of a purely ecclesiastical enclave or 'close' around the new cathedral, may have been part of a carefully considered plan aimed at bolstering the church of Lincoln's independence from royal control.

As we have already noted above, at the same time that Alexander was in the process of withdrawal from his barony at Lincoln there were radical changes in the layout of the castle. Sometime after about 1100 the former Roman West Gate was abandoned and the present West Gate was begun as part of the creation of the new earthwork and wall along the west side of what was to become a much smaller enclosure. Similarly the pottery dates from the excavations under the Observatory Tower suggest that it was not constructed until the middle of the century.[85] These two results taken together strongly suggest that the campaign of construction of both the earthworks of the present enclosure and the masonry walls with which the banks are topped, belongs to the period between 1100 and c.1150, although, as we have also seen, it might have been the result of two consecutive campaigns. Consequently the construction of the present reduced castle was approximately contemporary with the withdrawal of the Bishop from the Upper City enclosure. The work on the new smaller castle would, presumably, have been the responsibility of the De la Haye family, who were the hereditary constables during this period,[86] indeed it may be that the rise to influence of the De la Haye family within the twelfth-century castle was itself a direct result of the Bishop's self-imposed withdrawal. They did not have a free hand in the castle, however, as their power was balanced (as the Bishop's had been before them) by that of the hereditary Sheriffs – Countess Lucy's father and husband, a situation discussed in Dr Dalton's paper below.

It was long ago suggested by Sir Francis Hill that, whatever the detailed circumstances, the fundamental reason for there being two keeps at Lincoln is this divided responsibility and the rivalries between the two lordships in the castle.[87] Both mottes have masonry towers, belonging to the central years

of the twelfth century. Today the twelfth-century tower on the Observatory Tower motte is almost completely invisible beneath subsequent rebuilds, but it is clear, both from an inspection of the modern fabric and from results of clearance work on the motte top to the south-east in 1985, that this was originally a large rectangular tower.[88] It may have been a chamber block separated from, but connected with, a suite of contemporary rooms (perhaps including a hall) which it is known lay inside the east curtain wall and which were recorded in some detail by Willson.[89]

The Lucy tower, however, represents a different type of residence. It is easily large enough to have contained a suite of chambers and a hall, possibly set one above the other, as the building was clearly originally of at least two storeys. These chambers, however, must have been mostly of timber, although there are small mural chambers still surviving in the stone turrets to east and west, where the building is connected to the curtain wall.[90] The Lucy Tower survives in a remarkably original state and it can be given a date in the 1150s by virtue of the lunette hood-moulding (now completely replaced; the original was recorded by Willson) which is identical to hood-mouldings from St Mary's Guildhall, the nave of Stow church and over openings in the lower stages of the west towers of the Cathedral.[91]

One of these two great towers, each containing lordly suites, would have been the headquarters, no doubt, of the Sheriff and the other, that of the Constable. It is not possible to confirm which was which, but the tower on the principal motte, (that is to say the principal symbol of lordship) has retained the name Lucy Tower, after Lucy wife of Ivo Taillebois – the Sheriff – and daughter of Thorold the first Norman Sheriff of Lincolnshire.[92] As the Sheriff was the officer with responsibility in the county for the implementation of Royal justice from the earliest period following the Conquest it would be entirely appropriate, symbolically, that the Sheriff's tower would occupy the early motte of lordship. Certainly, the Sheriff would seem to have a stronger claim to hold the older and more dominant motte in the castle than the Constable, whose role may have risen to significance only once the present reduced enclosure had been created, and once the Bishop had withdrawn from his feudal responsibilities in the Castle. The arguments over which tower belonged to which lordship are complex, however, and are considered in greater detail by Paul Dalton and Pamela Marshall below.

In addition to the two suites of lordly chambers, which we can suggest were formed around and on top of the two mottes, it is clear that both the East and West gates of the new enclosure contained large chambers above them. That above the East Gate can now only be inferred, as it was entirely reconstructed during the thirteenth century and only the inner order of the twelfth-century gate arch itself along with lengths of flanking wall can be seen.[93] The presumed chamber over this gate, however, may well have been connected to the buildings along the east curtain wall to the south, between the gate and the Observatory Tower, and thus it may be that the Constable held direct access to this key gateway. Similarly, at the West Gate there were clearly chambers both above the gate arch and to the south and north as well – although a description and a dating of these will have to await the publication of the 1983-88 excavations.[94]

Although its size was greatly reduced from what it had been in the eleventh century, the new castle still enclosed a great space within its new walls. Furthermore, the structures we have identified so far as belonging to the new twelfth-century castle were all located around the curtain wall and it is, perhaps, unlikely that the interior space created by the massive new enclosure would have been entirely empty. From at least the seventeenth century there were two great buildings here; one was a major hall in which the shire courts sat, and the other was an administrative and/or prison building.[95] Although we have little idea of the original date of the buildings reported at these later periods, we can suggest, perhaps, that such buildings would have been needed from the twelfth century onwards to fit the castle for its role in the administration of justice. Certainly one of them might have been the 'great hall' mentioned by name in 1327 and 1335.[96] Thus, as at the shire castles at Leicester and Oakham (to take nearby examples), there may have been a great public hall in the centre of the bailey from the time of the construction of the present castle in the early twelfth century.

The classification of the present Lincoln Castle has always caused scholars with an interest in taxonomy great difficulties. Until recently, the castle could have been seen as a simple motte and bailey, with a second motte added later at the south-eastern corner. However, now that we are suggesting that the motte is likely to belong to a period prior to the construction of the bailey, the twelfth-century bailey itself could be viewed more as a ringwork, which happened to have been constructed adjacent to a pre-existing motte. Certainly the enormous earthwork banks topped with stone walls are more reminiscent of twelfth-century castles like Oakham or Castle Rising, but to suggest that Lincoln is a case where the motte is earlier than the ringwork, is to reverse the generalisation put forward in his study of ringworks by David King.[97] Even so we seem to have enough evidence to make the proposal, and the general lesson to be drawn might be that such classifications should not become strait-jackets when more complex and interesting developmental histories can be explored.

Summary.

The recent work on Lincoln Castle's West Gate, and on the archaeology of the Upper City more generally, has resulted in a radical change in our understanding of the layout and character of the early phases of this castle. We can now propose that there were in fact two entirely different castles established here in the century following the Conquest. The first, founded in 1068, was an emergency measure, the symbolic re-occupation of an existing enclosure – formerly the Upper Roman City – which had been, we may suspect, the Anglo-Scandinavian *burh* of Lincoln. Building work must have been quite extensive, focusing on re-edification of the Roman gatehouses and the construction of the motte below the Lucy Tower, but by far the largest and most impressive building project within the castle, according to this new interpretation, would have been the great tower in stone built by Remigius adjacent to, or part of, his new cathedral.

This first castle proved unsuitable, however, no doubt partly because it was wasteful of potentially valuable commercial land, but it also seems clear that the Bishop was not happy with the arrangement whereby he held the principal secular lordship within the shire castle alongside other barons. He finally divorced himself from the Castle in the early 1130s and this was one of several actions taken in the early decades of the twelfth century which was to result in a smaller, more conventional shire castle – albeit one which continued to have a divided lordship (divided now between the Constable and the Sheriff). A new circuit of defences was built around the earlier motte and two suites of seigneurial accommodation were constructed at the Lucy Tower and the Observatory Tower, as well, perhaps, as a public hall or halls in the centre of the bailey.

This twelfth-century castle was not greatly altered subsequently. The West Gate was reconstructed in the thirteenth century, perhaps as the result of expenditure recorded in 1233/34,[98] and this may have represented a final phase of re-edification and repair following the so-called 'Fair of Lincoln' in 1217. A more major aspect of this campaign of re-fortification was probably the upgrading of the defences along the eastern wall. Here, it seems likely that a great new tower was added, now known as Cobb Hall, which forms the

subject of the study below by Dr Renn. At the same time the East Gate was comprehensively rebuilt (although it was not completed until after 1227). It was provided with a barbican (only demolished in 1791) and bartizans, probably of the fourteenth century. These later alterations, of course, emphasise the castle's function as the judicial centre for the county but we have only a little architectural evidence that the important seigneurial residence in the Observatory Tower was upgraded during the later medieval period, and none that such rebuilding occurred at the Lucy Tower. Probably Lincoln, like so many other shire castles, became the residence only of lesser officials in the justice system. From the thirteenth century onwards the Earldom of Lincoln itself was held by great magnates who had many castles and other residences[99] and, although such lords did visit Lincoln on numerous occasions, they invested in accommodation in their other holdings – at Bolingbroke in Lincolnshire for example. Indeed it may have been the case that, when John of Gaunt (who held the Earldom of Lincoln) brought his entourage to Lincoln in 1386, he stayed, not in his castle on the hill, but as a family guest in the house of his vassals the de Suttons in Wigford.[100]

Acknowledgements

This paper is one of several which have arisen from stimulating discussions with Dr Alan Vince during the course of his work on Lincoln in recent years. It is built on work which is substantially his and I am very grateful for the help and advice with which he has provided me. Mick Jones has also been most helpful in guiding my thinking about the Roman city and in allowing me access to the records of CLAU. Dr Richard Hall has also been generous with his time and advice on various aspects of the *burhs* of the 'Five Boroughs'. David Roffe also kindly read through the text and provided me with several key observations. I am also grateful for Dr Derek Renn's comments and those of Philip Dixon and Phillip Lindley. As always I am very grateful for Paul Everson's trenchant views and tolerant criticism. The plans were drawn by Mr David Watt.

Notes

1. The published engraving, from the south-west, is dated 1726, and is dominated by the Lucy Tower, but this was worked up from one of a series of drawings in the brothers' *Lincolnshire Sketchbook*, (Oxford, Bodleian Library, Gough Ms., Lincs 15, f.6r-7r, 13r; 14r, 17v, 51r).

2. The earliest scholarly discussion, in 1782, between Sir Henry Englefield and Edward King focused on the date and purpose of the West Gate. The bibliography for Lincoln Castle in D. J. Cathcart King, *Castellarium Anglicanum* (London and New York, 1983), pp.261-62 is valuable. The bibliography in D. M. Short, *A Bibliography of Printed Items Relating to the City of Lincoln*, Lincoln Record Society, 79 (Woodbridge, 1990) is weak on archaeological material – see entries 799-822.

3. For a brief biography of Edward Willson see H. M. Colvin, *A Biographical Dictionary of English Architects 1660-1840* (1954), pp.678-79.

4. The bulk of the Willson Collection is deposited in the Society of Antiquaries of London (Ms.786) whilst a number of important portfolios are amongst the manuscript collections at the Cathedral library. Willson's principal publication on the castle was the paper he gave to the 1848 meeting of the Archaeological Institute at Lincoln: E. J. Willson, 'Lincoln Castle, notices of its History and the existing remains; illustrated by a plan from actual survey', *Memoirs Illustrative of the History and Antiquities of the County and City of Lincoln communicated to the Annual Meeting of the Archaeological Institute of Great Britain and Ireland held at Lincoln, July 1848* (1850), pp.280-92.

5. The most important contribution of the twentieth century was undoubtedly made by Lincoln's principal historian Sir Francis Hill: J. W. F. Hill, 'Lincoln Castle: the Constables and the Guard', *Associated Architectural Societies' Reports and Papers*, 40 pt 1 (1930), pp.1-14; J. W. F. Hill, 'Danish and Norman Lincoln',

Associated Architectural Societies' Reports and Papers, 41 pt 2 (1933), pp.7-22; J. W. F. Hill, *Medieval Lincoln* (Cambridge, 1948); J. W. F. Hill, *Lincoln Castle: Official Guide* (Lincoln, 1969).

6. Details of the watching briefs undertaken since 1970 by the City of Lincoln Archaeology Unit and its predecessors are to be found in the Lincoln Urban Archaeological Database (UAD).

7. *The Anglo-Saxon Chronicle*, edited by G. N. Garmonsway (1953), p.202. See also *The Ecclesiastical History of Orderic Vitalis*, edited by M. Chibnall, 6 vols (Oxford, 1969-80), p.218 and also C. G. Harfield, 'A handlist of castles recorded in the Domesday Book', *English Historical Review*, 106 (1991), pp.371-92, although this paper takes a literalistic view of the 166 houses destroyed when the castle was built.

8. *The Lincolnshire Domesday and the Lindsey Survey*, edited by C. W. Foster and Thomas Longley, Lincoln Record Society, 19 (Horncastle, 1924), 7, no.25.

9. The new castle at Warwick, only displaced four houses, Stamford only five properties, Wallingford a mere eight houses, whilst Cambridge Castle, like Lincoln, a motte established within a small Roman enclosure was larger, displacing twenty-seven houses. The castle at Canterbury displaced thirty-two houses, Exeter (probably) displaced forty-eight, but the only one of the these early castles in *Domesday Book* which came anywhere near Lincoln was the very large castle at Norwich which, despite its large size – displacing ninety-eight houses, plus fifteen *burgenses* – was still only two-thirds the area of Lincoln, D. F. Renn, *Norman Castles in Britain* (second edition, London and New York, 1973), p.32.

10. See discussion in Hill, *Medieval Lincoln*, pp.53-56, for example. Also C. Mahany and D. Roffe, 'Stamford, The development of an Anglo-Scandinavian Borough' in *Anglo-Norman Studies V. Proceedings of the Battle Conference* edited by R. A. Brown (1982), pp.198-219, esp. p.215. Because Hill was trying to fit the houses into the area covered by the present Castle, he arrives at a density of occupation in the upper city which has simply not been demonstrated so far by the results of excavations.

11. The UAD is a computerised database curated by Lincoln City Council.

12. The view that the Roman Upper City was to be considered as a part of the early Castle was first expressed, though not fully discussed, in H. Elliott and D. A. Stocker, *Lincoln Castle* (Lincoln, FLARE and Lincolnshire County Council, 1984).

13. A further discussion of this evidence is contained in M. J. Jones, D. Stocker and A. Vince, *The City by the Pool, Assessing the Archaeology of the City of Lincoln*, edited by D. Stocker, Lincoln Archaeological Studies No.10 (Oxford, 2003), chapter 9. The principal evidence and those conclusions which related directly to the development of the Castle were published as a note in D. Stocker and A. Vince, 'The early Norman Castle at Lincoln and a re-evaluation of the original west tower of Lincoln Cathedral', *Medieval Archaeology* 41 (1997), pp.223-33.

14. For the 1983-89 excavations, and for a study of the architectural development of the gate tower, see the interim reports in D. A. Stocker, 'Lincoln Castle', *Archaeology in Lincoln 1982-1983*, Annual Report of the Lincoln Archaeological Trust, 11 (Lincoln, 1983), pp.18-27 and M. Otter, 'Lincoln Castle, West Gate', *Lincoln Archaeology 1988-1989*. First Annual Report of the City of Lincoln Archaeological Unit (Lincoln, 1989), pp.13-16.

15. Dr Vince and the author are very grateful to Ms Jane Young for discussing her preliminary assessment prior to publication. It is anticipated that a full report on the dating of the pottery from the West Gate excavations will be provided in the excavation report currently being prepared by the City of Lincoln Archaeology Unit.

16. For example at the churches at Upton and Marton in Lincolnshire. See also J. Taylor and H. M. Taylor, 'Herring-bone masonry as a criterion of date', *Journal of the British Archaeological Association*, third series, 27 (1964), pp.4-13.

17. Stocker and Vince, 'The early Norman Castle', p.224, Fig.9b.

18. N. Reynolds, 'Investigations in the Observatory Tower, Lincoln Castle', *Medieval Archaeology*, 19 (1975), pp.204-05; see also Marshall, this volume, below.

19. The pottery from the Observatory Tower motte is a locally made ware of the mid twelfth century, J. Young and A. G. Vince *et al.*, *The Corpus of Anglo-Saxon and Medieval Pottery from Lincoln*, forthcoming.

20. The Roman gates were the subject of a detailed study by F. H. Thompson and J. B. Whitwell, 'The gates of Roman Lincoln', *Archaeologia*, 104 (1973), pp.129-207.

21. A full account of its discovery and further references are in Thompson and Whitwell, 'The gates of Roman Lincoln', pp.194-200. See also Elliott and Stocker, *Lincoln Castle*, chapter 7. It is worth recording the possibility that what was discovered in 1836 was actually a Norman, or partly Norman gate. We have evidence that, although the

other three Roman gates retained some Roman fabric, they were all substantially repaired and added to by the Normans, and there is no reason to think that similar re-edification works were not necessary to the Roman west gate also. Now that the date of the bank in which the gate house was buried can be dated to after *c*.1100, we do have a context in which such Norman re-edification of the Roman gate could have taken place. Nothing was recorded in the gate's fabric, however, which points strongly towards a Romanesque rather than a Roman date, and the voussoirs recorded in 1983 are certainly Roman (Stocker, 'Lincoln Castle').

22. H. L. Turner, in *Town Defences in England and Wales* (1971), pp.21-25, suggests that there was little interest in the fortification of towns until the end of the twelfth century – a point apparently confirmed by archaeological review, C. Drage, 'Urban castles', in *Urban Archaeology in Britain* edited by J. Schofield and R. Leech, CBA Research Report No.61 (1987), p.120. The original gate towers at York must be amongst the earliest purely civic gatehouses known and these are presumed to date from the twelfth century, RCHME, *The City of York, volume two, The Defences* (1972), pp.10-11. Furthermore we should note that there is no suggestion that the earlier Roman gatehouses in the same approximate locations of Bootham Bar, Micklegate Bar and of the early gate north-west of Monk Bar were reused at that date.

23. A view from the west by Nathan Drake of *c*.1730 now in the Usher Art Gallery (Fig.2) and a second view from the east by the Buck brothers made in 1723 (Bodleian, Gough Ms., Lincs 15, f.19v).

24. Unfortunately the excavations of the medieval layers in 1960 were undertaken with machinery and the results have proved hard to interpret, Thompson and Whitwell, 'The gates of Roman Lincoln', p.150 n.2.

25. Thompson and Whitwell, 'The gates of Roman Lincoln', p.132.

26. Thompson and Whitwell, 'The gates of Roman Lincoln', pp.150, 157-58; M. Blackburn, C. Colyer and M. Dolley, *Early Medieval Coins from Lincoln and its Shire c.770-1100*, The Archaeology of Lincoln, VI-1 (1983), pp.21-22. A coin of Cnut *c*.1030-35 was reportedly discovered in the foundation trench of the north tower of this new structure, but the assumption made in the excavation account that this must have been lost before *c*.1040 is no longer tenable – it could easily have been incorporated in a foundation deposit of *c*.1070. It must also be said that fragments of late twelfth- and thirteenth-century ceramic were also reported from these foundations, and this great mixture of material from this deposit is probably the result of the adverse circumstances under which it was recorded. It is probably wisest to regard the date of these of these foundations as unproven archaeologically.

27. *The Registrum Antiquissimum of the Cathedral Church of Lincoln*, edited by C. W. Foster and K. Major, 10 vols (Lincoln Record Society, 1931-73), i, p.34, no.49.

28. Stocker and Vince, 'The early Norman Castle', p.226.

29. The gatehouse was the subject of excavations in 1954 reported in Thompson and Whitwell, 'The gates of Roman Lincoln', pp.185-94.

30. For a review of the depictions of the Newport Arch in topographical drawings from the early eighteenth century see C. N. Moore, 'The Newport Arch – a reconsideration' in M. J. Jones, *The Defences of the Upper Roman Enclosure*, The Archaeology of Lincoln, VII-1 (Lincoln, 1980), pp.56-60. Moore discusses the likely form of the gate and whether or not the topographical drawings provide any evidence for the barbican which Thompson and Whitwell thought they could detect.

31. Thompson and Whitwell, 'The gates of Roman Lincoln', p.187.

32. The interpretation of the Roman and medieval South Gate has been the subject of great confusion over the years (see Thompson and Whitwell, 'The gates of Roman Lincoln', p.200; Jones, *Defences of the Upper Roman Enclosure*, p.28). First, it seems likely that in the later medieval period there were two gate arches on Steep Hill, C. P. C. Johnson and A. G. Vince, 'The South Bail Gates of Lincoln', *Lincolnshire History and Archaeology*, 27 (1992), pp.12-16. It seems that it is only the northern of these two arches which stands on the site of the Roman gatehouse. A further explanation of the history of the gatehouse is presented by Mr Jones in Jones *et al.*, *The City by the Pool*, pp.63-65, and the account here rests on that work and I am grateful to Dr Vince and Mr Jones for discussing the matter with me.

33. Johnson and Vince, 'The South Bail Gates of Lincoln', pp.12-13; S. Jones, K. Major, J. Varley and C. Johnson, *The Survey of Ancient Houses in Lincoln IV: Houses in the Bail: Steep Hill, Castle Hill and Bailgate* (Lincoln, 1996), pp.21-24.

34. Johnson and Vince, 'The South Bail Gates of Lincoln', pp.12-13. S. Jones *et al.*, *Survey of Ancient Houses IV*, p.21.

35. P. J. Drury, 'Aspects of the origins and development of Colchester Castle', *Archaeological Journal*, 139 (1982), pp.391-401.

36. D. A. Stocker, 'The pre-history of conservation', in *Reconstruction and Regeneration. The Philosophy of Conservation* edited by D. Kincaid, Proceedings of the IHBC Canterbury Conference 1997, (Canterbury, 1998), pp.6-12. Since this paper was first written Professor Anthony Quiney has emphasised that the west tower of Remigius' cathedral is also highly dependent on Roman models, A. Quiney, '*In hoc signo*, the west front of Lincoln Cathedral', *Architectural History*, 44 (2001), pp.162-71.

37. Sir C. Peers, *Richmond Castle* (thirteenth impression, 1977).

38. Jones, *Defences of the Upper Roman Enclosure*.

39. Thompson and Whitwell, 'The gates of Roman Lincoln'.

40. D. A. Stocker, 'Excavations to the south of Lincoln Minster 1984 and 1985 – an interim report', *Lincolnshire History and Archaeology*, 20 (1985), pp.15-19, esp. p.17.

41. Stocker and Vince, 'The early Norman Castle', p.231, and n.32.

42. Jones *et al.*, *The City by the Pool*, pp.178-79. A postern is reported in this area south of the Minster in 1224-27 in a document in the Vicars Choral Chartulary (LAO, VC 2/1 no.217) but Stanley Jones *et al.* believe this refers to the east gate of the Bishop's palace (see S. Jones, K. Major and J. Varley, *The Survey of Ancient Houses in Lincoln II: Houses to the South and West of the Minster* (Lincoln, 1987), pp. 65-66).

43. D. F. Petch, 'Excavations in Lincoln, 1955-58', *Archaeological Journal*, 117 (1960), pp.40-70; Jones, *Defences of the Upper Roman Enclosure*, p.27; Stocker and Vince, 'The early Norman Castle', p.226.

44. UAD; Stocker and Vince, 'The early Norman Castle', pp.224-26.

45. Jones *et al.*, *The City by the Pool*, pp.196-204. I am grateful to Dr Vince for discussing this interesting building with me in some detail.

46. The date of the transfer was refined to within two years by Hill, *Medieval Lincoln*, pp.64-65, more recently discussed in D. Owen, 'Introduction: the English church in eastern England, 1066-1100', in *A History of Lincoln Minster* edited by D. Owen, (Cambridge, 1994), pp.1-13.

47. R. D. H. Gem, 'Lincoln Minster: *ecclesia pulchra, ecclesia fortis*', *Medieval Art and Architecture at Lincoln Cathedral*, The British Archaeological Association Conference Transactions for the year 1982 (1986), pp.9-28.

48. This case is discussed in greater detail in Stocker and Vince, 'The early Norman Castle', pp.227-32 and by Quiney '*In hoc signo*'. Work by the author and others on alternative explanations for the Remigius' tower is underway in 2004 and it is already clear that the first floor halls probably ran east-west and not north-south as initially proposed. Survey work is being undertaken by David Taylor of Nottingham University.

49. Sir Francis Hill thought that the Observatory Tower motte was likely to be the older, but this seems to have been mostly because he presumed that the mound beneath the Lucy Tower was the same date as the tower which now sits on top of it: Hill, *Medieval Lincoln*, pp.82-86. This view was followed by R. A. Brown, H. M. Colvin and A. J. Taylor, *The History of the King's Works*, volume II, *The Middle Ages* (1963), p.704. More recent opinion has been consistently in favour of the Lucy Tower motte being the earlier, following Reynolds' excavations in 1974 (Reynolds, 'Investigations in the Observatory Tower').

50. This argument is made in greater detail in Jones *et al.*, *The City by the Pool*, pp.175-76, 210-12, and is outlined in Stocker and Vince, 'The early Norman Castle'.

51. At least this is the implication which has sometimes been drawn from the 1726 engraving by Buck which seems to show the mound made of alternate bands of limestone and earth. The motte at Carisbrooke, for example, was constructed in this way, P. Barker and N. Higham, *Timber Castles* (1992), p.154.

52. Reynolds, 'Investigations in the Observatory Tower'.

53. See also M. J. Jones and C. J. Bond, 'Urban defences', in *Urban Archaeology in Britain* edited by J. Schofield and R. Leech, CBA Research Report No.61 (1987), pp.81-116; C. Drage 'Urban castles' and N. J. G. Pounds, *The Medieval Castle in England and Wales. A Social and Political History* (Cambridge, 1990), pp.207-15. The most thorough account of the Five Boroughs, however, is R. A. Hall, 'The Five Boroughs of the Danelaw: a review of present knowledge', *Anglo-Saxon England*, 18 (1989), pp.149-205.

54. Pounds, *The Medieval Castle*, pp.207-15 and useful diagram at Fig.8.5.

55. Mrs Armitage lists ten, tenth-century *burhs* which subsequently had mottes placed within them, E. S. Armitage, *The Early Norman Castles of the British Isles* (1912), pp.26-27, a further listing is provided in Jones and Bond, 'Urban defences' and such lists are discussed by Dr Parsons in his paper below.

56. Amongst the midland *burhs* only Lincoln has produced much excavated evidence – summarised in Hall, 'The Five Boroughs' – but this is almost all from the Lower City.

57. This view was most clearly stated by Armitage, *Early Norman Castles*, chapter II) – 'We see that the main idea of the borough was the same as that of the prehistoric or British "camp of refuge", in that it was intended for the defence of the society and not of the individual. . . . It was a town, a place where people were expected to live permanently and do their daily work. It provided a fostering seat for trade and manufactures, two of the chief factors in the history of civilisation. The men who kept watch and ward on the ramparts, or who sallied forth in their bands to fight the Danes, were the men who were slowly building up the prosperity of the stricken land of England.' (*Ibid.* pp.29-30). This appreciation has been tacitly followed by many subsequent writers.

58. Although Torksey appears in Jones and Bond's lists with a question mark, there is no evidence that the beach-market at Torksey was defended ('Urban defences', pp.93-97).

59. Jones *et al.*, *The City by the Pool*, pp.204-07, 230-34.

60. C. Colyer, B. J. J. Gilmour and M. J. Jones, *The Defences of the Lower City. Excavations at the Park and West Parade 1970-2 and a discussion of other sites excavated up to 1994*, The Archaeology of Lincoln, VII-2, CBA Research Report No.114 (1999). Jones *et al.*, *The City by the Pool*, pp.204-07. I am grateful to Dr Vince for his advice on this point.

61. D. Owen, 'The Norman Cathedral at Lincoln', *Anglo-Norman Studies*, 6 (1984), pp.188-99, esp. p.189. Bischoff draws attention to the fact that the grant of burgage tenure payments for individual citizens in 1130 did not apply to the Upper City. This area, then, was **not** an area of standard burgage tenure prior to 1130, J. P. Bischoff, 'Economic Change in Thirteenth Century Lincoln: Decline of an Urban Cloth Industry' (unpublished doctoral thesis, Yale University, 1975).

62. *The Lincolnshire Domesday and the Lindsey Survey*, edited by C. W. Foster and Thomas Longley, Lincoln Record Society, 19 (Horncastle, 1924), p.xxxii. This entry is discussed in Hill, *Medieval Lincoln*, p.46 and in S. Jones, K. Major and J. Varley, *The Survey of Ancient Houses in Lincoln III: Houses in Eastgate, Priorygate, and James Street* (Lincoln, 1990), pp.50-51.

63. Discussed in Hill, *Medieval Lincoln*, p.96.

64. R. Morris, *Churches in the Landscape* (1989), pp.195-96, 204-05.

65. For *Bardolfhalle* see Hill, *Medieval Lincoln*, pp.105-06; D. Roffe, 'An Introduction to the Lincolnshire Domesday', *The Lincolnshire Domesday* (1992), pp.1-42, esp. p.27; S. Jones *et al.*, *Survey of Ancient Houses IV*, pp.126-28. I owe this observation on the relevance of the De la Haye family holding to David Roffe. It would be very pleasing to be able to associate *Bardolfhalle* with the North Gate, that is to suggest that it was one of the chambers fashioned out of the remains of the Roman gate now represented by Newport Arch. Many such manorial court halls were located in chambers above gatehouses, and it is this court function which has ensured the survival of many gatehouse buildings, when the buildings to which they originally gave access have disappeared. But unfortunately, this does not seem to have been the case with Newport Arch, as *Bardolfhalle* is known to have been in the parish of St Clement whilst the western part of the North Gate seems to have been in the parish of St Paul-in-the-Bail in the thirteenth century, S. Jones *et al.*, *Survey of Ancient Houses IV*, p.126.

66. *The Peterborough Chronicle of Hugh Candidus*, ed. W. T. Mellows, trans. C. Mellows and W. T. Mellows (revised edition, Peterborough, 1980), pp.44-45. Derek Renn accepts Armitage's view (*The Early Norman Castles of the British Isles*, p.185) that the motte was built by Thorold as part of the campaign against Hereward in 1070, *Norman Castles*, p.30.

67. E. King, 'The Town of Peterborough in the early Middle Ages', *Northamptonshire Past and Present*, 6 (1980), pp.187-95; D. Mackreth, 'Recent work on monastic Peterborough', *Durobrivae*, 9 (1984), pp.18-29; D. Mackreth, *Peterborough History and Guide* (Stroud, 1994), pp.13-15, 21; C. Hart, *The Danelaw* (1992), pp.627-30 and Fig.24.1. Although only the north and east sides of the enclosure have been demonstrated through excavation, a reconstruction following the lines of the later precinct boundaries to west and south would give a total area of more than thirty-five acres for the enclosure. Similar circumstances may have prevailed at several other major church sites in the first generation following the Conquest at towns whose enclosures were also dominated by ecclesiastical communities such as Chichester, Rochester and Worcester, for example. The same may also be true of less prominent church communities set within earlier enclosures, such as those at Dover, Pevensey and Hastings (on which see A. J. Taylor, 'Evidence for a Pre-Conquest origin for the chapels in Hastings and Pevensey Castles', *Studies in Castles and Castle Building* (1985), pp.233-40).

68. It is also worth pointing out that the castles at Cambridge and Huntingdon, reported to have been built in this campaign (see Mahany and Roffe, 'Stamford', p.216), are also key locations controlling river access to the Fens, and access to the interior from the Fenland waterways. Along with Peterborough and Lincoln, castles control four of the five the principal navigations inland, along the rivers Witham, Nene, Ouse and Cam, which might have formed potential routes of counter-invasion by Hereward's Danish allies. On the fifth route, via the Welland past Stamford, the castle may also have been established as part of this defensive campaign as Abbot Thorold sought refuge there in 1070 when Hereward attacked Peterborough, D. Roffe, 'The Castle History', *Stamford Castle and Town, South Lincolnshire Archaeology*, 2 (1978), p.15; Mahany and Roffe, 'Stamford', p.216.

69. For Hereward's rebellion and the campaign against Peterborough see *De Gestis Herwardi Saxonis*, ed. and trans. T. A. Bevis (March, 1982), pp.32-33. For Taillebois see Hill, *Medieval Lincoln*, pp.92-93.

70. A marginal note in the continuation of Hugh Candidus' Chronicle states that the *castellum* at Peterborough was destroyed by Abbot Martin of Bec (1133-55). This may be a reference to the abandonment of the motte as part of the Anarchy settlement, Mackreth, *Peterborough History*, pp.28-29.

71. A point first made at length by Mrs Armitage, *Early Norman Castles*, chapter II and frequently discussed since.

72. Although there can be no doubt of the military intent and capacity of mottes in both Normandy and England, this does not preclude their also possessing great symbolic value. Evidence for the symbolic meaning of the motte was discussed in R. Allen Brown, *English Castles* (third edition, 1970), p.35, and the point is well made by Barker and Higham's recent survey of mottes in Ireland which shows that a considerable number have either very modest buildings on the summits, or occasionally, no buildings at all. In such cases, clearly, the mound, the symbol of lordship, was more important than the practical function of the buildings on top, Barker and Higham, *Timber Castles*, pp.75-77.

73. This argument was put forward most convincingly by Brian Davison, 'Early earthwork castles: a new model', in *Château Gaillard. European Castle Studies* 3, edited by A. J. Taylor, Proceedings of the Conference at Battle, Sussex 19-24 September 1966 (Chichester, 1969), pp.37-47.

74. Points made, for example, by Allen Brown, *English Castles*, pp.37-39.

75. One of the reasons given for the need to remove the Cathedral at Old Sarum from within the Castle/Hill fort was the inconvenience of running a cathedral community within a defended area, RCHME, *Ancient and Historical Monuments in the City of Salisbury*, volume 1 (1980), p.16.

76. Hill, *Medieval Lincoln*, pp.87-99.

77. The manning of the Castle and the role of the Bishop's twenty knights is discussed in Hill, 'Lincoln Castle: the Constables and the Guard' and Hill, *Medieval Lincoln*, pp.86-88. See also Stocker and Vince, 'The early Norman Castle', p.226. Recent excavations at Newark have done much to elucidate the castle to which Alexander moved his knight's service. It seems that the Bishops already had a fortified establishment there, but Bishop Alexander completely replanned the complex, and on a 'palatial' scale, – P. Marshall, 'The twelfth-century castle at Newark', *Southwell and Nottinghamshire. Medieval Art Architecture, and Industry. British Archaeological Association Conference Transactions*, XXI (1998), pp.110-25.

78. *Registrum Antiquissimum*, i, p.34, no.49; Stocker and Vince, 'The early Norman Castle', p.226.

79. Gem reported some evidence that there might have been a structure immediately to the north of the cathedral west front, 'Lincoln Minster', pp.9-28. The proposal that the west front itself contained the Bishop's halls is made in Stocker and Vince, 'The early Norman Castle', and a more substantial study is in preparation. Work subsequent to 1997 has shown that any halls at first floor would have been aligned east-west and not, as originally surmised, north-south.

80. *Registrum Antiquissimum*, i, pp.86-87, no.137.

81. By way of comparison, for example, the secular role of the Abbot of Peterborough, who provided sixty knights at the comparable castle there, probably came to an end during the same period, under Abbot Martin of Bec (1132-54).

82. For Alexander himself see A. G. Dyson, 'The monastic patronage of Bishop Alexander of Lincoln', *Journal of Ecclesiastical History*, 26 (1975), pp.1-24 R. A. Stalley, 'A twelfth-century patron of architecture: a study of the buildings erected by Roger, Bishop of Salisbury', *Journal of the British Archaeological Association*, third series, 34 (1971), pp.62-83. For Henry of Blois, see G. Zarnecki, 'Henry of Blois as a patron of sculpture', in *Art and Patronage in the English Romanesque* edited by S. Macready and F. H. Thompson, Society of Antiquaries of London Occasional Paper (New Series) VIII (1986), pp.159-72; N. Riall, *Henry de Blois, Bishop of Winchester: A Patron of the Twelfth-Century Renaissance*, Hampshire Papers, 5 (1994).

83. M. Chibnall, *Anglo-Norman England 1066-1166* (1986), p.69.

84. The development of church politics in this period has been recently surveyed in C. Harper-Bill, *The Anglo-Norman Church* (Bangor, 1992), esp. pp.24-37.

85. Reynolds, 'Investigations in the Observatory Tower'.

86. Hill, *Medieval Lincoln*, pp.87-91.

87. Hill, *Medieval Lincoln*, pp.177-181. See also C. Coulson, 'The castles of the Anarchy', in *The Anarchy of King Stephen's Reign*, edited by E. King (Oxford, 1994), pp.67-92.

88. An interpretation of the phasing of the masonry in the tower is provided in Reynolds, 'Investigations in the Observatory Tower'. In this analysis, however, dates are given to walls on the basis of their inclusion of various re-used architectural details, which have clearly been inserted during the re-edification of the tower in the nineteenth century. Not all of these details are of twelfth-century date, however, and the presence of later medieval mouldings may well suggest that the tower was altered in the late medieval period.

89. Willson, 'Lincoln Castle, notices of its History', p.289; evidence discussed in Elliott and Stocker, *Lincoln Castle*, chapter 3.

90. Evidence described in (for example) Willson, 'Lincoln Castle, notices of its History', p.228; discussed in Elliott and Stocker, *Lincoln Castle*, chapter 4.

91. Willson, 'Lincoln Castle, notices of its History', p.287; D. A. Stocker, *St Mary's Guildhall, Lincoln. The Survey and Excavation of a Medieval Building Complex*, The Archaeology of Lincoln XII-1 (1991), p.83 (Nos 82133 and 82164).

92. For Countess Lucy see Hill, *Medieval Lincoln*, pp.92-99. The application of the name 'Lucy Tower' to the tower on the western motte may not be continuous – see Marshall below.

93. For the East Gate see Elliott and Stocker, *Lincoln Castle*, chapter 6. A plan was made and full photographic recording was undertaken at this gate, including the buried remains of the barbican towers, in 1986. The records were deposited in the CLAU archive (CEG 86).

94. See also Donel and Jones below.

95. The earliest post-medieval reference to the courtyard buildings seems to be that made in a survey of 1608, but many plans and surveys follow – references in Elliott and Stocker, *Lincoln Castle*, chapter 9.

96. Hill, *Medieval Lincoln*, p.99; Brown, Colvin and Taylor, *The History of the King's Works*, II, p.705.

97. D. J. Cathcart King and L. Alcock, 'Ringworks of England and Wales', in *Château Gaillard. European Castle Studies* 3, edited by A. J. Taylor, Proceedings of the Conference at Battle, Sussex 19-24 September 1966 (Chichester, 1969), pp.90-127.

98. In 1233/4, £54 6s.4d. was spent on repairs to this gate – Brown, Colvin and Taylor, *The History of the King's Works*, II, p.705; Stocker, 'Lincoln Castle', p.25.

99. J. G. Nichols, 'The descent of the Earldom of Lincoln . . .', *Memoirs illustrative of the History and Antiquities of the County and City of Lincoln communicated to the Annual Meeting of the Archaeological Institute of Great Britain and Ireland held at Lincoln, July 1848* (1850), pp.253-79.

100. D. A. Stocker, ' "A very goodly house Longging to Sutton . . ." a reconstruction of "John of Gaunt's palace", Lincoln', *Lincolnshire History and Archaeology*, 34 (1999), pp.5-15; S. H. Rigby, ' "John of Gaunt's palace" and the Sutton family of Lincoln', *Lincolnshire History and Archaeology*, 35 (2000), pp.35-39. See also A. Goodman, *John of Gaunt. The Exercise of Princely Power in Fourteenth-Century Europe* (1992), pp.308-09.

The Early Topography of Lincoln Castle

Michael Thompson

Although we have had fine historians of Lincoln such as the late Sir Francis Hill, and Dorothy Owen, the castle has been very reluctant to give up the secrets of its early development. I am going to speculate a little on this period in the hopes that it will stimulate research on some very puzzling aspects of the castle's early history.

First, attention may be directed to the general method of entry to shell keeps in castles. It is an almost invariable rule in the surviving cases that the steps were against one of the two abutting walls of the bailey: Windsor, Farnham, Arundel, Pickering, Eye, Carisbrooke and so on. Possible exceptions like York, where Clifford's tower is a monumental quatrefoil structure, perhaps originally were not so. Obviously two crossings of the motte ditch for the bailey walls to link up with the keep on top were more economical than three but the main reason no doubt was that the wall parapet or palisade overshadowing the steps gave protection and shelter for those using them.

At Lincoln the modern steps to the Observatory tower are against the curtain wall but those leading to Lucy's tower are in the middle, unrelated to the two abutting walls (Figs 1 and 2). The doorway is clearly twelfth-century in date and so, even if the steps are a late eighteenth-century reconstruction, the original entry was presumably on this line. It might be that this is an exception to our rule but more likely it is a relic of when the earliest enclosure wall formed its eastern side. If so, an extension of its eastern wall should show this line, and if ruled out on the plan one can see that it reaches the Cobb Hall tower at the north-east corner of the castle (Fig.3) The present structure there dates from c.1200, but clearly this corner has always made a sharp angle. Such a line divides the castle into two unequal parts: a larger one on the west formed more or less by straight lengths, and a smaller curved and less regular part on the east. The western part appears like a regular, laid-out motte and bailey while the eastern seems an afterthought. It is here proposed tentatively to refer to the western part as the 1068 or original castle and the eastern part as the annex.

In the last century G. T. Clark noticed that the north and west walls of the castle differed markedly from the east wall, their herring-bone masonry making them appear more ancient.[1] The well-known charter of King Stephen in the 1140s[2] in which the two towers (*turres*) or mottes were referred to, as well as the division of the castle between the king and the earl, suggests some original internal division within its walls. The complicated history of the two families in the castle descended from Colswein and Thorold, described by Sir Francis Hill,[3] prompts the same thought. The case for some early division is not without basis, quite apart from my suggestion as to how it came about.

The foundation of the castle by the king on his way back from York in 1068 is recorded by Orderic Vitalis[4] and is well documented in one version of the Anglo-Saxon Chronicle.[5] This I suggest comprised the western section of the castle just

Fig.1. View of north-east side of Lucy tower and its mound showing entry steps and door, south-east curtain wall, abutting it and prison wall (A. E. Thompson).

Fig.2. View looking up to Lucy tower doorway (A. E. Thompson).

referred to. Its motte was not set on the Roman wall to the south of the site but further back on the line of vision from both above and below. It presumably bore a Bayeux-tapestry style type of superstructure and had associated domestic buildings below. The west side followed the line of the Roman wall to the Roman West gate which was deliberately included on the circuit and perhaps was intended to be the main access (Fig.4). Why was it that after a short period this gate was abandoned and buried under a huge earthen bank? One explanation is that the castle was turned from back to front so its principal entry was now on the east not the west.

Bishop Remigius, who had accompanied Duke William in his 1066 army, bringing with him a group of knights and apparently promised a bishopric as his reward, had been awarded the see of Dorchester-on-Thames.[6] The soldier-bishop with the authority and support of the king (but hostility of the archbishop of York) had added Lindsey to the see which was placed under Canterbury and transferred the episcopal seat to Lincoln in 1072 or 1073. Construction of the cathedral started straight away in the south-east corner of the upper town. The construction of the annex to the castle could have been a response to this, the main gate being placed to face the west end of the cathedral, in such a way that a clear processional way existed between the two. There was then no St Mary Magdalene church (it had stood on the site of the cathedral),[8] no Exchequer Gate and no Close wall creating obstructions (Figs 5 and 6). A processional way was required because if the bishop was living in the annex then the elaborate treatment of the west front of the cathedral would have reflected the important function it performed for the bishop's ceremonial entry.[9]

The transference of the see had a significantly strategic motive for the bishop owed sixty knights' fees, forty-three of

which had been enfeoffed by 1135, and probably twenty of which formed the main part of the Lincoln castle guard.[10] The bishop's special relationship with these knights that he provided for the king is demonstrated by a writ of 1130-33 allowing Bishop Alexander to transfer a third of the king's knights (that is those in the castle) to his own newly-erected castle at Newark, as if they were his own knights.[11] If he had been living with them in the castle this anomaly would be at once intelligible.

In 1130-33 – that is at more or less the same time – Bishop Alexander was authorised to occupy the Roman East Gate and the tower over it (*portam de Estegate cum turri*).[12] This was in effect a sort of keep so he would have been moving from one castle to another, since we can hardly assume that he would have had two 'palaces' within the Close at the same time, and the charter of the 1140s leaves no doubt that he was not then in the castle. He built three other castles on his manors which is a fair indication of his interests. The site north of a non-monastic cathedral was not a usual one for a bishop's palace and Bishop Alexander was authorised by King Stephen in 1137 to construct a house south of the upper town wall through which he was permitted to make an *introitus* to reach the cathedral.[13] As a fuller grant or confirmation was made by Henry II to his successor, Bishop Robert II in 1157, it is not clear when the actual move was made.

This may be contrasted with the *exitus*, allowed by a writ of Henry I to Ranulf le Meschines, Osbert the Sheriff and Picot (the other provider of castle guard) authorising Bishop Bloet to make a gateway through the wall 'of my Castle' provided the wall was not weakened. It was to be done at his own expense[14] and he seems to be treated almost like a repairing tenant and no right of way is mentioned, which one would expect if he was going to treat the castle as a

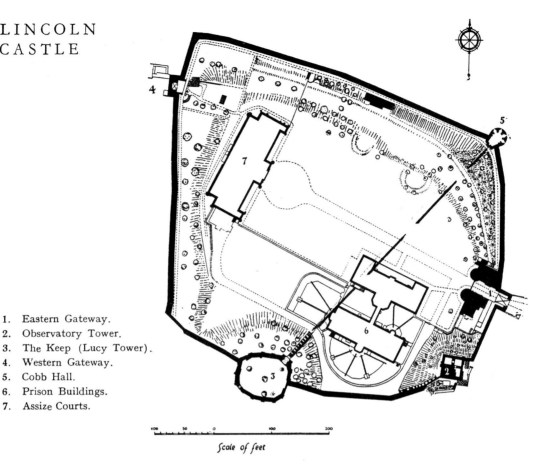

LINCOLN
CASTLE

1. Eastern Gateway.
2. Observatory Tower.
3. The Keep (Lucy Tower).
4. Western Gateway.
5. Cobb Hall.
6. Prison Buildings.
7. Assize Courts.

Scale of feet

Fig.3. Plan of castle with broken line showing suggested course of eastern side of castle as designed in 1068 (Lincolnshire County Council plan).

thoroughfare. As this writ is the main positive evidence for believing that the bishop was living in the castle and it is a short one it is worth quoting in full:

> H. rex Anglie. Rannulfo Meschino. Osberto vicecomiti et Picoto filio Colsueni. et omnibus baronibus suis de Lincolnia. salutem. Sciatis me concessisse Roberto episcopo Lincolnie ut faciat exitus in muro castelli mei ad sua necessaria facienda ad domum suam. Ita tamen ne murum propter hoc debilitetur. Testibus. Alano de. Linc. et Osberto vicecomite. apud Lundonias.

The editor dates it 1101-15. To construct a gate with external bridge over a large ditch is a major operation and since there was a perfectly good gate into the town it must mean an exit to the country outside; I see no reason to doubt that the present West Gate was the result. The Latin only makes good sense if '*ad domum suam*' is referring to a house already in the castle. At other cathedrals the palace of the bishop was always within the Close and Foster's suggestion that the bishop lived in his '*maneriolum*' outside and commuted so to speak is difficult to sustain.[15] It was intended surely, and the form of the existing West Gate implies it, that the bishop should have a dignified entry without having to pass through the Close.

A medieval bishop of Lincoln had perhaps a dozen or more houses on his manors between which he constantly travelled only occasionally visiting the see palace. He required an external entry and most other see palaces had one. Indeed an elaborate second gateway such as the West Gate at Lincoln Castle tends to confirm that the castle has been a bishop's palace, since one would not expect to find such a handsome second gateway in a layman's castle.

Another puzzle at Lincoln is the long delay between the Conquest and the 1130s before the creation of the earldom. It must have been contemplated from an early stage since *Domesday Book* refers to an earl that did not yet exist.[16] Stenton thought that the clerk was making provision for an earl when one was created. At Durham the bishop moved into the royal castle, which became his permanent residence, only when Earl Waltheof had been executed by William I.[17] The bishop could not exercise the earl's powers if there was an earl, and so conversely there could not be an earl while the bishop was exercising some of an earl's powers by living in the castle. That Henry I saw the bishop to some extent in that light is suggested by the writ at the beginning of his reign when his brother Robert was threatening to claim the throne.[18] The writ is addressed to the bishop first and then the royal officers in the castle as if the bishop fell in some sense into the same category. It guaranteed their rights and privileges but required them to take an oath of allegiance to him. When the bishop was moved out of the castle to the East Gate in the 1130s the way was clear for the creation of an earl; Stephen appointed William de Roumare, a son by her third husband of the Countess Lucy, as earl of Lincoln in 1141.[19]

The question of whether the first bishops lived in the castle is not solely academic for, if my proposal is right, it resolves several very difficult problems of the castle's early history. However, it is time to return to more solid survivals and reconsider the sequence of development of the various parts of the castle.

Fig.4. *Drawing in Gentleman's Magazine in 1836 showing Roman West Gate before its collapse and Norman West Gate.*

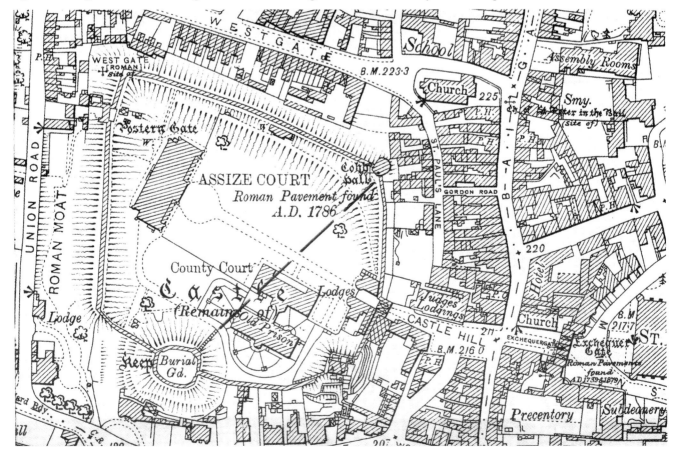

Fig.5. *Part of OS 1907 25in. sheet showing castle with earthworks, the supposed 1068 castle bank and the later East Gate facing the west end of the cathedral with later medieval obstructions between.*

Fig.6. Aerial view of castle from west showing Lucy tower on right, Cobb Hall tower on left, back of the East Gate and the west front of the cathedral (Cambridge University Collection of Air Photographs: copyright reserved).

The 1068 castle consisted of the motte beneath Lucy's tower with an attached bailey, formed of straight banks, roughly triangular in shape with acute angles at the Roman West Gate and the present site of the Cobb Hall tower. The huge earthworks must have been enlarged more than once and the Roman gate was presumably buried when the annex was added probably in the 1070s. The stone East Gate would be an original part of the addition as also a motte at the south-east corner beneath the present Observatory tower. The authority for the bishop to build the West Gate (assuming it is correctly identified) refers to the castle wall so it must have existed by *c.*1110 at least on the north and west sides (with herring-bone masonry). It was set on top of a wooden palette of criss-cross timbers.[20] Possibly the original east wall was built of stone. The West Gate followed shortly after 1100 and, not long after, Lucy's Tower, the shell keep. The elusive Countess Lucy who died in *c.*1136 had as her third husband Ranulf Meschines, earl of Chester and hence her title. We have the authority of Stephen's charter that she built or strengthened a tower and so the shell keep might be say *c.*1125 in what I would regard as the king's part of the castle.[21]

The lack of communication between the wall-walk on the east side and the shell keep puzzled King in the eighteenth century,[22] and it is possible that the annex was not yet walled. The structure on top of the Observatory tower motte was rebuilt presumably as a consequence of Stephen's twelfth-century charter and yet again in its present form in the fourteenth century. The Cobb Hall tower is an impressive horseshoe-shaped building with fine vaults probably to be identified with royal works in 1200.[23] The postulated division

separating the annex had perhaps been swept away before this in the works of 1190 on the defences.[24]

Much of this sequence is only controlled guesswork and clearly large missing parts can only be resolved by excavation. The postulated east side of the first castle needs checking by a section north of the prison. Where were the domestic buildings? There would be two sets on the theory suggested here, king's and bishop's. What is the real sequence in the huge earthworks, so distinctive a feature of the castle which rendered any normal lay-out of domestic buildings impossible? The motte below Lucy's tower may hold evidence on the original super-structure and its date. Recent excavations on the motte below the Observatory tower have yielded some very puzzling results.

Nicholas Reynolds in the early 1970s dug within the tower.[25] He found an inner masonry face descending with offsets below the present one and becoming increasingly irregular as it descended (Fig.7). This was filled up with a 'core' of rubble, deliberately laid and, in the excavator's view, of the same date as the enclosing wall face. The 'core' seemed to pass under the face at one point but if this had fallen in it would be quite indistinguishable from the 'core'. If there was a rock-cut well at the bottom and parts of the masonry fell away, as in the huge shaft at Farnham in the centre of the motte,[26] it might look like this in the upper levels (Fig.8). The excavation only reached a depth of 2.4 metres (8 feet) so it may not have reached an earlier motte, let alone the original ground surface. It was too unsafe to proceed but without a full section and the horizontal dimensions of the original

27

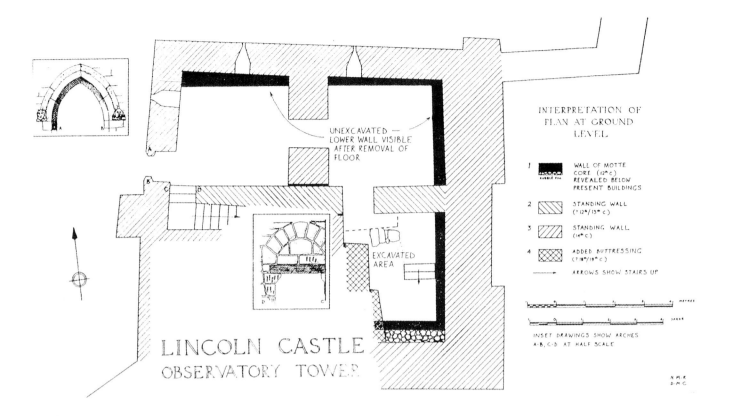

*Fig.7. Plan by N. Reynolds of top of shaft excavated by him in Observatory tower (*Medieval Archaeology, 19 (1975), p.202).

structure no real interpretation is possible. The twelfth-century pottery in the 'core' might belong to a deliberate filling of an abandoned collapsed well. We do have the information in the charter of Stephen that two *turres* already existed in the 1140s and so the earliest motte would be much earlier, even of Remigius, forming the bishop's *donjon*, as I have suggested.[27]

Dr Dorothy Owen has written: 'The site of the first bishop's dwelling in Lincoln is something of a mystery';[28] if the suggestion put forward here is right this would no longer be true. There is more conjecture than one would wish and circumstantial evidence is never conclusive so it may prove to be wrong. Nevertheless at Lincoln Castle we are short of a working framework or hypothesis either to knock down or confirm.

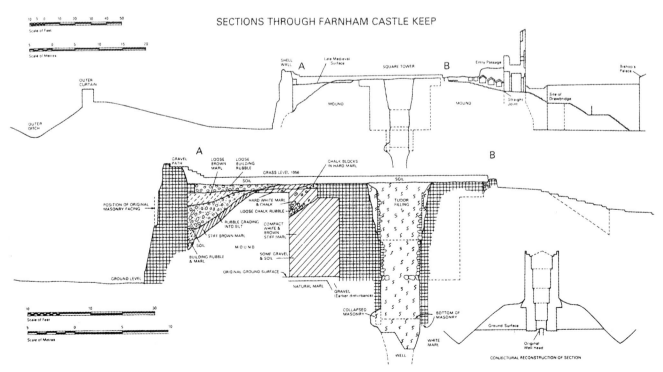

Fig.8. Section, plan and reconstruction of well shaft and tower above found at Farnham Castle, Surrey (M. W. Thompson).

Summary chronology

It may be helpful to draw up a summary chronology of events as envisaged in this paper.

1068. The castle was ordered by the Conqueror to be erected in the south-west corner of the upper Roman town, the Baile. It comprised a motte, with a bailey to the north, with corners on the Roman West Gate and the present site of Cobb Hall tower.

1072. The See was transferred from Dorchester-on-Thames to Lincoln and the cathedral started in the south-east corner of the Baile.

An annex with its own motte was added to the east side of the castle to house the bishop. The Roman West gate, if used, was now abandoned and buried under a bank.

1080s. The west end of the cathedral was constructed, acting as a terminal for a processional way from the East Gate of the castle. The castle curtain wall was erected on a wooden mattress on an earlier bank.

c.1110. Bishop Bloet was authorised to construct the new West Gate that still exists.

c.1125. Lucy Tower, a shell keep, was built on the western motte.

c.1130. Bishop Alexander was authorised to occupy the Roman East Gate tower.

Knights were transferred from the royal castle at Lincoln to the bishop's castle at Newark.

1137-57. The Roman wall south of the south transept was broken through and the palace (*domus*) erected on its present site.

c.1141. The first Earl of Lincoln was created.

1140s. A collapsing well at the centre of the eastern motte was filled in by the earl and the tower was constructed; it was reconstructed in the fourteenth century.

1160. The East Hall of the palace was constructed.

c.1200. The later West Hall was built.

c.1200. Cobb Hall tower was erected in the castle and the dividing wall in the castle removed.

c.1300. A Porch and door for the bishop was built on the south transept.

1316, 1318 Licences to crenellate[29] for the construction of the Close wall and its subsequent raising, so that the castle was completely cut off from the cathedral.

Notes

1. G. T. Clark, *Medieval Military Architecture in England* (1884), ii, p.197.
2. W. Farrer, *The Lancashire Pipe Rolls* (Liverpool, 1912), pp.367-68.
3. J. W. F. Hill, 'Lincoln Castle: the Constables and the Guard', *Associated Architectural Societies' Reports and Papers*, 40 pt 1 (1930), pp.1-14, esp. pp.5-8; J. W. F. Hill, *Medieval Lincoln* (Cambridge, 1948), pp.82-89.
4. *The Ecclesiastical History of Orderic Vitalis*, edited by M. Chibnall, 6 vols (Oxford, 1969-80), ii, p.218.
5. *The Anglo-Saxon Chronicle*, edited by G. N. Garmondsway (1953), p.202
6. *Giraldi Cambrensis, Opera*, edited by J. F. Dimock (Rolls Series, 1877), vii, pp.14-75; *William of Malmesbury, De Gestis Pontificum Anglicanum*, edited by N. Hamilton (Rolls Series, 1870), pp.312-13.
7. *Symeonis Monachi Opera Omnia*, edited by T. Arnold, 2 vols (Rolls Series, 1882-85), ii, p.219.
8. *Giraldi Cambrensis*, ed. Dimock, pp.193-94.
9. F. Saxl, 'Lincoln cathedral: the eleventh century design for the West front', *Archaeological Journal*, 103 (1947), pp.105-18.
10. Hill, 'Lincoln Castle: the Constables and the Guard', pp.4-6.
11. *The Registrum Antiquissimum of the Cathedral Church of Lincoln*, edited by C. W. Foster and K. Major, 10 vols (Lincoln Record Society, 1931-73), i, p.35, no.51.
12. *Ibid.*, p.34, no.49.
13. *Ibid.*, pp.54, no.87; pp.86-87, no.137.
14. *Ibid.*, pp.20-21, no.21.
15. *Ibid.*, p.268.
16. *The Lincolnshire Domesday and the Lindsey Survey*, edited by C. W. Foster and Thomas Longley, Lincoln Record Society, 19 (Horncastle, 1924), p.xxxi.
17. M. W. Thompson, 'The place of Durham among Norman episcopal palaces and castles', in *Anglo-Norman Durham 1093-1193*, edited by D. Rollason, M. Harvey and N. Prestwich (Woodbridge, 1995), pp.427-36.
18. *Registrum Antiquissimum*, p.47, no.73.
19. G. E. Cokayne, *The Complete Peerage of England, Scotland, Ireland . . .*, revised edition by V. Gibbs *et al.*, 13 vols (1910-59), vii, 668-69.
20. Clark, *Medieval Military Architecture*, ii, pp.196-97.
21. Hill, *Medieval Lincoln*, pp.86-95.
22. E. King, 'Observations on ancient castles', *Archaeologia*, vi (1782), pp.261-65.
23. R. A. Brown, H. M. Colvin and A. J. Taylor, *The History of the King's Works*, volume II, *The Middle Ages* (1963), pp.704-05.
24. *Ibid.*, ii, p.704.
25. N. Reynolds, 'Investigations in the Observatory Tower, Lincoln Castle', *Medieval Archaeology*, 19 (1975), pp.201-05.
26. M. W. Thompson, 'Recent excavations in the keep of Farnham castle Surrey', *Medieval Archaeology*, 4 (1960), pp.81-94.
27. Farrer, *The Lancashire Pipe Rolls*, pp.367-68.
28. D. M. Owen, 'Historical survey, 1091-1450', in *A History of Lincoln Minster*, edited by D. M. Owen (Cambridge, 1994), p.123.
29. *Calendar of Patent Rolls*, 1316, p.436; 1318, p.257.

Urban Castles and Late Anglo-Saxon Towns

David Parsons

Introduction

The purpose of this paper is to discuss some late Anglo-Saxon fortified towns, precursors of the urban castle of the Norman period, and the way in which motte and bailey structures were superimposed on them after the Conquest. Selected sites in southern and midland England will be discussed in some detail to illustrate the historical context of the development of the castle at Lincoln and to provide topographical parallels for it. The underlying premise is that for at least two centuries before the Norman Conquest the basic unit of defence was the town: the erection of urban castles as an addition to existing fortified towns or as an alternative to 'whole town' fortifications represented more a change of emphasis than a totally new departure.

Towns as fortresses: documentary evidence

The earliest systematic evidence that towns played a significant part in military strategy in England is given by the *Anglo-Saxon Chronicle* in several entries for the Alfredian period. The first reference occurs, indeed, in the reign of King Alfred's brother and predecessor Æthelberht (king of Wessex 860-66), when in an unspecified year 'a great pirate host landed and stormed Winchester'.[1] In 866 the Vikings occupied York, and on 21 March the Northumbrian levies stormed the city, but despite forcing an entry suffered heavy losses and were compelled to make peace (*s.a.*867). The following year the Vikings over-wintered in Nottingham; a combined force of Mercians and West Saxons approached the fortification, but 'there was no serious engagement' and a peace was concluded (*s.a.*868). In 874 three kings with 'a great host' left Repton for Cambridge, where they remained for a year (*s.a.*875). It is implied, rather than stated, that they occupied the town itself. Meanwhile, in Wessex, the Vikings got into Wareham, where they were evidently besieged by an Anglo-Saxon force; the following year, under cover of a peace agreement, they evaded the English and occupied Exeter (*s.a.*876). King Alfred pursued them, but could not overtake them before they were 'in the fortress where they could not be got at' (*s.a.*877). In 884 a Viking army, after some continental adventures, besieged Rochester, which the inhabitants defended until Alfred came to their relief the following year (*s.a.*885). Two years later Alfred himself occupied London and put the ealdorman Æthelred in charge of it (*s.a.*886). In 893 Exeter was again the target of a Danish force, which besieged it, and once more King Alfred came to the rescue; in the same year Chester, a 'deserted Roman site' was taken by the Vikings, and the English besieged the town for two days, pursuing something of a scorched earth policy:

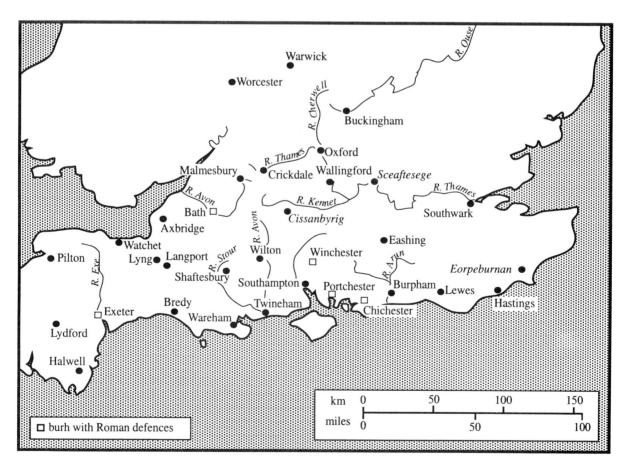

Fig. 1. Location of the Burghal Hidage forts. (Source: N. P. Brooks. 'The unidentified forts of the Burghal Hidage', Medieval Archaeology, 8 (1964), pp.74-90, Fig.21.)

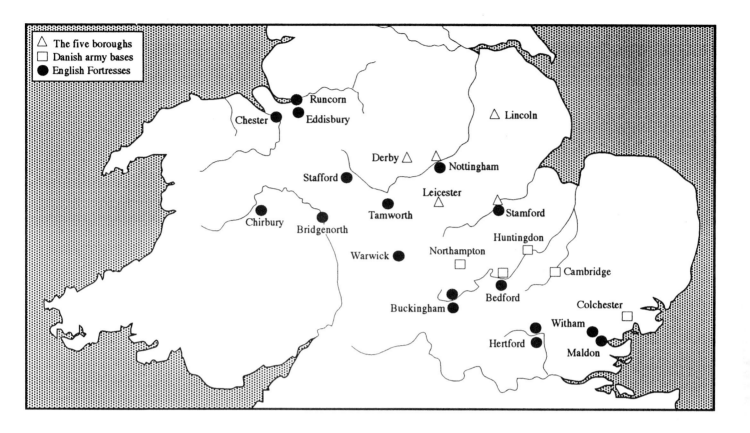

Fig.2. Location of Mercian forts and fortified towns in the early tenth century (After Wainwright 'Æthelflæd, Lady of the Mercians' (as note 9), Fig.2).

they 'seized all the cattle in the vicinity ... burnt up all the corn, and with their horses ate all the neighbourhood bare' (*s.a.*894). During the campaigns of the first quarter of the tenth century, Æthelflæd, Lady of the Mercians, captured Derby, but at the cost of four thegns, who lost their lives 'within the gates', and in the following year took Leicester 'by peaceful means' (*s.aa.*917, 918 (version C)). Subsequently Edward the Elder occupied Nottingham and repaired the defences; two years later he built a second fortification on the south bank of the river, connecting it to the first with a bridge (*s.aa.*922, 924), having previously erected a second fort at Stamford, though there is no mention of a bridge in this instance (*s.a.*922). The list of Edwardian and Æthelflædan fortifications could be further extended from the *Chronicle* record (for example, Buckingham and Towcester), though it is a moot point whether the more minor sites like these were truly urban; this objection could also be held to apply to some of the towns mentioned above, for instance Derby. Nevertheless, the general point is clear: urban or proto-urban sites were regarded as the unit of defence and the tactical targets of the Viking forces.

A similar pattern emerges in the course of the renewed Danish invasions in the late tenth and early eleventh centuries. In 997 (*s.a.*) the Danish army harried south Wales and the West Country, making two Burghal Hidage forts[2] a particular target: at Watchet they 'wrought great havoc by burning and killing people' and at Lydford they similarly 'burned and slew everything they met'. Two years later a 'sharp encounter' resulted in the capture of Rochester. In 1003 (*s.a.*) two more Burghal Hidage towns were the subject of the Danes' attentions: Exeter and Wilton. The first was 'utterly laid waste' and the latter burnt to the ground, after which the Danish army moved on to Salisbury. This was long before the foundation

of the modern town and the Danes' objective must have been Old Sarum, a former Iron-Age hillfort.[3] Thetford and Norwich, the episcopal, and thus by implication urban, successors of North Elmham, were looted and burnt down in 1004, while Wallingford, another Burghal Hidage fort, suffered the same fate two years later. So did Oxford in 1009, following unsuccessful attacks on Canterbury and London. In the next year Thetford was burnt once again and Cambridge, which a century before had been a Viking stronghold, was similarly destroyed. Then in September 1011, after a three-week siege, the Danes occupied Canterbury, capturing Ælfheah (Alphege) the archbishop, the story of whose subsequent martyrdom, burial at St Paul's, London, and eventual restoration to Canterbury is well known.[4]

The fortified towns of Wessex

This rehearsal of the catalogue of attacks on towns is not to deny the frequency of pitched battles in the open countryside or at sea, but to demonstrate that towns were an important factor in military campaigns of the later Anglo-Saxon period. The strategic significance of the fortified town in pre-Conquest warfare was recognised, if not actually brought about, by the provisions of the document known as the Burghal Hidage (Fig.1). The earliest surviving text appears to date from the reign of Edward the Elder (899-924), but it is widely accepted that the arrangements it describes are likely to have been introduced by Alfred the Great.[5] The Hidage gives details of a defensive system largely confined to the Kingdom of Wessex, in which the unit of defence was the *burh* or fortified town,[6] whose hinterland was assessed to determine its contribution to the maintenance and defence – and perhaps the original construction, in some cases – of the surrounding

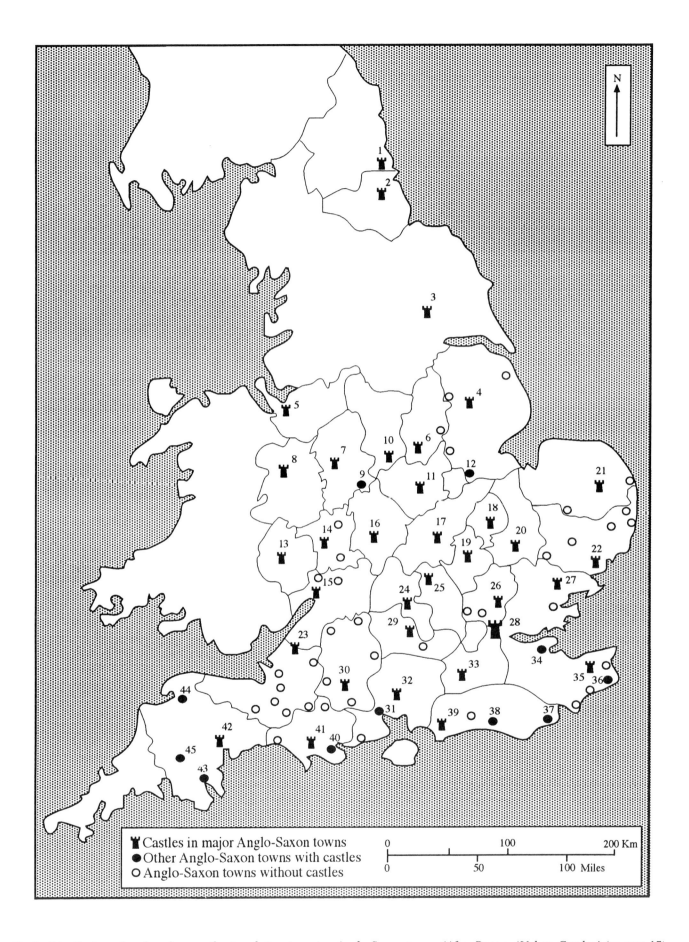

Fig.3a.Distribution of early urban castles in relation to major Anglo-Saxon towns (After Drage, 'Urban Castles' (as note 17),
    Fig.52).

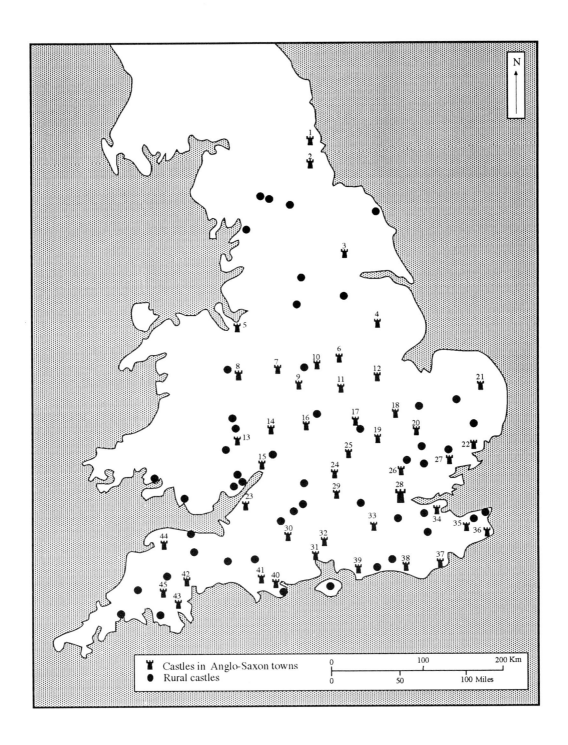

Fig.3b.Distribution of early urban castles in relation to contemporary castles in rural locations (After Drage, 'Urban Castles' (as note 17), Fig.54).

KEY FOR FIGS 3a and b

1. Newcastle, 2. Durham, 3. York, 4. Lincoln, 5. Chester, 6. Nottingham, 7. Stafford, 8. Shrewsbury, 9. Tamworth, 10. Derby, 11. Leicester, 12. Stamford, 13. Hereford, 14. Worcester, 15. Gloucester, 16. Warwick, 17. Northampton, 18. Huntingdon, 19. Bedford, 20. Cambridge, 21. Norwich, 22. Ipswich, 23. Bristol, 24. Oxford, 25. Buckingham, 26. Hertford, 27. Colchester, 28. London, 29. Wallingford, 30. Old Sarum, 31. Southampton, 32. Winchester, 33. Guildford, 34. Rochester, 35. Canterbury, 36. Dover, 37. Hastings, 38. Lewes, 39. Chichester, 40. Wareham, 41. Dorchester, 42. Exeter, 43. Totnes, 44. Barnstaple, 45. Lydford

rampart and ditch. Where these still survive, there is often a close correlation between the length of the defensive circuit and the calculated footage based on the Hidage assessment. In the case of Winchester, for example, the correspondence is particularly close.[7] Towns such as Winchester and Exeter, along with such smaller sites as Portchester, had masonry walls from the beginning, since they reused the existing Roman defences. In other cases, for example Burpham and Lydford, ramparts appear to have been built specifically to make the sites defensible. Towards the end of the Anglo-Saxon period ramparts were being replaced by stone walls, for example in Oxford and Wareham.[8] In some towns, such as Wareham, Wallingford, Oxford and once again Winchester, part of the internal street pattern survives to bear witness to the fairly sophisticated planning of such fortified centres (see below and Figs 4 and 5).

Urban defences north of the Thames

A defensive system similar to that of Wessex was developed in the Midlands during the tenth century, when it was used in a strategic manner against the Viking armies in the reconquest of the Danelaw by Edward the Elder and his sister Æthelflæd. The beginnings of this development can be seen already in the Burghal Hidage. The earliest surviving version of this document includes the Mercian towns of Oxford and Buckingham, which did not come under the control of the West Saxon king until 911 and 914 respectively. Their inclusion in what is essentially a West Saxon document shows that the system established in Wessex was being extended into the south Midlands at this time. The surviving medieval

manuscript versions of the Hidage also add, as an appendix to the main list, Warwick and Worcester, which lay even deeper in Mercian territory. Evidence for further fortified towns in Mercia comes from another document known as the Mercian Register, parts of which were incorporated into the *Anglo-Saxon Chronicle*. As long ago as 1959 F. T. Wainwright drew attention to the significance of these towns in the recovery of the Danelaw by the English.[9] Most of the identifiable places (shown but not named in Wainwright's figure 2) lay in a double line close to or behind the established frontier with the Danelaw, placed to confront the equivalent Viking fortresses to the north and east of it (Fig.2). The line stretched from Maldon and Witham in Essex to the neck of the Wirral peninsula. This 'fortress system had ... an offensive value'[10] and was instrumental in the reconquest of the Danelaw. Town defences now had a more positive and strategic military role. In two cases, at Hertford and Buckingham, pairs of forts were established on either side of the river, presumably with a bridge between them, an arrangement for which there are Carolingian parallels on the continent. The plan of the later castle at Hertford and its surroundings suggests very strongly the layout of its late Anglo-Saxon predecessor: a roughly circular area divided by the river, as shown in a map published by Turnor,[11] could represent two D-shaped enclosures with the river forming the straight side of each. Single examples of such enclosures are known at Repton and elsewhere. Bedford is another example of paired fortifications with a river between them, but here the English fort occupied one side of the river and its Danish counterpart the other. In other cases the spatial relationship between English and Danish fortresses is less close.

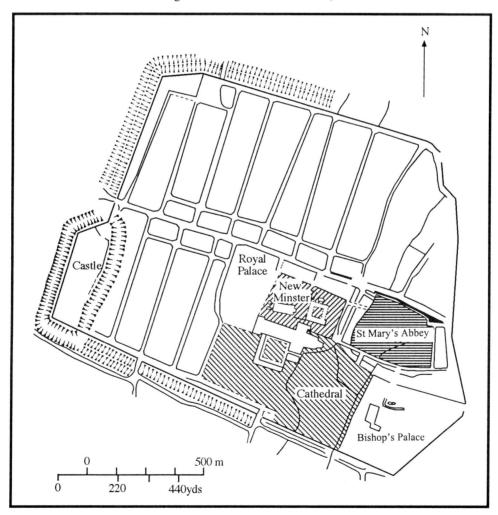

Fig.4. Plan of Winchester, c.1100, showing Anglo-Saxon street pattern and site of Norman castle (Source: Biddle, ed., Winchester in the Early Middle Ages *(as note 7), Fig.26).*

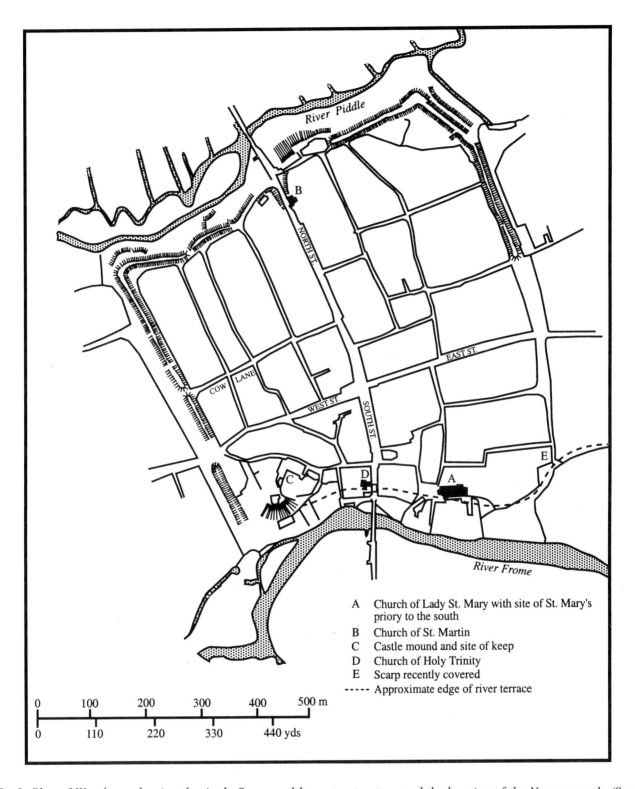

Fig.5. Plan of Wareham, showing the Anglo-Saxon and later street pattern and the location of the Norman castle (Source: RCHME 'Wareham West Walls' (as note 24), Fig.46).

Of these post-Alfredian fortified towns, some – like a number of West Saxon *burhs* – developed out of Roman walled towns, for example Worcester and Gloucester in English Mercia. Rather more of the fortifications on the Danish side of the frontier had Roman origins: Colchester, Cambridge, Leicester and Lincoln. The remaining towns on either side of Watling Street were post-Roman creations, surrounded by ramparts and ditches rather than stone walls. They are less well attested archaeologically than those in Wessex, though rescue excavations in the late 1960s identified part of the rampart and an entrance to the Edwardian town of Tamworth,[12]

and comparable discoveries have been made in the ensuing thirty years in other Mercian towns. These include Hereford, a town not involved in the Edward/Æthelflæd campaigns of the 910s,[13] and Northampton, one of the Viking centres, where excavation in early 1996 revealed for the first time a section of the pre-Conquest and medieval defences on the south-west of the town and adjacent to the motte-and-bailey castle.[14] A recent evaluation of all the information relating to Northampton castle includes archaeological evidence for the superimposition of the castle on the Saxo-Norman town.[15] The defensive circuits of these towns typically consisted of a

35

rampart and ditch, with internal timber structures shaping and stabilising the rampart, as for example at Tamworth.

The superimposition of castles after the Norman Conquest

By the end of the Anglo-Saxon period a considerable number of such forts and towns with defensive circuits had come into being. In their paper on urban defences Jones and Bond list 124 sites; of these 32 were of Roman origin; 68 were defended towns and 24 were forts of Anglo-Saxon or Anglo-Scandinavian origin.[16] All but a handful of these were located in England south of the Humber. Omitting the 24 burghal forts, dismissed by the authors as being 'of no later urban

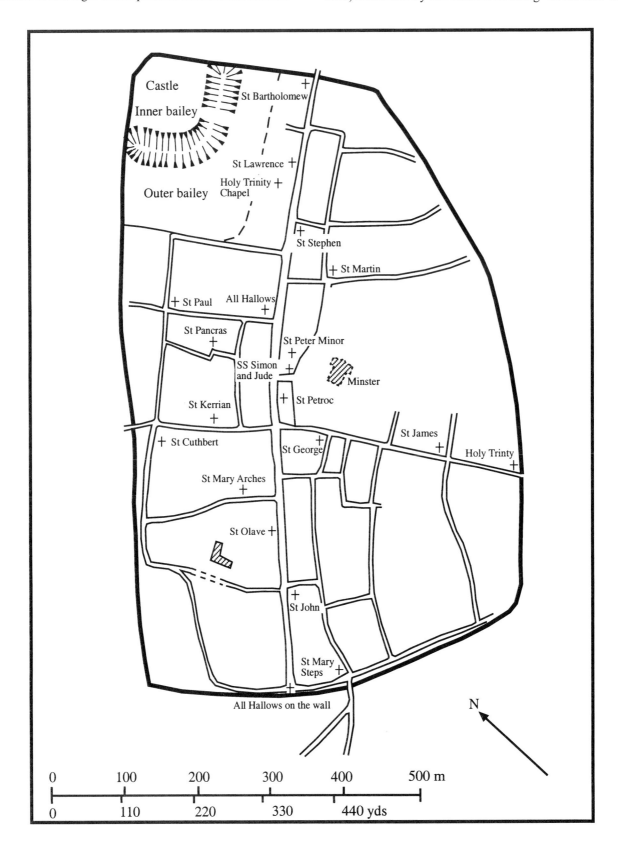

Fig.6. Plan of Exeter, showing the Anglo-Saxon and later street pattern and the location of the Norman castle (Source: Allan et al. 'Saxon Exeter' (as note 26), Fig.128).

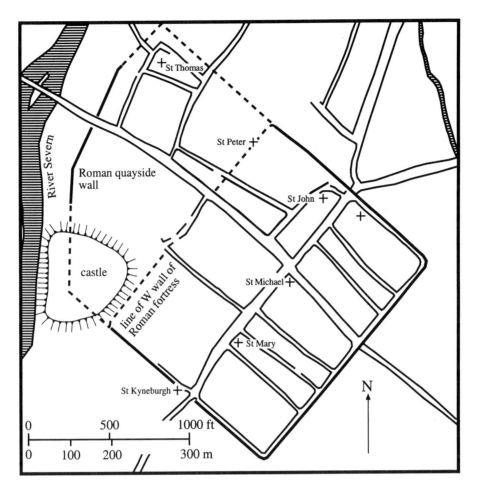

Fig.7. Plan of Gloucester, showing the Roman town, the Anglo-Saxon extension and the location of the Norman castle (Source: VCH Gloucestershire, 4 (as note 27), Figs 2 and 4).

significance', more than half of the pre-Conquest towns attracted a motte-and-bailey castle in the early Norman period. In an important paper in the same CBA Research Report, Drage discusses this development, noting that some of the earliest recorded Norman castles are to be found in an urban context.[17] He lists and maps forty-five castles in the principal pre-Conquest towns,[18] many of which later became county towns. In many cases these are the only pre-Conquest town in their respective counties to be furnished with a castle after the Conquest (Fig.3). The counties along the south coast, however, have two or more urban castles: two in Dorset and Hampshire, three in Kent and Sussex, and four in Devon. The area which was formerly Wessex is also notable for the number of Anglo-Saxon towns which did *not* acquire a Norman castle. Drage sees the urban castles as a distinct group, most of them of royal foundation, and their purpose as the domination of routes as well as the control of the inhabitants of the respective towns. Most important for the present purpose, however, is his recognition that urban castles were frequently located at the edge of the town, their 'peripheral location ... determined in part by the re-use of existing defences'.[19] He notes the abandonment of early mottes – Dane John at Canterbury and Boley Hill at Rochester – in favour of new sites just within the town defences, and the use of the corner of Roman defences in non-urban situations at Pevensey and Burgh Castle (to which Portchester might also be added) as evidence of the preference for this kind of position for the construction of castles in the post-Conquest period.

The erection of a motte and its attendant earthworks necessarily had a disruptive effect on the topography of a town. The destruction of houses and the displacement of their inhabitants is recorded in Domesday Book for eleven towns.

The number of houses or sites affected ranges from a mere four or five at Warwick and Stamford through figures in the teens and twenties at Canterbury, Gloucester, Norwich,[20] Huntingdon and Cambridge, to fifty-one in Shrewsbury and a massive 166 in Lincoln, the significance of which will be discussed below. In several other cases there is archaeological and topographical evidence for the effect of castle-building. In Norwich an Anglo-Saxon church and its cemetery appear to have been destroyed by the construction of the north-east bailey,[21] while excavations in Winchester revealed considerable destruction in the previously fully occupied quarter of the town, including the obliteration of a north-south street and part of the intramural street of the late Anglo-Saxon planned town,[22] though in this case there is no Domesday reference to the events (Fig.4). The disruption of the Anglo-Saxon street pattern and the realignment of the streets around the castle are clear from the plan of the town in the Norman period,[23] as well as from the present-day topography.

In towns where the pre-Conquest street pattern is well represented in the present-day topography the realignments caused by the imposition of a castle can be seen very clearly. At Wareham, Dorset, the interior of the town is divided into four unequal areas by the principal streets, which intersect at right angles a little to the south of the geometrical centre point of the town (Fig.5).[24] The north-western 'quarter', between West Street and North Street, preserves the Anglo-Saxon layout, with a back lane (Cow Lane) parallel to West Street, three north-south streets roughly parallel with North Street, and an intramural street inside the line of the ramparts. A similar pattern is faintly discernible in the two 'quarters' east of North and South Streets, but later developments in these areas have led to some adjustment of the Anglo-Saxon layout;

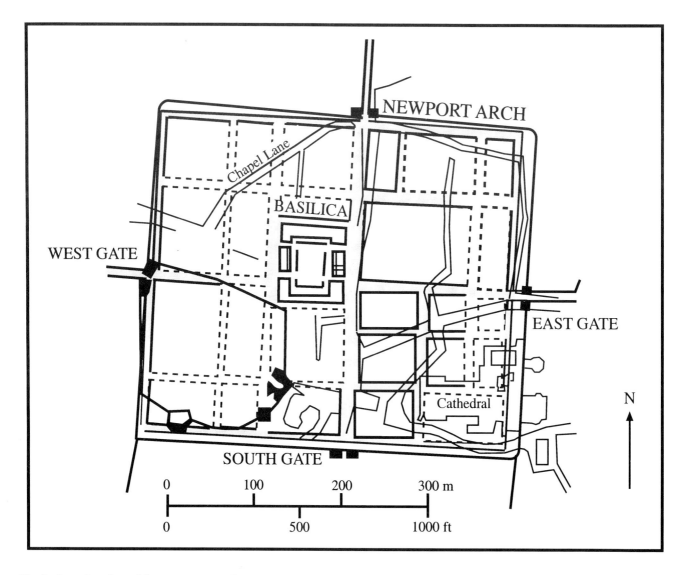

Fig.8. Lincoln: plan of the upper town, showing the site of the castle in relation to the Roman defences and street pattern; cathedral and modern streets shown in faint line (After J. S. Wacher, Towns of Roman Britain, *2nd edition (1995), Fig.57).*

nevertheless the present street pattern is still basically a rectilinear one. This is not true of the fourth 'quarter', which lies in the angle between West and South Streets. A small motte built in the south-west corner of the town has almost completely obliterated the pre-Conquest street pattern. Instead, the two main secondary streets in this area describe arcs of two circles concentric with the motte; the more northerly arc has in addition caused a minor deflection in the line of West Street. These streets probably represent the inner and outer lines of the castle defences. At all events, it is clear that the construction of the castle had a profound effect on the topography of the south-western 'quarter' of Wareham.

The evidence at Wallingford, in the historic county of Berkshire, is comparable, though the detail of the Anglo-Saxon street pattern is less well established. In the south-east quarter of the town a grid of streets survives, which may represent substantially the pre-Conquest layout. In the south-west quarter little remains, though the west side of the market may follow the line of an original back street. The north-west quarter was largely occupied by a Benedictine priory in the Middle Ages, but is now mostly open, and with one small exception no streets survive. In the north-east quarter a huge motte-and-bailey castle has obliterated not only any earlier streets but also the Anglo-Saxon defences on the north side, and possibly on the east as well. To the west, the castle site has encroached upon the northern end of the north-south axial

street (Castle Street), whose route has been diverted into the north-western quarter, where it makes use of what may have been the Anglo-Saxon back street. Excavations in 1966 and 1968 produced evidence of houses of tenth-century and later date which had been cut or forced to realign by the construction of the outer defences of the castle in the mid twelfth century. Parish boundaries within the town respect the east and south sides of the castle site.[25]

There is similar evidence at Exeter, a West Saxon *burh* of Roman origin, where the modern street pattern reflects several elements of the Anglo-Saxon layout (see Fig.6). The main axial streets are still clearly identifiable, and to a lesser extent several of the secondary streets and parts of the back lanes.[26] This pattern is all but obliterated by the castle, which occupies a significant area (about 40%) of the northern 'quarter', though short sections of the secondary streets are still recognisable and the line of the back lane can be suggested with some confidence.

Outside Wessex similar evidence occurs at Gloucester (Fig.7). As at Winchester and Exeter, the Anglo-Saxon town grew up within the walls of its Roman predecessor. To the south and east of Southgate and Northgate Streets, the axial route that runs from south-west to north-east, a street grid comparable with that at Wareham has survived in the present street plan, but little remains in the other half of the Roman enclosure. By the end of the tenth century the town had extended beyond the Roman north-west wall, and the Anglo-Saxon defences took in an irregular area, whose shape was largely determined by the course of the River Severn. After the Conquest a castle was built between the original western corner of the Roman town and the obtuse western angle of the Anglo-Saxon extension. The earlier topography of this part of Gloucester is unknown, and no Anglo-Saxon streets have been identified in the areas adjacent to the castle, namely the western half of the western quarter of the Roman town and the western part of the Anglo-Saxon extension.[27] The implication is that the construction of the castle was responsible here, as elsewhere, for the obliteration of the evidence for occupation in both the Anglo-Saxon and Roman periods.

Elsewhere north of the Thames such detailed evidence for the internal layout of towns does not exist, but in several cases it is possible to appreciate in more general terms how post-Conquest castles have affected the local topography. On the Danish side of Watling Street a number of towns, including Lincoln, had Roman predecessors. At Cambridge, before the town sprawled south and east across the river, the nucleus of the settlement was the Roman *Duroliponte*,[28] which covered an area on either side of the present road to Huntingdon and Ely to the north-west of St Giles's church.[29] An early castle, built in 1068, occupied much of the eastern half of the enclosed area; its motte was placed almost centrally in the south-eastern quarter and its remarkably rectilinear bailey spread across the east-west axial road into the north-eastern quarter.[30] Another Danelaw town with Roman origins, Leicester, was of sufficient importance to be counted as one of the Five Boroughs, though there is no firm archaeological evidence for its occupation during the Anglo-Scandinavian period.[31] The north, east and south walls of the Roman town were reused by the medieval town, however, which may argue for continued – if only partial – occupation through the Anglo-Saxon and Anglo-Scandinavian periods. The line of the western defences can only be conjectured, and the exact position of the south-western corner, where the Norman castle was built, cannot be determined. If the southern wall of the town and the conjectured line of the western defences are produced as straight lines, then the castle motte appears to have been built just outside the enclosed area, though much of the bailey lies inside the south-west corner of the town. It is possible, however, that the line of the western defences swung outwards, following the course of one of the branches of the River Soar. If this was the case, it would have intersected with the line of the southern wall at a point just under or even beyond the motte, so that the motte would have occupied the 'classic' corner position.[32]

Lincoln: the town and its castle (Fig.8)

The mention of the Danish Five Boroughs leads to a consideration of Lincoln itself and the topographical context for the castle erected after the Norman Conquest. Leicester is in fact a closely comparable example, with its Roman defences and its castle constructed in and around the south-west corner of the enclosed area. The other three Danish Boroughs do not, however, offer evidence which could throw any light on the development of Lincoln castle in the Norman period. Neither Stamford nor Nottingham has a Roman origin. Although nothing remains of the original castle at Stamford, its site lies close to the south-west corner of the Anglo-Scandinavian town. However, since the circuit of the town is poorly defined in archaeological terms, it is impossible to be certain whether the castle was outside or inside the enclosure.[33] It does not directly guard the present river crossing, which is true of some others of the castles discussed above, but it has been suggested that the original crossing – the eponymous ford – was immediately to the east of the castle site.[34] At Nottingham a new Norman town grew up to the west of the

pre-Conquest one, with which the castle has no direct relationship.[35] At the last of the Five Boroughs neither the Anglo-Saxon name for the settlement (Northworthy) nor the Danish name (Derby) suggests that the Roman Little Chester (*Derventio*) was reoccupied, though some Anglo-Scandinavian material has been discovered during excavation outside the fort. It is impossible to make any firm statement about the topography of the pre-Conquest town, and no Norman castle appears to have been constructed there.[36]

Apart from Leicester, then, the territory of the Five Boroughs does not provide instructive *comparanda* for Lincoln and its castle. The closest parallels lie further south, mainly in English Mercia or Wessex. The southern Danelaw towns of Roman origin are not strictly comparable; at Cambridge the castle does not occupy a corner site in the strict sense, while at Colchester the keep has a much more central position in the town, and although the outer bailey is contained by the town wall it is well away from the nearest (north-eastern) corner.[37] Just across Watling Street in English Mercia, the castle at Towcester lies to the north-east of the present town centre, but its relation to the Edwardian *burh* and that of the *burh* to the Roman town are problematic. Farther west, Gloucester is more closely comparable with Lincoln, though it is not a 'classic' example because of the expansion of the town beyond its Roman walls before the superimposition of the castle. South of the Thames, Canterbury is a possible example, though the polygonal plan of its defences makes the position of its castle less relevant to the Lincoln situation. The closest comparative examples are undoubtedly Winchester and Exeter, which have been discussed above, and Chichester, where something of the Anglo-Saxon topography can be reconstructed from the present street pattern. The castle occupies the classic position in the north-east corner of the enclosure, obliterating the earlier street pattern in the familiar way.[38]

The castle at Lincoln occupies a position analogous to those of the three southern examples just cited, but exceptionally incorporates the west gate of the Roman town in its own defensive circuit (Fig.8). The evidence of Domesday Book clearly indicates that its construction caused a major disruption, but this has not yet been demonstrated archaeologically. The extent of the disruption must have been far greater than that in any other town, according to the Domesday record. The number of houses affected in Lincoln, 166, is more than three times the next largest number (51) at Shrewsbury. These figures have to be taken seriously. In most cases they are not round numbers, which makes it difficult to dismiss them as 'formulaic' (*pace* Jones and Donel elsewhere in this volume), and Domesday Book, as a fiscal document, had an interest in numerical accuracy. If Michael Thompson's interpretation of the extent of the first (1068) castle is correct (above pp.23-24) an extraordinary number of properties must have been crowded into a relatively small area. It seems hardly credible that, if the interior of the town had been so densely settled, archaeological evidence for it would have remained undiscovered. It may be that some, perhaps many, of the properties affected by the construction of the castle were outside the walls. As the paper by Jones and Donel (below, pp.43) makes clear, a great earth bank was added to the Roman defences on the west side of the town, and it is not unreasonable to postulate an extra-mural settlement here, which would have been buried by the bank. It is interesting to note Jones's suggestion that earlier structures may lie buried beneath the northern bank of the castle, though these will have been intra- rather than extra-mural.

There is also evidence for a post-Roman street running diagonally between the north and west gates, and another, between the west and south gates, is suspected (below, pp.43). If these streets date from the period of Anglo-Scandinavian occupation or, having been developed earlier, survived it, then the street pattern of Lincoln was totally at variance with that of the typical 'planned' town of southern England, such as Winchester or Wareham. To this extent Lincoln is unique among the former Roman towns resettled and refortified in the Anglo-Saxon period. With the 'modernisation' of the defences in the Norman period, however, Lincoln becomes more closely comparable with other fortified towns that had a Roman origin. The Roman wall forms the basis of the defensive circuit, and the castle is added in one corner; the motte (in the case of Lincoln, exceptionally two mottes) and bailey begin to influence the further development of the street pattern (for example, the course and position of Westgate). In the south-west quarter the castle arrested any further development of the town, which eventually transgressed its Roman bounds on the opposite (eastern) side as a result of the expansion of the cathedral. This episode of Lincoln's development belongs, however, to the ecclesiastical rather than to the military history of the town.

Notes

1. *s.a.*860; in most cases the years ascribed to the annals are not those of the (modern) calendar years in which the several events took place. Translations of Chronicle entries are taken from *The Anglo-Saxon Chronicle*, trans. G. N. Garmondsway (1953).

2. These were fortified towns or proto-urban settlements forming a defensive system in central southern and south-western England, which is documented by a text known as the 'Burghal Hidage'; see the description below and nn.5-6.

3. The *Chronicle* version of the place-name in this entry is *Searbyrig*, while MS A has *Searobyrg* in the annal for 552. In her edition of the *Chronicle* Dorothy Whitelock notes 'It is believed that references to *Searoburh* apply to Old Sarum, rather than the present Salisbury' (*The Anglo-Saxon Chronicle*, edited by D. Whitelock with D. C. Douglas and S. I. Tucker (1961), p.12, n.7). Quite apart from Old Sarum's revival as a fortified site, it is interesting to note that after the Norman Conquest it became a bishop's seat. Since the Council of Windsor in 1072 decreed that diocesan sees should be in towns, and removed bishoprics from rural centres such as North Elmham, it follows that Sarum must have been accorded urban status, presumably on the strength of its surviving prehistoric fortifications. The tendency to equate military and urban can be found as far back as Bede; see D. Parsons. *Books and Buildings*, Jarrow Lecture for 1987 (Jarrow, 1988), p.17.

4. See *Anglo-Saxon Chronicle, s.aa.*1012, 1023, and, for example, the discussion in D. Rollason, *Saints and Relics in Anglo-Saxon England* (Oxford, 1989), pp.158, 176.

5. A good summary description of the system attested by the Burghal Hidage is given by J. D. Richards, *Viking Age England* (1991), pp.52-55, with references to publications on specific sites on p.133; see also D. Hill, *An Atlas of Anglo-Saxon England* (Oxford, 1984), p.85 and Figs 147-53; and for a more detailed discussion of the document D. Hill, 'The Burghal Hidage: the establishment of a text', *Medieval Archaeology*, 13 (1969), pp.84-93. On the dating and attribution of the document see now D. N. Dumville, *Wessex and England from Alfred to Edgar* (Woodbridge, 1992), pp.24-27.

6. There is no exact equivalent in modern English for the word *burh*, which is variously translated as 'fort', 'fortress' or 'town', depending on context. Several of the *burhs* did not later develop as towns in the present sense of the word; the important point, however, is that the fortifications were associated with normal settlement sites in contrast to the later motte-and-bailey castles, which were specialist military installations, not themselves settlement sites and capable of existing independently of settlement. This distinction is obscured when 'fort' or 'fortress' is used to translate *burh*.

7. *Winchester in the Early Middle Ages: an edition and discussion of the Winton Domesday* edited by M. Biddle, Winchester Studies 1 (Oxford, 1976), pp.272-73.

8. For an overview of early towns in the southern counties of England, see J. Haslam, *Anglo-Saxon Towns in Southern England* (Chichester, 1984).

9. F. T. Wainwright, 'Æthelflæd, Lady of the Mercians', in *The Anglo-*

Saxons ...*, edited by P. Clemoes (1959), pp.53-69.

10. *Ibid.*, p.58.

11. *[Victoria] History of the County of Hertford*, vol.3, edited by W. Page (1912), facing p.490.

12. J. Gould, 'First report of the excavations at Tamworth, Staffs, 1967 – the Saxon defences', *Transactions of the Lichfield and South Staffordshire Archaeology and Natural History Society*, 9 (1967-68), pp.17-29; and 'Third report of the excavations at Tamworth, Staffs, 1968 – the western entrance to the Saxon borough', *Transactions of the Lichfield and South Staffordshire Archaeology and Natural History Society*, 10 (1968-69), pp.32-42.

13. R. Shoesmith, *Hereford City Excavations*, vol.2: *excavations on and close to the defences* (1982).

14. A. Chapman, 'Excavation of the Town Defences at Green Street, Northampton, 1995-6', *Northamptonshire Archaeology*, 28 (1998-99), pp.25-60.

15. B. L. Giggins, 'Northampton's Forgotten Castle', (unpublished MA dissertation, University of Leicester, 1999), p.80.

16. M. J. Jones and C. J. Bond, 'Urban defences', in *Urban Archaeology in Britain* edited by J. Schofield and R. Leech, CBA Research Report No.61 (1987), pp.81-116; see lists A to F, pp.95-98, and Fig.45 on p.93.

17. C. Drage, 'Urban Castles', in *Urban Archaeology in Britain* edited by J. Schofield and R. Leech, CBA Research Report No.61 (1987), pp.117-32; on castles generally, see now O. H. Creighton, *Castles and Landscapes* (2002), chapter 7, esp. pp.139-51, is particularly relevant to the subject of this paper.

18. *Ibid.*, Fig.52 with key on p.119.

19. *Ibid.*, p.119.

20. Ninety-eight properties are described as being *in occupatione castelli*, though this does not necessarily imply that they were all destroyed.

21. B. Ayers, *Excavations within the north-east Bailey of Norwich Castle, 1979*, East Anglian Archaeology, no.28 (Dereham, 1985).

22. M. Biddle, ed., *Winchester in the Early Middle Ages*, pp.302-03.

23. The late eleventh-century and twelfth-century town and its castle are shown in varying degrees of detail *ibid.*, Fig.26 facing p.470, Fig.27 facing p.489 and Fig.32 facing p.558.

24. Royal Commission on Historical Monuments (England), 'Wareham West Walls', *Medieval Archaeology*, 3 (1959), pp.120-38; plan of the town Fig.46 on p.121.

25. G. Astill, 'The Towns of Berkshire', in Haslam, *Anglo-Saxon Towns in Southern England*, pp.53-86. Wallingford is discussed on pp.73-79, with a plan of the town, Fig.29, on p.75. The excavations are briefly reported in the Medieval Britain sections of *Medieval Archaeology*, 11 (1967), p.284, and 13 (1969), p.255.

26. J. Allan, C. Henderson and R. Higham, 'Saxon Exeter', in Haslam, *Anglo-Saxon Towns in Southern England*, pp.385-411, esp. Fig.128.

27. *[Victoria County] History of Gloucestershire*, vol.4, edited by N. M. Herbert (1988), pp.8, 245; plan of town *c*.1000, Fig.2 on p.6; plan of town with castle *c*.1500, Fig.4 on p.68.

28. For this form of the name, rather than the *Durolipons* of the older literature, see A. L. F. Rivet and C. Smith, *Place-names of Roman Britain* (1979), pp.351-52.

29. The location of the church just outside the likely position of the Roman south gate is potentially significant and could point to an Anglo-Saxon or Anglo-Scandinavian origin for St Giles's.

30. *Atlas of Historic Towns*, edited by M. D. Lobel, vol.2 (1975), pp.2-5 and Map 2.

31. Evidence for the Five Boroughs, both documentary and archaeological, has been reviewed by R. A. Hall, 'The Five Boroughs of the Danelaw: a review of present knowledge', *Anglo-Saxon England*, 18 (1989), pp.149-206; for Leicester, see pp.163-68.

32. R. Buckley and J. Lucas, *Leicester Town Defences: excavations 1958-1974* (Leicester, 1987); plan of medieval Leicester, Fig.27 on p.58.

33. Royal Commission on the Historical Monuments of England, *The Town of Stamford* (1977); Hall, 'The Five Boroughs', pp.193-200.

34. Hall, 'The Five Boroughs', p.193.

35. *Historic Towns. Maps and Plans of Towns and Cities in the British Isles, with Historical Commentaries from Earliest Times to 1800*, edited by M. D. Lobel, vol.1 (Oxford, 1969); Hall, 'The Five Boroughs', pp.187-93.

36. Hall, 'The Five Boroughs', pp.153-63.

37. For outline plan see Drage, 'Urban Castles', Fig.53 no.3.

38. J. Munby, 'Saxon Chichester and its predecessors', in Haslam, *Anglo-Saxon Towns in Southern England*, pp.315-30; area of castle shown, but not identified, in Fig.108.

Archaeology at Lincoln Castle: Before and After 1068

Lisa Donel and Michael J. Jones

Introduction and Pre-Norman Archaeology.

Michael J. Jones

(a)   Background

In terms of human occupation of its site, the castle at Lincoln, like the historic City as a whole, is a palimpsest not only of the past 900 years, but also of the previous millennium. Beneath the banks and lawns, and some of the existing buildings, are traces, surviving in various states of repair, of structures associated with the life of both the castle and of the pre-Norman history of Lincoln. Only a small fraction of this vast resource has yet been investigated: we could learn a great deal from a sustained programme of excavations. On the other hand, the ethos of today is first to establish what survives and assess its importance, then to manage its preservation for future generations to enjoy, rather than to spend resources on destroying it – for that is what archaeological excavation involves. The emphasis of effort in urban archaeology has moved away from large-scale excavation work to the survey of standing remains, analysis of previous discoveries, and non-destructive or only marginally damaging methods of site evaluation, in all cases making increasing use of sophisticated computer technology.

This paper is concerned both with what we know of the site in the period before the castle was built, and what we have been able to learn about the castle's history from investigations in the past twenty years or so.

(b)   The Pre-Norman site: its history

It is still possible to come across statements that hard evidence exists for a pre-Roman hill-top fort at Lincoln. These are based on misleading evidence of what were originally considered to be Iron Age postholes, but later confirmed as solution holes of geological origin, and an unfortunate tendency to equate the second syllable of Lindum with '-dunum', indicating a hillfort. As far as we can tell at present, the main focus of pre-Roman occupation at Lincoln appears rather to have lain close to the river.[1] On the other hand, it is still conceivable that a hilltop enclosure, with a ritual rather than political or settlement function, may have existed in the same period: but no structural evidence has as yet come to light.

Lincoln first became a major settlement in the mid first century AD with the establishment of a legionary fortress on the hill-top by legio IX Hispana. The Roman army may have been in the Lincoln area before AD50, but the pottery dating from the site suggests a Neronian foundation, that is after AD54. It may be that the uphill base was the second site, replacing an earlier fortress to the south of the river.[2]

On departing to set up the York fortress in c.AD71, the Ninth Legion was replaced by legio II Adiutrix, a supplementary legion from the Rhine, but this legion, too, soon moved on, to Chester. By AD80, only a caretaker garrison can have been left, but within a decade or so the former fortress had become a colonia, a self-governing community consisting largely of retired legionaries, who had the status of Roman citizens. The colonia was also the highest status awarded to provincial communities, with a constitution modelled on that of Rome, a town council and annual magistracies. The new colonists were encouraged to see that the physical manifestation of their city reflected its privileged status, by providing it with a range of public works in addition to domestic accommodation. The legionary fortress's grid layout provided a framework which could be developed for these purposes.

Lincoln did indeed realise the ambitions set for it, with an impressive forum and basilica (civic centre), public baths, drains and sewers amongst those remains so far identified.[3] The city also seems to have been successful in commercial terms, spreading well beyond even its extended fortifications. It may have been a combination of its colonial status – by then less significant – and its economic prosperity which caused it to be selected in the early fourth century to be one of the four capitals of the re-ordered province, and, probably in conjunction, to have been given its first bishop, Adelfius, in time to attend the Christian Council at Arles in AD314.[4]

Yet by the mid fifth century, this urban prosperity, and the substantial population which went with it, had been lost, a victim of the collapse of the Roman system in Britain. The former city probably reverted to a semi-rural economy, and may have been the centre of a small independent kingdom before becoming an essential central place of Anglo-Saxon Lindsey by c.600.[5] It may have retained or at least regained some political and ecclesiastical importance, but it was to be a further three centuries before an urban revival can be discerned. Archaeological excavations across the city are elucidating the sequence of reoccupation.[6] The old upper enclosure, containing the early church of St Paul in the Bail, may have remained under separate (royal?) control until the end of the tenth century or even until after the Norman conquest (see Stocker, this volume, pp.15-16).[7]

By the time of the castle's foundation, the city had developed into one of the most thriving in England with a population in excess of 5,000 and extra-mural suburbs: this much is clear from documentary and archaeological evidence (Fig.1). Some wealthy figures had houses here. The Domesday Survey records that the construction of the castle in 1068 involved the clearance of a large number of households from its site. Whether the actual figure, of taxable units of 'notional household' space – often represented in the modern literature as the equivalent of 166 houses – can be accurately converted into population size or not, it does indicate a closely built-up area. Mike Thompson's view of the size of the first castle[8] would indicate even more intensive occupation. Yet the recent suggestion that the original castle was in fact the former upper Roman enclosure resolves the discrepancy, we believe, more convincingly.[9]

(c)   The Pre-Norman site: archaeological potential

The remains of this first thousand or so years of Lincoln's history include archaeological deposits, principally of the Roman and late Saxon periods, which can be up to two metres deep but are in places much shallower. Apart from the structural evidence, the occupation and rubbish layers contain artefacts which can illuminate social and economic aspects of contemporary life.

LATE ANGLO-SAXON LINCOLN : c.1000

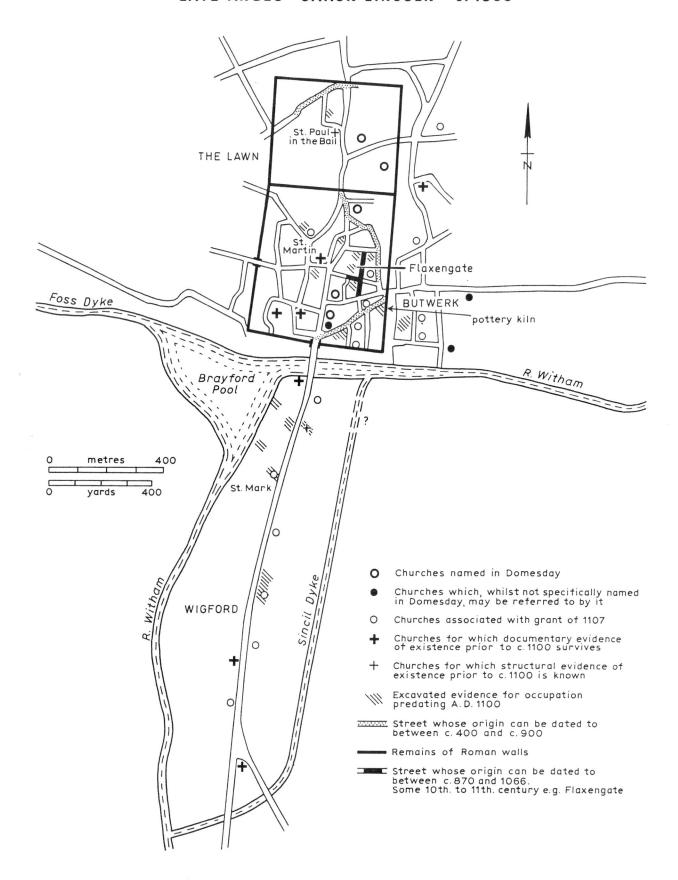

Fig.1. Plan of the Anglo-Scandinavian city, c.AD1000 (from An Historical Atlas of Lincolnshire *edited by S. Bennett and N. Bennett, 1993).*

The fortifications are of obvious interest, since the castle itself made use of the western and southern walls of the upper enclosure, though in differing ways – no new bank was provided on the south side. Investigations at several sites have shown the Roman defensive sequence to be a complex one, from the earth and timber legionary rampart to the considerable scale of the late Roman wall, bank and ditch (Fig.2).[10] This was such a formidable obstacle that it largely survived throughout the medieval period and as a result has influenced the layout of the city to the modern day. No definite evidence for a late Saxon refurbishment has come to light, and only cosmetic changes may have been necessary to keep the Roman defences in commission. Their suggested re-use[11] would strengthen the idea that they survived in a good state in this area.

The discovery in 1836 of a Roman gate immediately north of the castle's west gate is well known from two contemporary depictions, and this gate's single carriageway plan was elucidated by Hugh Thompson.[12] The construction of an earth bank over these walls, either in 1068 or, as now seems more probable from the pottery dating of the bank as excavated in the 1980s (see below), in the early twelfth century, had to take account of the greater height of the gate tower than that of the adjacent walls. The Norman gate with its revetment walls was then a useful device to cope with the discrepancy in bank height between the banks to north and south. This functional explanation for the change in bank level means that there is no need to postulate a pre-Norman tower structure, which was once suggested as the explanation. To the north of the castle, the Roman deposits are in places close to the modern ground level and in places have almost disappeared: it may be that some of the later Roman and Anglo-Saxon deposits (if these latter ever existed, in view of the likely use of the enclosure as a royal reserve) were removed, either to help create the castle bank in the Norman period, or to fill the ditch after it was sold off by Charles I. Roman and possibly Anglo-Saxon remains may therefore survive in particularly good condition in the lower part of the northern bank of the castle, near to its north-west corner.

During the life of the Roman legionary fortress, which was built of timber, part of its *principia*, or headquarters building, encroached into the north-east corner of the site later occupied by the castle, and the same is true of the subsequent *colonia* forum.[13] Other Roman public buildings may also lie beneath the castle, but the greater part of the site is likely to have been covered by domestic buildings, initially rows of timber barracks, and subsequently housing for the colonists. It would be of considerable interest to examine the military-civilian transition at Lincoln, for work at the two other early *coloniae* in Britain, Colchester and Gloucester, has shown that some of the barracks were first adapted rather than being rebuilt on a new civilian plan.[14] There does seem to have been a delay in introducing classical style houses into Romano-British cities, but from the late second century they became much more common. The mosaic pavements which have come to light during building operations at the castle are probably to be associated with town-houses of late second- to fourth-century date (Fig.4).[15] A number of streets crossed the site, some provided with underground drains.

Since we know so little about the buried archaeology of Lincoln Castle, it would be surprising if it had yet told us anything of the intractable period between the end of Roman Britain and Viking settlement. There are hints of occupation belonging to this period from the site of St Paul in the Bail, to the north-east of Cobb Hall, where two timber churches were built on the forum courtyard at a date between the late fourth and early seventh centuries, with an associated burial ground.[16] Moreover, the largest group of eighth- to ninth-century pottery from the city to date was recovered from the grounds of the former Lawn hospital, immediately west of the castle. Area excavation of contemporary deposits within the castle grounds, could (if well-preserved) add considerably to our understanding of this obscure epoch. We know that Roman buildings were becoming ruinous as they were neglected – although some survived in part for many centuries – and that the old street system was largely being lost, but that new rights of way, some of them diagonal routes linking the Roman gates, were appearing. One of these may still survive partly as Chapel Lane, whose line changed as it joined the medieval street of Westgate: it linked the north and west Roman gates; alternatively, it may have served St Clement's Church. Another street may have linked the west gate to the south gate (on Steep Hill) across the later site of the castle.

When the population had re-established itself, with property rights also in place, new streets such as these were less likely. Rather, over much of the walled area, a new grid was imposed, in some cases using the Roman Ermine Street as a base line. The castle site would be an ideal place to study this changing topography, but as yet the potential evidence remains untouched. It also offers an opportunity for testing the hypothesis that this was a royal preserve before the Norman Conquest, so that the remains of tenth-century timber houses, with their cottage industries and evidence for technology and trade, ubiquitous in other parts of the town, might not occur here.[17]

In this brief review, I hope that I have been able to demonstrate Lincoln Castle's considerable potential for archaeological research into the late prehistoric period, Roman fortress and *colonia*, early to middle Saxon periods, and late Saxon town – as well as the earliest Norman arrangements. What we still have to establish is the extent to which deposits survive beneath the ground. This is something which is best considered together in the light of archaeological work at the castle, and an account of that now follows.

Lincoln Castle – A Review of Archaeological Investigation 1974-95.

Lisa Donel

Several excavations, evaluations and watching briefs have been undertaken at Lincoln Castle in the past twenty-five years. Some were carried out in response to work linked to service repair or installation, and some to stability investigations, but the greatest area of concentration of work was carried out in preparation for the opening of the West Gate.

This part of the article deals with examples of all types of work that have been carried out at Lincoln Castle. More detailed description is confined to those excavations which produced the most important results, but this account must remain for the most part an interim summary. We still have to obtain the resources to allow us to produce definitive reports on some of these discoveries, although work on the largest element, the West Gate, is now in progress.

1. The West Gate area

Excavations and survey on and around the West Gate took place initially in 1982-83, and subsequently from 1986 until 1992. The builders of the first castle made use of the remains of the Roman west wall, and may have rebuilt the Roman gate and tower,[18] and in due course incorporated them into the twelfth-century bank. Several alterations to the West Gate itself took place subsequently, but it was both the need to renew the thirteenth-century strengthening arch (Fig.6) and the plan to reopen the gate which occasioned the excavations here. The 1982-89 work was designed to reduce the level to that of the medieval road and gateway in advance of the re-opening.

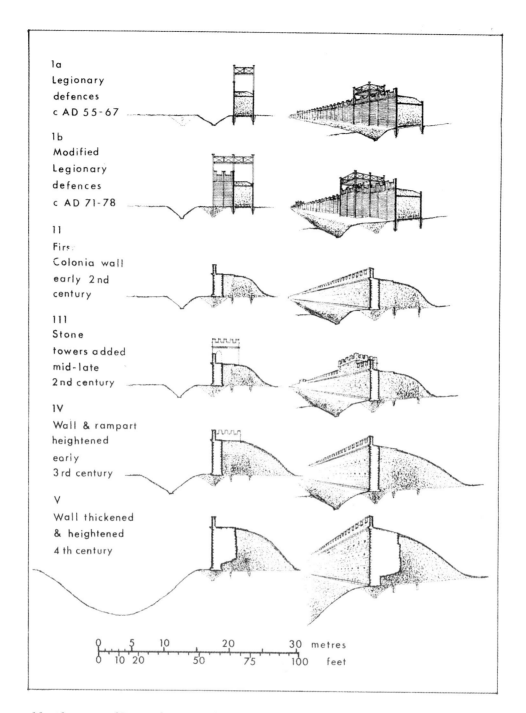

Fig.2. Sequence of fortifications of Roman legionary fortress and Upper City (D. R. Vale).

The West Gate was surveyed in 1982 and limited excavations were carried out on various areas outside the gate.[19] These showed that the earthen bank had been revetted by a stone wall on either side of the gateway. The twelfth-century stone gate was constructed to give direct access to the countryside, perhaps for the cavalry,[20] or in case the city was captured by an enemy. Its plan included not only the visible gate-tower but also an outer barbican, and subsequently a tower was added on the north side. As the use of the castle as a fortification declined, the gate was in disuse by c.1500.

Between 1986 and 1989, excavation was carried out inside the west gate (Fig.5).[21] Almost three metres of modern dump were removed to reveal the medieval gateway. Part of the original Roman city wall was discovered in a pit, immediately beneath the Norman road surface which ran into the castle from the gate. This wall was aligned with the Roman gateway, whose voussoir arches (having collapsed forward) still survive beneath the ground in the bank to the north of the Norman

gate. Clearance of the vegetation on the outer scarp of the bank immediately north of the medieval gate uncovered some of those voussoirs which had been exposed previously in 1954. They were subsequently re-covered. Inside the gate-arch, the medieval road level was uncovered for the full width of the bank, and structures to the north and south were uncovered in the process (Fig.7). They are described below.

The earliest stone gate was a two storey structure, apparently barrel vaulted, and probably constructed in the early twelfth century. In the Norman period, the roadway dipped sharply to the east on entering the castle (perhaps following the slope of the truncated Roman rampart). Inside the bank, to the south of the road, lay a contemporary building with arrow-loop windows overlooking the carriageway (Figs 5 and 8).

Various alterations to the gate had been carried out either contemporaneously with, or earlier than, the insertion of the portcullis and reinforcing arch in about 1233-34. Among these

Fig.3. Reconstruction drawing of Roman upper west gate (D. R. Vale).

operations was an extension to the east of the rear passage walls; and the building to the south of the roadway was extended out on to the carriageway. At least two periods of passageway walls were found to the east of the gate, extending the gate structure a further twelve metres or so, with other structures of indeterminate function attached (see plan, Fig.5). The road level also rose during the twelfth to fourteenth centuries, so that the original slope to the east was levelled out, possibly as a result of numerous repairs and re-surfacings as well as of deliberate dumping. As a result, the building south of the road became buried to a depth of over 1.5m; a replacement was provided on its north side (Fig.9).

Pottery dating suggests that disuse of the gateway probably occurred in the mid fourteenth to early fifteenth century. Rubbish, rubble and silt built up over the latest road surface and a single adult skeleton was buried in the road: presumably it was no longer a major thoroughfare. Subsequently, a blocking wall was built across the narrowest point of the gate, and at some point in the sixteenth to seventeenth centuries, the gateway was partially blocked by new walls. The interior thus formed was used as a bronze foundry, partly for bell casting, during the seventeenth to eighteenth centuries.[22] A photogrammetric survey was subsequently undertaken, by the Institute of Advanced Architectural Studies at York University, of the whole standing structure, including the walls uncovered during excavation.

The Lawn Link

The final stage of the project to re-open the West Gate and to provide a link to the Lawn across Union Road was achieved in 1992-93, in time for the official opening in April 1993 by Sir Jocelyn Stevens, the then Chairman of English Heritage, which had financially supported the project.

Prior to the commencement of any construction work, English Heritage required that certain preliminary works be carried out on the external face of the West Gate. Two trial pits were excavated in May 1992 by Geotechnical Services for Allott and Lomax, Consulting Engineers, in the back garden of Castle Cottage. Their purpose was to examine the deposits uncovered directly in line with the West Gate, on the line of the proposed bridge. Archaeologists were present to record the excavation in order to report on any archaeological implications.

The lack of any real dating material and the small size of the trial pits made the archaeological analysis of this geotechnical investigation difficult. It was impossible to determine whether the pits cut into the lower slope of the bank, or actually cut the ditch itself, or merely cut later deposits. There was no indication of a previous bridge structure, or structures, nor any evidence that natural subsoil had been reached as one might assume if the lower part of the castle bank was excavated. Previous excavation at the Lawn, c.100m to the west, reached the natural subsoil at 63.12m OD. The tops of the pits at the castle were over a metre below this and 1.8m deep (60.68m OD).

Following the decision to re-open the trench originally excavated in 1983 immediately outside the West Gate (rather than excavating a new trial pit), the Archaeology Unit was then asked to examine the stratigraphic sequence exposed, with special reference to the material at the base of the trench.

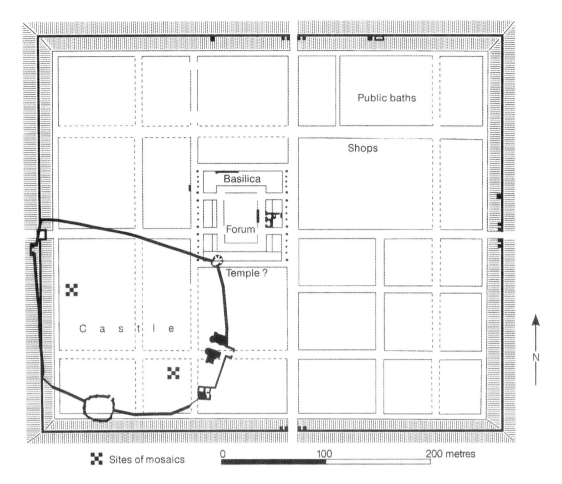

Fig.4. Plan of Roman Upper City, showing locations of mosaic pavements discovered during construction of the courts and prison extension (D. Watt, copyright English Heritage).

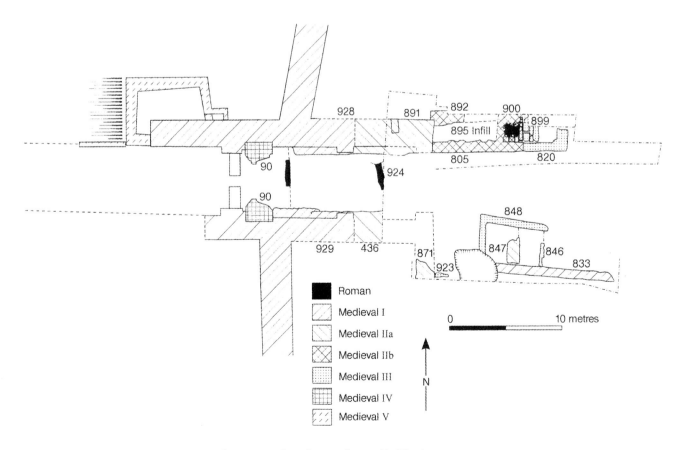

Fig.5. Plan of west gate excavations, showing medieval gate phases (D. Watt).

Fig.6. Interior of west gate prior to excavations and repair.

The 1983 trench had originally been cut from about two metres above the foundation level. However, some erosion had taken place since the excavations. There was no evidence to indicate that any of the present infill material was associated with the medieval gate itself. The 1983 excavation had been cut approximately 0.40m into the foundations under the misconception that the underlying layer was natural limestone brash. This supposition was proved incorrect as the excavation moved westwards revealing a more substantial foundation approximately two metres to the west of the gate entrance. It was now thought possible that this platform may have extended across the whole of the area. During the bridge construction work in 1992-93 it was discovered that the 'foundation platform' was actually a layer of debris probably created when a great crack in the foundations below the West Gate was repaired. There was no associated dating evidence.

In 1992-93 the Unit also carried out a watching brief on the ground-works associated with the Lawn Link and opening of the West Gate. Lying to the west of the North Tower was a modern lean-to structure that had been used as a workshop. Examination showed that the eastern wall of the lean-to had been built on to an existing stone structure. Stepped footings discovered to the west of the standing walls of the medieval tower may provide one explanation, in that the wall may have been built on to part of this footing which, originally, would have stood several courses higher and extended directly back to the North Tower behind the lean-to. Another possibility is that there was another chamber adjoining the tower on its west and that the lean-to wall was built onto an earlier wall of this chamber. The clean, clear-edged nature of the footings at the base of the North Tower appear to show that they had never been open to the elements but were covered by an earth

(and turf?) layer. The footings seemed to have been constructed in stages: definite divisions between blocks of masonry from north to south indicated as much.

The watching brief also allowed access to the ditch which was shown to have been dug into the natural rock. The presumed bridge had not crossed the ditch: rather, a wall faced on one side only appeared to represent a revetment for a causeway allowing access into the castle at this point.

2. The Stabilisation Survey

Extensive work has also been carried out during a major investigation into the stability of the banks and walls of the entire castle. This was undertaken on behalf of Lincolnshire County Council, by Allott and Lomax, Consulting Engineers. Following slippage on the west and south-west banks in the 1980s, a survey involving trenching and boreholes was carried out to determine the best means of preserving the earth banks and the stone walls. In over a dozen trenches, no example of exactly the same constructional details was seen, either of the banks or the foundations of the walls themselves, although a general pattern was clear, and the banks and walls appeared to be of one date and of one general sequence of build (Fig.10). The variations must be due partly to the differential utilisation of natural or secondary material.

There was no evidence for an earlier wooden phase of the castle (this is not to say that it did not exist), the stone walls being built directly on to the mound, and then earth mounded up against them. Some attempt was made to counteract subsidence by the construction of wooden frames upon which the walls were built. The most surprising of these construction methods was at the Lucy Tower, where the walls appeared to have no real foundations, merely an average of three courses of stone, and sat directly on a mound comprising large boulders separated only by large pockets of air. Presumably these are the stones visible on Buck's engraving which suggests a structure of large stones alternating with bands of earth. There was no evidence for a previous wooden structure, but as no work has been carried out inside the tower, it is possible that the present tower may have been keyed into an earlier, smaller keep whose foundations remain intact.[23]

Following the stability investigations, certain areas were listed as priority areas for remedial works, the most crucial area being the west bank, which had already suffered some slippage. Work was carried out to re-grade part of the bank and stabilise it by the insertion of soil nails and a netting "skin". Next, the bank was replanted with a variety of low shrubs that are reinforcing its stability. Recording of the remedial works produced no new information about the medieval monument.

3. Service Trenches 1991-92 (Fig.11)

At a number of locations inside the castle, new, updated services were installed at different locations to serve the current functions of the site. As a condition of the works, it was usual for there to be archaeological test-pits and/or a watching brief, and these resulted in a number of discoveries, which are described below according to their various locations.[24]

The Crown Court area

The evidence from pits to the east and north of the Crown Court suggested that the area around the building underwent much disturbance through landscaping and levelling during the eighteenth and nineteenth centuries. Presumably, extensive works were involved in the construction of the Crown Court in the 1820s and its predecessor. Although artefacts from both

Fig.7. Excavations in progress inside the west gate, showing the road-surface and emerging structures either side (cf. Fig.5).

Roman and medieval date were discovered, none came from securely dated stratigraphy. Finds were intermixed with later material and later deposits overlain by layers containing material from earlier periods. This phenomenon is likely to have resulted from deep ground disturbance. Should early archaeological deposits survive intact here, they probably lie at much greater depth than those seen during the service works.

No remains earlier than the post-medieval period were encountered. At the northern end of the trench (Fig.11, no.1) was a limestone and mortar surface, partly cobbled, which disappeared beneath the east and west sections but measured three metres from north to south. It is possible that this surface may represent a path either leading up to the existing Court building or its predecessor. It clearly predated a graveyard to the north-east of the building (Fig.11, no.2; see below) as graves were found cutting into the surface and through two overlying layers of clay. These graves, which were not deep, and probably therefore of post-medieval date, may represent part of a debtors' graveyard, or possibly one for felons and outlaws. Many of the skeletons had been badly disturbed, but in some places the preservation of complete skeletons and associated grave goods (coffin nails, coffin handles, clothing buttons, *etc.*) was good. All the skeletons lay on an east-west alignment with the heads to the west/north-west. Five complete skeletons and the remains of another possible five were identified, together with mixed remains totalling approximately twelve other individuals. All were recorded and reburied in the same area in which they had been found.

To the west of the graves was a line of large limestone blocks which may represent the remains of a boundary wall.

Whether this wall was contemporary with the graves or earlier is hard to prove. However, if it was standing during the life of the cemetery, it would have effectively created a barrier between at least two of the areas of graves. The presence of burials so close to the Crown Court does seem an oddity, and probably suggests that it represents an earlier eighteenth-century graveyard which was displaced by the construction of the new nineteenth-century Crown Court.

Area north of the former Prison building

A service trench close to the former prison building revealed a compact layer of limestone fragments intermixed with sand and mortar. Its depth ranged from *c*.60cm at the west to *c*.20cm at the east, appearing to level out, and ending *c*.5m from the former Prison building. It is possible that it represents part of the exercise yard created for the prisoners in the nineteenth century. Evidence of a courtyard surface was identified during the excavation of trial pits.[25]

To the north of the former prison, an east-west wall was recorded directly in front of the building (Fig.11, no.3). Only 2.2m of its length was visible, up to 1m wide. Both faces were of well cut limestone, enclosing a rubble and mortar core. There were six courses of stonework still remaining. Unlike most of the deposits recorded during this project, dating material was available for the clay which sealed the wall. This layer has been provisionally dated, by pottery, to the thirteenth century. As neither the mortar nor the stonework appeared to be Roman, it is probable that the wall represents part of a medieval stone structure. It is impossible to determine, from present evidence, whether the wall was part of a building,

Fig.8. Norman structure to the south of the early roadway inside the west gate; looking east (cf. Fig.5).

Fig.9. Steps leading to building on north side of road (visible to left).

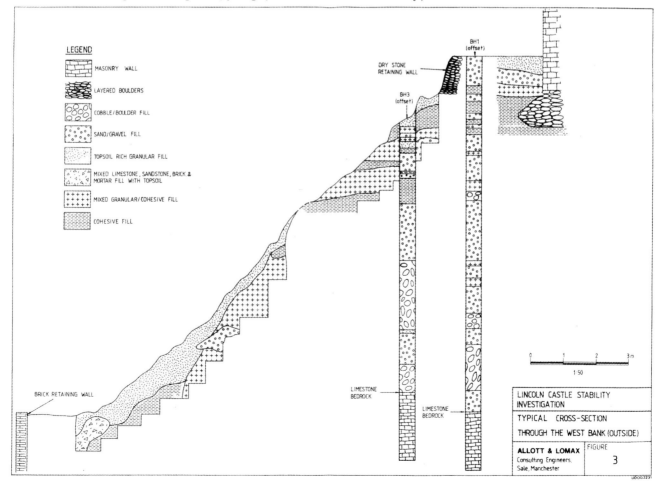

Fig.10. Typical cross-section through Castle bank (by courtesy of Allott and Lomax).

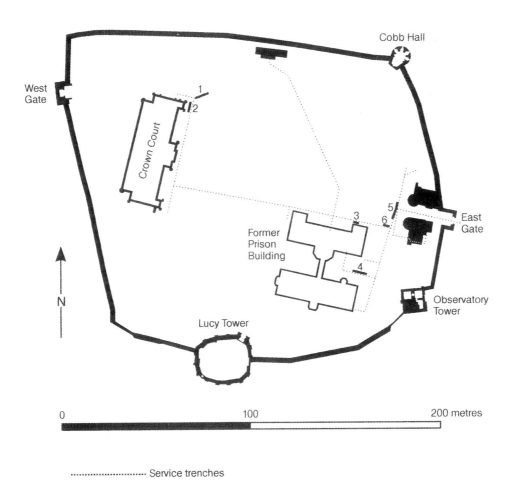

Fig.11. Plan of the castle showing locations of discoveries made during the cutting of service-trenches.

perhaps part of one of the two medieval halls, or some form of boundary wall within the castle.

This work confirmed that the area adjacent to the former Prison contains some relatively undisturbed archaeological deposits.

East Gate to Observatory Tower

A service trench cut from inside the East Gate in the roadway towards the Observatory Tower (Fig.11, no.6) disturbed a number of limestone slabs lying east to west across the trench, which may have been part of a courtyard or roadway. Also encountered was a partial east-west burial lying in the east-facing section. The proximity to the East Gate entrance does make this burial a curiosity (*cf.* that found during excavations at the West Gate, above).

Another unexpected find was a limestone wall aligned east to west across the trench directly in front of the East Gate (Fig.11, no.5). Herringbone construction in its upper courses may have suggested that it was medieval, but post-medieval tile in its core and mortar of probable nineteenth-century type indicate a more recent date. It is possible that the wall may belong to an earlier structure and all that was seen was a later repair, but the wall did lie directly in the centre of the modern entrance. It seems strange that a wall would be constructed in such an obstructive position at any time of the castle's history, but the 1833 plan of the castle shows that Turnkey's house may have lain partly beneath the present roadway.

A service trench in the Prison Chapel courtyard revealed a north-south stone wall constructed from medium and large limestone blocks, standing eight to ten courses high with possible stepped footings to the west (Fig.11, no.4). It was sealed by another wall constructed of red brick, also aligned north-south. It is possible that the brick wall was part of an outbuilding associated with the former Prison. Stone walls and other features were also revealed: most again may belong to the earlier prison building.

4. Other Research

Lincoln Castle is unusual in having at least two mottes; the Lucy Tower on the south-west corner and the Observatory Tower on the south-east. In 1974 work was carried out within the latter tower which was interpreted as proving that it was the later of the two, possibly having been constructed in the mid twelfth century.[26]

In 1986 a sloping masonry feature was uncovered in the course of restoration of the north wall. It appeared to be a single course thick, of mortared rubble, extending down the bank from the outer face of the wall. It was re-examined in 1990 during the Stabilisation Survey and identified as a possible room attached to Cobb Hall, its entrance probably being through a now blocked doorway on the west side of Cobb Hall.[27]

The East Gate

David Stocker recorded visible remains of the East Gate in the 1980s and was able to suggest its plan (Fig.12).[28] Excavations in 1990 outside the gate revealed the northern part of the southern barbican tower. Its position was subsequently marked on the ground in the cobbled area outside the gate. Plans to display the southern side of the tower, much of which survives below the modern ground surface, have yet to come to fruition. Remains of the northern tower also survive.

Discussion.

M. J. Jones

We have been able to describe, only briefly, tantalising glimpses into the medieval and Roman periods from many of the sites excavated. It is evident that the late eighteenth and nineteenth century was the major period of activity that involved deep disturbance and resulting damage to earlier remains, owing to the construction of the various court and prison structures. The constantly reversed stratigraphy found in so many of the sites is evidence of this disturbance. Yet it is likely that outside these areas there are still intact deposits at depths of three metres and more which have the potential to provide valuable information on the earlier history of the site.

Lincoln Castle deserves detailed study. Not only is little of its potential yet realised; it also awaits full reports on previous work. There are positive signs of progress: work on the West Gate excavations is now moving forward,[29] and a Conservation Plan has now been produced.[30] One of its recommendations is the need for a photogrammetric survey of the whole monument. Should a large-scale excavation programme ever become possible (and this is only a remote possibility), there is plenty of scope within the grounds for an imaginative presentation of the results. Nowhere in Lincoln does another site exists which offers the opportunity for revealing the

Fig.12. Reconstruction drawing of the east gate with its barbican towers added (Tig Sutton).

sequence of habitations from the mid first century AD – Roman barracks, Roman town-houses, Anglo-Saxon occupation and whatever changes took place in the Viking period, and Norman and medieval structures. As long ago as 1983, one of us (MJJ) suggested that it would be an exciting prospect to uncover these remains over several years, with the dig itself forming a visitor attraction, and subsequently to create an archaeological park consisting of reconstructions of these houses. It remains an unlikely prospect.[31]

One important initiative *has* reached fruition – the creation of an Urban Archaeological Database for the City of Lincoln. This incorporates all known records of archaeological finds, mapped using Geographical Information Systems, so that all finds can be plotted three-dimensionally. It is now possible to produce 'deposit models' indicating the depths at which remains of individual periods are likely to be found – if at all: of course there is a possibility that earlier building work, both stone quarrying and deep foundations, has removed much of the evidence. Perhaps new non-destructive methods such as ground-penetrating radar can help show us whether this is really the case. These new methods represent vital advances in terms of managing the monument's archaeology and could also allow research problems to be addressed. The preparation of an Urban Assessment has followed, and has set a research agenda for each era of the city's history.[32]

Let us hope that we can move forward from here and stimulate further interest in what the site holds: there is so much to be gained for both scientific knowledge and public appreciation alike.

Acknowledgements

The work reported on here was largely undertaken by staff of the City of Lincoln Archaeology Unit or its predecessor organisations, with funding provided by Lincoln City Council, Lincolnshire County Council, the Manpower Services Commission Community Programme, and English Heritage. The paper in its present form was prepared for publication by M. J. Jones, with co-operation from Lisa Donel, and helpful comments from both Phillip Lindley and David Stocker.

Notes

1. M. J. Darling and M. J. Jones, 'Early settlement at Lincoln', *Britannia* 19 (1988), pp.1-56. See now Michael J. Jones, David Stocker and Alan Vince, *The City by the Pool, Assessing the Archaeology of the City of Lincoln*, edited by David Stocker, Lincoln Archaeological Studies No.10 (Oxford, 2003), which supersedes some of the statements here.

2. M. J. Jones, 'Lincoln', in *Fortress Into City*, edited by G. Webster (1988), pp.145-66, see p.146. See also note 1 and Michael J. Jones, *Roman Lincoln. Conquest, Colony and Capital* (2002).

3. M. J. Jones, 'Roman Lincoln: changing perspectives', in *The Coloniae of Roman Britain: new studies and a review*, edited by H. R. Hurst, Journal of Roman Archaeology, Supplementary Series, 36 (1999), pp.101-12.

4. M. J. Jones, 'The latter days of Roman Lincoln', in *Pre-Viking Lindsey*, edited by A. G. Vince, Lincoln Archaeological Studies No.1 (Lincoln, 1993), pp.14-28.

5. K. Steane and A. G. Vince, 'Post-Roman Lincoln: archaeological evidence for activity in Lincoln in the 5th-9th centuries', in *Pre-Viking Lindsey*, edited by A. G. Vince, Lincoln Archaeological Studies No.1 (Lincoln, 1993), pp.71-79; Jones *et al.*, *The City by the Pool*, chapter 8.

6. A. G. Vince, 'Lincoln in the Viking period', *Proceedings of the International Congress of Viking Studies 1997* (2001), pp.157-79.

7. D. Stocker and A. Vince, 'The early Norman Castle at Lincoln and a re-evaluation of the original west tower of Lincoln Cathedral', *Medieval Archaeology*, 41 (1997), pp.223-33.

8. Mike Thompson, this volume, p.23, above.

9. Stocker and Vince, 'The early Norman Castle'; *cf.* D. A. Stocker, this volume.

10. M. J. Jones, *The Defences of the Upper Roman Enclosure*, The Archaeology of Lincoln, VII-1 (Lincoln, 1980).

11. D. A. Stocker, this volume, pp.9-13.

12. F. H. Thompson and J. B. Whitwell, 'The gates of Roman Lincoln', *Archaeologia*, 104 (1973), pp.129-207, see Fig.3.

13. Jones, *Roman Lincoln*; Jones, 'Roman Lincoln: changing perspectives'.

14. P. Crummy, 'Colchester', in *Fortress Into City*, edited by G. Webster (1988), pp.24-47; P. Crummy, 'Colchester: making towns out of fortresses and the first urban fortifications in Britain', in *The Coloniae of Roman Britain: new studies and a review*, edited by H. R. Hurst, Journal of Roman Archaeology, Supplementary Series, 36 (1999), pp.88-100; H. R. Hurst, 'Gloucester', in *Fortress Into City*, edited by G. Webster (1988), pp.48-73; H. R. Hurst, 'Topography and identity in *Glevum Colonia*', in *The Coloniae of Roman Britain: new studies and a review*, edited by H. R. Hurst, Journal of Roman Archaeology, Supplementary Series, 36 (1999), pp.113-35.

15. I. A. Richmond, 'The Roman City of Lincoln', *Contributions to the Archaeology of Lincolnshire and Lincoln being the report of the Summer Meeting at Lincoln 1946*, Archaeological Journal, 103 (1946), pp.26-56, esp. p.39.

16. M. J. Jones, 'St Paul-in-the-Bail, Lincoln: Britain in Europe?', in *Churches Built in Ancient Times: Recent Studies in Early Christian Archaeology*, edited by K. Painter, Society of Antiquaries/Accordia Centre, (1994), pp.325-47; also discussed in Jones *et al.*, *The City by the Pool*, chapters 7 and 8.

17. Jones *et al.*, *The City by the Pool*; Vince, 'Lincoln in the Viking period', n.6.

18. Stocker, this volume, p.11, above.

19. D. A. Stocker, 'Lincoln Castle', *Archaeology in Lincoln 1982-1983*, Annual Report of the Lincoln Archaeological Trust, 11 (Lincoln, 1983), pp.18-27; H. Elliott and D. A. Stocker, *Lincoln Castle* (Lincoln, FLARE and Lincolnshire County Council, 1984).

20. Marshall, this volume, p.54 and Fig.2, below.

21. C. J. Guy, 'Castle West Gate', *Archaeology in Lincolnshire 1986-1987*, Annual Report of the Trust for Lincolnshire Archaeology, 3 (Lincoln, 1987), pp.23-25; P. Miles, 'Castle West Gate 1987', *Archaeology in Lincolnshire 1987-1988*, Annual Report of the Trust for Lincolnshire Archaeology, 4 (Lincoln, 1988), pp.21-24; M. Otter, 'Lincoln Castle, West Gate', *Lincoln Archaeology 1988-1989*. First Annual Report of the City of Lincoln Archaeological Unit (Lincoln, 1989), pp.13-16.

22. J. E. Mann, *Lincoln Castle, West Gate Archive Completion, Stage 1*, City of Lincoln Archaeology Unit Archaeological Report No.411, (2000). There is a detailed report in preparation.

23. L. Donel, *Lincoln Castle: Stability Survey*, City of Lincoln Archaeology Unit Archaeological Report No.13, (1992).

24. L. Donel, *Castle-Lawn Link*, City of Lincoln Archaeology Unit Archaeological Report No.2, (1992); L. Donel, *Lincoln Castle Service Trenching: Archaeological Recording Report*, City of Lincoln Archaeology Unit Archaeological Report No.59, (1993).

25. L. Donel, *Lincoln Castle Services: Evaluation Report*, City of Lincoln Archaeology Unit Archaeological Report No.12, (1992).

26. N. Reynolds, 'Investigations in the Observatory Tower, Lincoln Castle', *Medieval Archaeology*, 19 (1975), pp.201-05; Elliott and Stocker, *Lincoln Castle*; but compare Marshall, this volume, below.

27. For which, see Renn, this volume, below.

28. Elliott and Stocker, *Lincoln Castle*, pp.22-24.

29. Mann, *Lincoln Castle, West Gate Archive Completion*.

30. C. Hayfield, *Conservation Plan for Lincoln Castle*, Lincolnshire County Council (2001).

31. M. J. Jones, 'Archaeology and tourism: the choice for Lincoln', *Archaeology in Lincoln 1982-1983*, Annual Report of the Lincoln Archaeological Trust, 11 (1983), pp.7-9.

32. Jones *et al.*, *The City by the Pool*.

Lincoln Castle: The Architectural Context of the Medieval Defences

Pamela Marshall

Introduction

The castle as an innovative building form has long been recognized as the 'badge' of the Norman Conquest.[1] Colvin puts the number of castles sanctioned by King William within a generation of his invasion of England at thirty-eight,[2] while Drage estimates over forty:[3] to these might be added Cardiff[4] and Newark.[5] Certain common factors governed the siting of these castles including, certainly, the control of important routes but also, and perhaps primarily, the governing of major concentrations of population.[6] Taking control of any existing administrative system was essential to the lasting success of the Conquest, and this centred on towns. The *Anglo-Saxon Chronicle* informs us that Lincoln castle was founded during the winter of 1068-69 after the king had pushed Norman control as far as York. The motive must have been partly strategic: a castle at Lincoln was necessary as a base to block unwanted movement to and from the north by the eastern route, and both Lincoln and nearby Boston were important ports.[7] But the choice of location must also be seen as a reflection of Lincoln's civic eminence at the time of the Conquest. In 1066 the Anglo-Scandinavian town housed a population exceeding 6000,[8] thriving on international trade and over-spilling its Roman boundaries into suburbs.[9] Almost from the beginning of the Norman occupation there are clues that it was singled out for special treatment. As early as 1072, plans were implemented to replace the old minster, or mother church of the county, with a new cathedral and to transfer the see from Oxfordshire.[10] By around the end of the eleventh century, special architectural attention had been afforded to the castle, which had been endowed with stone walls – rare at that period – as well as gates. In the words of Allen Brown: 'The juxtaposition of castle and church, the twin pillars of feudal lordship ... at Lincoln is on the grand scale, so that one thinks, as one was meant to think, of God and Caesar, Church and State, and the Two Swords of lay and ecclesiastical authority.'[11]

With this thought in mind it is all the easier to accept David Stocker's and Alan Vince's recent reinterpretation of the *Domesday Book* entry regarding the upper enclosure of the Roman city, known as the Bail.[12] The compilation of a comprehensive database by the City of Lincoln Archaeology Unit, charting archaeological interventions in the city, has made it easier to understand changes in land use over time. *Domesday Book* refers to the destruction of 166 houses directly in connection with establishing the castle.[13] Stocker and Vince have pointed out that, in view of what we now know about settlement in the Bail *c*.1066, the area now covered by the castle site could not have supported so many dwellings. The number, however, accords well with the whole Bail. The

archaeological record also suggests that by the time of the Conquest, this part of the city had been given over to an elite ecclesiastical enclave, including some high status residences. Their conclusion that the Norman conquerors took over the entire upper Bail as a special area of the city is convincing, particularly as the Bail retained separate administrative distinction until 1835. Their interpretation of what the Normans did with it is less so. Stocker and Vince go on to argue that the entire Bail area was treated as the first Norman castle, the Lucy Tower motte being the only feature of the later castle to be built at that time, and that not until *c*.1075.[14] According to their model, the castle bailey as now defined was not enclosed before *c*.1100. This requires some examination. It would be in the interests of the new establishment, on finding an elite, high-status enclave, whether secular or ecclesiastical in nature, to assume control of it: this was policy. In a small manor the thane's residence would typically be subsumed into a castle, as for example at Goltho (Lincolnshire) or Sulgrave (Northamptonshire) and the church, which was often adjacent, would be rebuilt as an outward sign of the new order in both church and state.[15] If the whole upper Bail was already established as an elite enclave, we see at Lincoln, writ large, the same process that we see elsewhere. However, that does not mean that a distinction was not drawn between ecclesiastical rights and secular domination. The Bail area encompassed a cathedral and three churches, which apparently all continued in use – quite an impressive complement of castle chapels. If Stocker and Vince's thesis is correct, the establishment placed in the Bail was not a castle under the normal definition of the word[16] and, moreover, it would have been unique in post-Conquest England.

Domesday Book may well record the complete annexation of the Bail. As far as the Domesday commissioners were concerned, their purpose was to record the tax potential of the upper city and to explain its basis. If their wording was loose, the relevant information was recorded as far as they were concerned. It is a big assumption to suppose from this that the whole Bail area was viewed as part of the castle in the ordinary way. It is far more likely that the elite ecclesiastical nature of the Bail was preserved under the new administration, and that the castle took its place within this enclave, defined from the start by its own ramparts. Even then, the castle was unusually large, a point explored below. The second part of Stocker and Vince's thesis – that the great west front of Remigius' cathedral was designed as one of the donjons of the castle, specifically to house the bishop[17] – falls outside the scope of this article but merits attention elsewhere.

Whatever the functional nature of the west end of Remigius's cathedral might have been, its remains stand as a testimony to the quality of its architecture and in the next century it was surpassed by a major rebuild set in train by Alexander the Magnificent. The work of both bishops is rightly viewed as symbolizing, not only the glory of God, but also the power and prestige of the Church. During the Norman period the secular architecture of the castle kept pace, in its own way, with its ecclesiastical neighbour. It was soon distinguished by stone walls and gatehouses, followed by a fine shell tower and a second motte and donjon. A parallel might be drawn with Norwich where, during the 1090s, William Rufus instigated the building of both a particularly prestigious great tower and a fine new cathedral.[18] Such architectural distinction seems to suggest that the city had been earmarked for royal favour, although in Lincoln's case this was later abandoned. Norman promotion of the castle, implied by its early architectural treatment, did not continue under the Angevin kings, for Lincoln was rather eclipsed by Nottingham in the neighbouring county, whose castle they evidently preferred.[19] Henry II spent nothing on Lincoln, even during the rebellion of 1173-74, compared with a total of £1,816 0s.3d. spent on Nottingham castle throughout his reign.[20] Richard I spent £101 3s.0d. at Lincoln,[21] mostly on repairs arising from a short siege in which the constable took the part of Count John against William Longchamp, the king's chancellor.[22] Recorded spending during King John's reign amounted to only £20 and damage done during a siege by Louis of France in 1217 fell to Henry III to repair.[23] He was the last monarch to attempt any improvement of the castle, spending a total of £548 6s.4d.,[24] a modest sum compared with the £2,464 19s.0d. he lavished on Nottingham castle.[25] Attention was given to the defences, focusing on the gates and the building of Cobb Hall, an angle tower at the north-east corner of the *enceinte*.[26] By the middle of the thirteenth century, Lincoln was not counted amongst the 'key' castles deemed to be essential for the defence of the country.[27] After 1270, no royal expenditure is recorded at Lincoln castle, the building being all but relinquished to the earls of Chester, and it began a steady decline. After 1335 it was considered to be incapable of defence and served only as the county court and gaol.[28]

Topography and plan of the castle

Lincoln was one of twelve castles of the immediate post-Conquest period to be sited within Roman towns[29] and the site was carefully chosen. Placed in the south-west quarter of the Roman Upper City and on the summit of a steep hill, it was well situated to dominate both the lower city to the south and open countryside to the north. It also controlled the main arteries of communication: Ermine Street, the Fosse Way, the river Witham and Fosse Dyke. As at the Tower of London, existing Roman defences were utilized on two sides. The western and southern ramparts followed the defensive enclosure of the Roman upper city, while banks and ditches to the east and north were created within the confines of the town (Fig.1). [30]

The castle occupied almost a full quarter of the Roman upper bail, covering 5.5 hectares (13.75 acres). While this area encompassed the defensive banks and ditches as well as a motte on the south side, it still left an unusually large, single

bailey (Fig.2a). Such vast enclosures were rare in urban castles, where space was generally restricted. They are perhaps related to the Norman use of cavalry, which proved such an effective element of their war strategy,[31] and it is significant that they occur at castles deemed to be of particular strategic importance. Such castles were seen as control bases from which sallies into the surrounding country could be made to subdue the population. William's castle at Nottingham, considered another vital link in any northern campaign,[32] also had a vast outer bailey (Fig.2d).[33] Here the natural topography of the site led to a triple ward design, but the total area enclosed was uncommonly large for an urban castle and was again likely to be connected with housing a division of cavalry and their horses.[34] Similar interpretations have been made of the outer baileys at Norwich[35] and Portchester.[36]

The closest parallels to the layout chosen at Lincoln are, in fact, in Normandy; at the ducal foundations in Caen (Calvados) and Gisors (Eure) (Figs 2c and 2b). Even larger in scale than Lincoln, Caen was founded only eight or nine years earlier, shortly before the Conquest, as part of Duke William's development of the town and its promotion to be the second seat of his duchy and capital of lower Normandy.[37] Lincoln, too, seems to have been chosen initially to act as administrative capital of the East Midlands. Bearing in mind that the barbicans and inner ward at Caen, with its great tower, were all later additions, its original form bears a marked resemblance to Lincoln. The layout of both of these castles is further reflected a generation later at Gisors, in the castle built by Robert de Belleme on the orders of William Rufus. Raised *c*.1096 at the eastern extremity of the duchy of Normandy, its purpose was to supplement a string of castles founded by the Conqueror to defend the Vexin from encroachment by France.[38] Caen, Lincoln and Gisors are notable for their single extensive baileys, each with two gates: one connected with the town and another giving swift access for troops and horses to the surrounding countryside. A castle's effectiveness could hinge on the latter for, in the words of Stephen Morillo, 'a castle whose garrison was restricted to within its walls was effectively neutralized as a force in war'.[39] While Caen is by

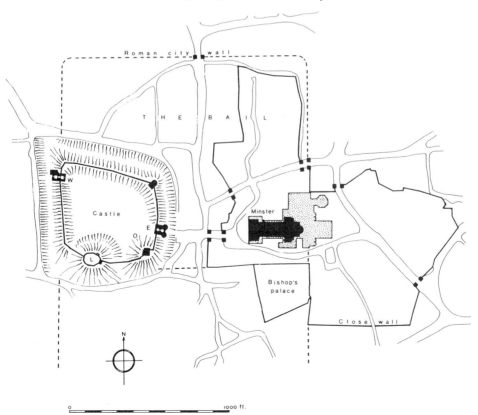

Fig. 1. Plan of Lincoln castle, showing its relationship to the Upper Bail of the town. After R. Gem.

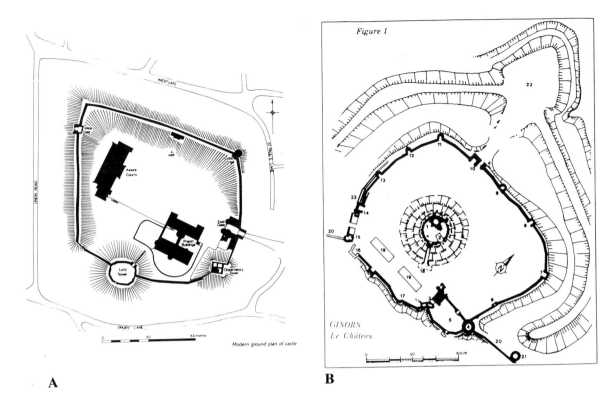

A

B

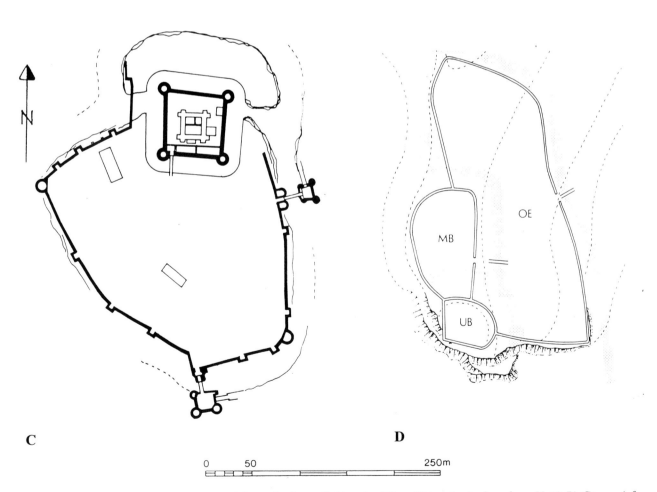

C

D

Fig. 2. Comparative plans of urban castles with large baileys: A) Lincoln (City of Lincoln Archaeology Unit) B) Gisors (after Toussaint) C) Caen: the barbican gates and inner ward at the end were later additions (after Salch) D) Nottingham (after Drage).

far the largest, the size of the *enceinte* at Gisors is almost identical with Lincoln and both these sites have mottes, the one at Gisors placed in the centre.

The line of the defences

The western rampart and ditch of Lincoln castle follow exactly the line of their Roman predecessors. On the south side there was probably only the remains of a wall with no ditch, for here the lower bail of the Roman city, built on the steep hillside, joined the upper bail which occupied the summit. Elsewhere, where Norman castles superseded Roman forts, such as Portchester (Hampshire) and Pevensey (Sussex), surviving Roman walls were reused. One assumes that those at Lincoln were in too poor a condition, for they were buried under the southern and western ramparts. Their encapsulation into the rampart material would have had the benefit of reinforcing the new earthworks, a goal more commonly achieved by the use of timber. At Norham Castle (Northumberland) erosion of the southern rampart of the outer ward has revealed a similar principle of stone reinforcing, albeit later in date. Here an arcade of roughly finished arches, buried in the earth bank, served the dual purpose of reinforcing the earthwork and forming the foundations of a stone curtain wall, which rose from its summit.[40] In 1836, subsidence of the rampart in the north-west corner at Lincoln revealed part of the Roman city west gate buried beneath it (Fig.3).[41] The thickening of the Norman earth bank at this point is more likely to have been caused by the burial of this substantial feature rather than by the creation of a third motte, as Stocker suggested.[42]

The southern line of defence overlooked the outer bail of the Roman town, where the land fell steeply away. An outer ditch was dug below a rampart in the south-east corner, but the bulk of the south side was occupied by a motte situated towards the south-west. This position maximized its visual impact on the town. Standing on the edge of a natural hill, it dominated the greater part of the settlement and would form a landmark both to shipping entering Brayford Pool from the river below and also to travellers entering the city from the south by the Fosse Way. Mottes and towers were deliberately sited so as to be visible from long distances, underlining the lordship they symbolized.[43] During the first third of the twelfth century, Lincoln's motte was crowned by a stone shell tower, which probably replaced a timber predecessor. A second, smaller, motte was added in the south-east corner before the middle of the century.

The curtain walls

Stone curtain walls were rare in the eleventh and early twelfth centuries, although there are other examples at Richmond (Yorkshire: 1071-89),[44] Rochester (Kent: 1088-89)[45] and Ludlow (Shropshire).[46] The use of the word *murus* in 1115 to describe the castle defences at Lincoln seems to confirm that the walls comprised more than palisades at this time.[47] Despite extensive restoration during the nineteenth century, there are places where the curtain walls still bear authentic herringbone masonry, a feature usually consistent with a date before 1100. We are also fortunate in having a description of the walls in 1848, before their mid nineteenth-century consolidation. After the castle had been purchased by the county, to house the

*Fig. 3. Engraving of 1836 showing the castle west gate on the right. The Roman west gate of the upper town is revealed beneath the Norman rampart of the castle (*Gentleman's Magazine, *1836).*

Assizes, extensive notes were made by E. J. Willson, the architect employed to consolidate the fabric.[48] He noted the presence of masonry laid in herringbone fashion, at a time when much more original herringbone work must have survived. In contrast with the cathedral, the masonry employed here was crude, but it should be remembered how rare stone curtain walls were at this time:

> The masonry of the castle walls, wherever the original facing remains, is very rude, the stones being laid together in unhewn masses; but the whole was so well grouted and filled up with good mortar that the substance of the work is mostly sound and firm.

Contrary to Stocker and Vince's claim that the walls and banks of the castle were built together around the turn of the twelfth century,[49] the presence of stone walls c.1100 argues in favour of the castle banks belonging to an earlier period of the castle's history. The ramparts would need to be well consolidated to provide a stable foundation for the walls. One might conceivably argue, though with little conviction, that on the south and west sides the burial of Roman walls within the bank might have provided a stable enough foundation to support curtain walls almost immediately (in a similar manner to the foundations found at Norham; see above). However, it would be virtually impossible to build a curtain wall in stone on newly erected banks, especially such massive ones, on the north and east sides. Where stone curtain walls were built on top of ramparts at Newark Castle, c.1130, the hard clay had had about sixty years to bed down before the wall foundations were laid.[50] In Lincoln's case, it would have been a source of some concern to the builders to raise walls on top of ramparts that were a mere thirty years old, let alone brand new. Indeed, there is evidence of that concern for, from Willson's observations and recording, we know that the foundations of the curtain walls were reinforced with timber (Fig.4):

> The extensive repairs [. . .] brought to light some curious particulars of their ancient form and construction. The bottom courses of masonry were found to have been set upon frames of rough timber, in which three or four parallel lines of beams were laid upon the rubble on which the walls were to be raised, and these lines were crossed, at short distances, by other beams to hold them in their right places. All this timber-work had decayed and fallen to dust in those parts that were discovered, but the cavities in the walls showed plainly the forms and sizes of the beams.[51]

Timber reinforcement was a method employed to hold a masonry structure to shape at least until the mortar had set firm, which could take up to a year. A timber framework was set into the masonry as the structure was raised: by the time it rotted away, its purpose had been served. Wilcox[52] notes the use of timber foundation reinforcement is to be found particularly where spreading or slippage of soft ground might have been expected, the longitudinal timbers preventing the walls from sinking unevenly, while the cross timbers arrested outward spread of the foundation material under the weight of the superstructure.[53] Foundation reinforcement had had a long history in Britain. It was used in the Roman forts of the Saxon shore during the third century and examples are known from Burgh Castle (Suffolk), Bradwell-on-Sea (Essex), Pevensey (Sussex) and Portchester (Hampshire).[54] Bushe-Fox's description of the timber element in the foundation arrangement at Pevensey sounds similar in essence to that used at Lincoln eight centuries later:[55]

> A trench was first dug and filled with chalk and flints, and the beams. which appear to have been framed together. were laid upon the surface of this, the space between them being packed with chalk. The masonry of the wall was built upon this foundation.

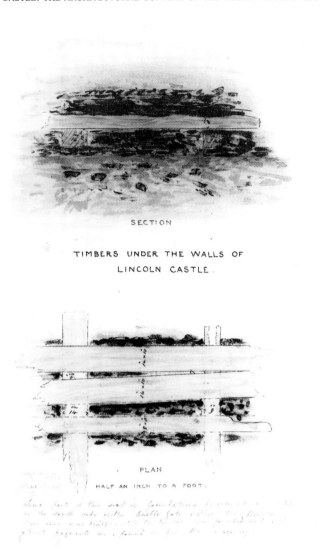

SECTION

TIMBERS UNDER THE WALLS OF
LINCOLN CASTLE.

PLAN

HALF AN INCH TO A FOOT.

Fig. 4. "Timbers under the walls of Lincoln Castle". Drawing by E.J. Willson, copyright Society of Antiquaries of London (MS 786/G, p.83.).

The method was used at Winchester Old Minster during the tenth century and at York Minster (1080), Richmond Castle (Yorkshire: 1071-89) and Sheffield Castle (c.1100) during the eleventh century.[56] At many other castle sites timber reinforcing has been noted in the body of walls as well as foundations, especially in shell towers or other situations where the wall was near the edge of a slope.[57] It was employed in shell towers at Lewes (Sussex) and Plympton (Devon), both built around the turn of the twelfth century and at Gisors (Normandy) c.1123-24. At Richmond (Yorkshire) it had been used to bind the Fallen Tower (ultimately unsuccessfully) to the east curtain wall at a point where the subsoil of blue clay was prone to expansion and contraction.[58] At Newark (Nottinghamshire) the method was utilized to bind the north-east curtain wall, which stood on an earlier rampart, into the east wall of the gatehouse, which had more substantial and secure foundations.[59] Although Willson only noted reinforcing in 'the lower courses', it would not be surprising to find that the walls at Lincoln, both in the shell tower and the *enceinte*, were similarly reinforced throughout.

The Gates

The entrances to Lincoln Castle represent two of the earliest examples in the country. The east gate, situated roughly in the centre of the eastern rampart, led directly into the town and the west gate, built beside the Roman west gate of the old town (Fig.3), gave that swift egress to open country which was essential for cavalry forces.[60]

The West Gate[61]

Excavations in 1982-83 showed that the west gate, built c.1100 (Fig.5a), superseded an earlier Norman gate, perhaps of timber, with stone foundations.[62] The gate tower comprised two storeys, the upper floor lit by two arrow loops, its simple square plan resembling other early examples at Exeter (Devon), Tickhill (Yorkshire), Peveril (Derbyshire), Prudhoe and Norham (both in Northumberland). Projecting forward of the line of the rampart, all these provided an entry passage to accommodate one or more gates and largely relied for defence on the outer ditch and a bridge which could be raised or withdrawn. At this early date first floor chambers were used solely for the defence of the entrance,[63] although domestic accommodation was to appear later in the century at Sherborne (Dorset c.1120), Newark (Nottinghamshire c.1135) and Barnard Castle (Durham c.1150). Although gate passages were normally ceiled in timber, at Lincoln there was originally a barrel vault,[64] which would have added to its security. At Exeter, where a more complete building has survived than at Lincoln, there were at least two storeys above the gate passage.[65] Access to the top floor of the gate tower was gained from the ramparts, via a ladder, to a platform set between projecting buttresses, and thence by a doorway in the centre of the rear elevation. We cannot tell how entry to the single upper floor at Lincoln's west gate was achieved, for the rear is very ruinous, but there might have been a similar arrangement. At Exeter a further doorway in the front elevation is interpreted as giving access to a platform between projecting buttresses, which would have placed defenders directly above would-be intruders.[66] At Lincoln, too, a doorway at the south end of the west wall at first floor level was used to defend the entrance. The lithograph, made in 1836, of the exposed Roman west gate (Fig.3) shows four substantial joist holes in the front of the castle west gate, now obscured by modern refacing. A timber platform of the Exeter type could have been cantilevered from these over the gateway in front of the building. However, the Lincoln defences were further elaborated by the addition of a barbican, an unusual feature

at this date, and one which underlines the prestige of the castle during the Norman period. It took the form of a rectangular enclosure with a further gateway at the west end.[67] The doorway in the front elevation of the gatehouse gave on to a barbican wall walk from which defenders would have an advantage over intruders who had breached the outer gate. The western gate of the barbican no longer survives and the south wall extends only 1.7m. The masonry in this short length matches the character of that used on the gate tower and it shares a chamfered plinth with the western tower arch: the two are undoubtedly of the same build. On the north side the barbican wall extends to over 9m. There are two distinct building breaks in it, attributable to modern refacing. One occurs about 1m from the gate tower, where the character of the masonry ceases to match that used on the gatehouse and the chamfered plinth comes to a sudden end.

Restoration work on the west gate costing £54 6s.4d was authorized in 1233-34 by Henry III.[68] The gate was apparently in a poor state, for the order states that the mined part should be completely demolished before rebuilding began. The thirteenth-century renovations seem to have made no attempt to rebuild the gatehouse properly, converting it into a gateway only. Norman work at the west end, which must have remained in relatively good condition, was retained and an additional pointed arch with chamfered mouldings was inserted east of the original archway, leaving space between the two to house a portcullis (Fig.5b). Of the eastern end of the building only the north wall remains, retained of necessity to act as a revetment to the wide rampart, which encompasses the Roman west gate. It may be that the gatehouse vault had collapsed, for the gate passage was restored with a timber ceiling, but it is more likely that the whole of the eastern end of the gatehouse was collapsing and was not rebuilt. Had it been, one might expect to find some evidence of change in the upper storey, which would almost certainly have been converted to domestic use at this date.

At the north-west corner of the west gate barbican, the foundations of a rectangular stone building were investigated by excavation in 1983-84 and proved to be medieval (Fig.6).[69] It was apparently a two-storey structure, for there are joist-holes for a floor, and a recess in the south-east corner has been interpreted as access between floors and the barbican wall-walk.[70] Its east wall was cut into the bank and the

Fig. 5a. The west gate of Lincoln Castle from the interior.

Fig. 5b. Detail of the west gate, showing the early thirteenth-century archway inserted to provide portcullis slot.

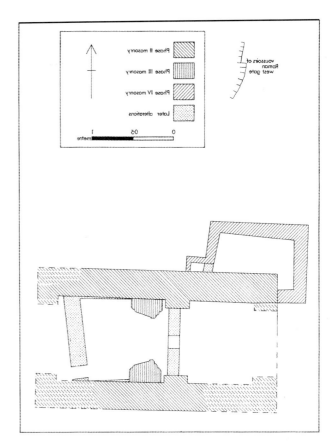

Fig. 6. Plan of the west gate (after Stocker).

excavations showed that the foundations of the north wing of the Norman barbican had been extended westwards to accommodate it. Its west wall rose out of the ditch, supported on a substantial masonry foundation. Unfortunately no dating evidence came to light, but Stocker thought it was likely to be late medieval and that it served as a further defence of the barbican, which was overlooked by the thickened north-west corner of the castle bank.[71]

The East Gate

The Norman east gate is encapsulated in later work (Fig.7a) but its original archway survives. It has a chamfered string course set very low; 2.8m below the springing of the arch, where it might be more commonly expected (Fig.7b). This survives well on the north side and its line can also be discerned on the south, although here it has been broken off. Its position suggests an early date: a similar feature can be found on the late eleventh-century gate-arch of Tickhill Castle (Yorkshire). Lincoln's east gate has been obscured by later alterations, but it seems likely that originally it was a simple opening in the wall facing the town. A parallel might be seen in the eleventh-century castle gate at Richmond (Yorkshire), also facing the town, which was later blocked and incorporated into the south wall of a great tower built c.1160.

Returning to Stocker and Vince's thesis about the development of the castle, the positioning of the east gate has

some relevance to their proposed topography of the Bail. They have shown that a large open space existed outside the castle's east gate, which could have served as a market place and parade ground.[72] It incorporated the surviving modern square called Castle Hill at its northern end and also the trapezoidal built-up area between Drury Lane and Steep Hill, which was encroached by Aaron the Jew by the end of the twelfth century (Fig.1). Clear spaces around castle walls were considered essential for defence,[73] and open spaces in front of castle gates became a common focus for markets: a similar feature can be seen at Nottingham. It is not, therefore, surprising to find that the orientation of Castle Hill respects that of the castle gate and the normal conclusion would be that the two features were laid out about the same time. There is no reason to suppose that this arrangement does not date from the immediate post-Conquest period. However, while Stocker and Vince have placed the erection of the castle's ramparts at a date no earlier than c.1100, they place the building of the castle's east gate even later, at c.1125, along with the setting out of Castle Hill. In fact, the surviving early stone portal is more consistent with a date of c.1100, or perhaps even earlier. The original castle, according to their model, consisted of the whole Bail, with the Lucy Tower motte in the south-west corner. They argue that Eastgate, the main Roman east-west artery of the Bail was diverted from its original true orientation so that it slanted south-west from the Bail's east gate in order to make a bee-line for castle motte. Logically, when the ramparts were built c.1100, according to their plan, one would expect the castle gate to respect the line of this road, but it is placed too far south and facing slightly away from its proposed line. It is difficult to imagine why the gate should ignore a road leading directly to the motte. A more straightforward sequence is that the castle ramparts were raised along with the Lucy Tower motte shortly after the Conquest, when Castle Hill was laid out in front of the castle's town gate. Stone walls and gates were built to replace timber predecessors c.1100, and Eastgate joined Bailgate (the main north-south thoroughfare), which itself gave on to Castle Hill. The work

Fig. 7a. The east gate of the castle, with the Observatory Tower in the background.

Fig. 7b. Original Norman archway of the east gate (north side).

of the City of Lincoln Archaeology Unit in the Bail has demonstrated that most of the Roman roads changed orientation after the Conquest, so Eastgate was not unique in this. Most notable amongst them is a road which has been dated to the period *c*.1075-1100. It describes a large curve from the south Bail gate, going north-east, then north-west. Stocker and Vince argue that its purpose was to link the parish churches of All Saints, St Paul and St Clement, but it also happens to follow the curve of the castle ramparts. In fact, it is likely that these dictated the course of the road.

In 1217 the castle was damaged during a siege by Louis of France and was repaired during the early years of Henry III's reign. Between 1217 and 1220 the Earl of Salisbury and the castellan, Nichola de la Haye, spent over £548 6s.4d. between them,[74] by far the largest recorded expenditure on the building. Although there is no specific reference to either of the gates before 1224, it is likely that improvements to the east gate began at this time, when a new emphasis was being placed on the gatehouse in military architecture.[75] In 1224-25 the sum of £20 was allocated to maintenance of the Lucy Tower, the east gate facing the cathedral and the addition of a barbican to it.[76] This sum seems too small to cover the extensive work carried out and perhaps refers to a plan already in train. The Norman portal was incorporated into a gate tower, in much the same way that the Constable's gate at Dover (Kent) elaborated upon a mural tower built by King John.[77] Housing for a portcullis was also provided, then a further archway was built forward of the Norman arch. The gate tower was not finished in 1227 when the Sheriff was ordered to have it completed.[78] At ground level, the new arch was flanked by the wing walls of the barbican, their wall-walks reached by twin round turrets rising from either side of the archway, the wall between them and above the arch being angled *en bec* (Fig.7a). Two further round towers were placed at the entry to the barbican.[79] It was perhaps to supply masons working on the barbican that an order was made in 1229 to make a lime kiln.[80] Little of this work remains: within the castle walls the west side of the gate tower has gone, replaced by Victorian buildings on either side of the former gate passage. By the thirteenth century the provision of accommodation in gatehouses had become common, as at Nottingham, Beeston (Cheshire) and the Black Gate at Newcastle-upon-Tyne. In 1782 Edward King reported the remains of 'one or two magnificent rooms above, in this tower; but no communication with them ... from the arched gate way beneath; the approach to them being from the walls within the castle'.[81] This description accords with Willson's mid nineteenth-century record of a narrow range of two storeys, described as galleries, between the east gatehouse and the area near the Observatory Tower motte, which he suggested had held 'a considerable mass of buildings'.[82] In 1848 the foundations of the inner walls of the gallery range were still discernible, with loop windows in the curtain wall and a round-headed wall recess in one of the upper rooms. Willson also records a circular staircase leading to a subterranean passage leading westwards into the bailey. Outside the east gate, the barbican and its towers were demolished in 1791.[83] The foundations of the south tower can still be traced on the ground and the vaulted ground floor chamber of its northern counterpart was discovered in 1883 when drains were excavated for the nearby Judges' Lodgings.[84] Of the entire complex only the east wall of the gate tower still stands, with its twin turrets of two storeys, a further floor having been lost. There were spiral staircases in each of the turrets and blocked doorways at first floor level originally gave on to the barbican wall-walk (Fig.7a).

The Lucy Tower (Fig.8)

The Lucy Tower motte dominates the south side of the *enceinte*, standing half inside and half outside the castle precinct, its base originally encircled by a ditch (Fig.1). On the exterior this was the only part of the southern defences to be thus protected because the ground fell so steeply away outside the south wall. On the interior the ditch formed a barrier between the motte and the rest of the bailey and was no doubt spanned by a drawbridge. The shell tower on its summit represents a fine example, despite having lost a full storey. In plan it forms an irregular polygon with pilaster buttresses at each angle. It stands on a well-made chamfered plinth of three courses, with rougher masonry and irregular-sized coursing on each of the faceted wall sections, tied together by good quality ashlar work on the buttresses. The architecture is closely paralleled by the shell keep at Gisors (Eure), where other resemblances to Lincoln have already been noted (above). The tower at Gisors was built by Henry I, almost certainly to replace an earlier timber building contemporary with the motte,[85] and a similar sequence would suit Lincoln. While a great deal of restoration took place in the mid nineteenth century, Willson records that stylistic details were replaced 'in exact accordance with the original work'.[86] The chamfered plinth and imposts, simple treatment of the main entrance and the style of decoration used on its hood-mould are all entirely compatible with a date of *c*.1125-35. Apart from its style, other factors point to Henry I as its instigator; it is unlikely to have been built during Stephen's reign and there is no recorded expenditure which would account for it after the accession of Henry II.

The internal diameter of the tower is roughly 26m x 20m and it was used in the nineteenth century as a cemetery for prisoners. Traces of joist-holes, which supported the floor of an upper storey, remain in the walls; both surviving traces and antiquaries' accounts attest that the tower was originally residential. It would have provided high status, secure accommodation, but there is insufficient evidence to determine the exact layout or function of individual rooms. There are

Fig. 8. The Lucy Tower sketched in 1784.

Fig. 9. Detail of the entrance arch to Lucy Tower.

no windows at ground floor level, but the range of timber apartments within would have surrounded a small courtyard, which would have acted as a light well. The main entrance is housed in a porch and faces north-east. The outer arch is round-headed and decorated only by a hood-mould (Fig.9). It has a chamfered impost, which continues as a string course on the facade. In the wall diametrically opposite this there is a postern gate facing south-west which gave on to the steep motte bank and a sharp descent into the moat below.[87] The Lucy Tower was also accessible from the wall-walks of each section of the south curtain wall, through porches or small forebuildings. The western porch housed a garderobe whose chute discharged into the motte ditch. In 1782 King recorded 'the remains of a passage or covered way' leading to the eastern side of the tower at wall-walk level. He also remarked that access could only be achieved by first ascending, then descending, a staircase inside the eastern forebuilding, where he also noted the existence of a well.[88] Willson described and drew a plan (Fig.10) of this forebuilding, which was destroyed in the mid nineteenth century:

> The lower story appeared to have been covered by a groined vault, springing from four small round shafts, placed in the angles. There was a chimney on the north side of this room, and a staircase adjoining to it which led to the upper story.[89]

The Observatory Tower

The smaller motte in the south-east angle of the *enceinte* bears a square stone tower showing work of the twelfth to fourteenth centuries which was added to during the nineteenth century and embellished by a turret. It is this later structure, built by a prison governor who was interested in astronomy, which has given the tower its present name. Above-ground remains of the medieval stone tower are fragmentary, but differences in the masonry suggest that the southern half of the west facade and the spine wall, which runs east to west, belong to a twelfth-century phase while most of the remaining walls were rebuilt during the thirteenth or fourteenth centuries.

The most interesting aspect of the tower was revealed by excavation in 1975 by Reynolds.[90] The removal of an earth floor laid during the eighteenth or nineteenth century revealed the remains of a staircase in the south-west quarter of the building and earlier wall faces on the north and east sides and

on part of the south side. These followed the same alignment as the later walls, which stand on top of them but were clearly independent of them. They were investigated to a depth of 2.4m and for the first 1.1m to 1.5m, they were found to be faced in ashlar with fine diagonal tooling. After this a slight offset occurred, then the stonework became rougher and cruder for a further metre, beyond which all attempts at coursing ceased. The rubble filling, which higher up formed the wall core, spread out to provide a foundation platform for the tower as a whole. Probing did not find the bottom of this

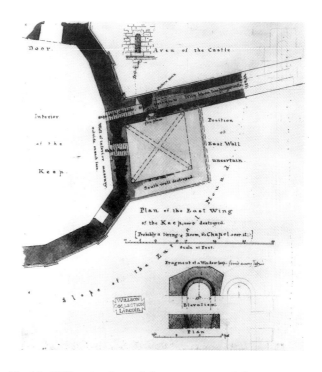

Fig.10. Willson's plan of the east wing of the Lucy Tower before its destruction in the mid nineteenth century. (Copyright, Society of Antiquaries of London, MS 786/G p. 69).

and the excavator inferred that it goes down to original ground level, forming a core inside the motte. Reynolds concluded that the Observatory Tower motte was designed from the beginning to support a square tower on its summit, its foundations being buried within the earthwork. He drew parallels with other mottes dating from the first half of the twelfth century, which have revealed masonry cores. At Totnes (Devon) a rubble-filled foundation 4.8 by 3.9m was traced to a depth of over 3m and was assumed to stand on the original ground surface.[91] At Farnham (Surrey) the stone tower was supported on a masonry core within the motte, although here the central portion was left open for use as a cellar and access to a well.[92] A motte was also found to enclose the basement of the tower at Ascot Doilly (Oxfordshire), having been raised with the structure.[93] Pottery recovered from Reynolds' excavation indicated that the Observatory tower motte was built during the twelfth century and the life span of the pottery did not preclude a date before the middle of the century.[94] He suggested that the superstructure of the tower might originally have been of timber, later replaced in stone, as Rigold proposed for the Totnes example.[95]

The Duplication of Mottes

Lincoln is unusual in having two mottes, each bearing the remains of a great tower. In England only one other castle, Lewes (Sussex), has a second motte, though there they are apparently contemporary. Although the precise relationship between towers and lordship is imperfectly understood, it can hardly be questioned that the former acted as visible symbols of the latter.[96] The link between building a great tower as a mark, even celebration, of status has been noted at Hedingham (Essex),[97] where the ceremonial and symbolic function of the building dictated its form.[98] Further investigation is needed into the historical background of sites like Lincoln, which have two mottes or towers. In western France, where cultural ties with England were strong throughout the twelfth century, dual towers of this date are slightly more numerous, though still uncommon. At Saint-Laurent-les-Tours (Lot) there is a twelfth-century donjon but another was added to the site, possibly as an outward sign of the division of the lordship which occurred in c.1360.[99] At Excideuil (Dordogne)[100] two donjons were also built, one during the twelfth century and the other around the turn of the thirteenth century. Contemporary twelfth-century towers stand adjacent to one another at Vernode (Dordogne)[101] and at Le Blanc (Indre).[102] However, perhaps the most significant example of the double donjon occurs at Niort (Deux-Sevres),[103] a city in Aquitaine, where the twin towers of about the 1160s seem to proclaim the dual lordship of Queen Eleanor, to whom the town belonged, and Henry II. Or, perhaps, of Eleanor and her son Richard, whom she was actively promoting as her prospective Aquitainian heir at that time. A possible explanation for building a second great tower at Lincoln might be the proclamation of Countess Lucy's hereditary constableship of the castle: hence the name of one of the towers; this, particularly against the uncertain background of the civil war.[104]

The name 'Lucy Tower' attached to the shell keep on the original castle motte has given rise to some confusion in the past concerning the sequence of the development of the two mottes, and it will be argued here that the name is still something of a misnomer. It used to be thought that this motte and tower were additions made by Lucy, countess of Chester, during the twelfth century while the Observatory Tower was taken to be the original motte of the eleventh-century castle.[105] It is now fully accepted that the so-called 'Lucy Tower' occupies the original motte of the eleventh-century castle, which was positioned by William the Conqueror's engineers to dominate the town most effectively. Reynolds' excavation proved that the Observatory Tower motte was a twelfth-century addition to the castle plan and the excavator took both motte and phase 1 tower to be contemporary. Nevertheless, the date of the motte and the motive for its construction remain the subject of some controversy.[106]

Lucy was a kinswoman (probably a daughter) of Thorold, and she was certainly married to Ivo Taillebois, both of whom were sheriffs of Lincoln.[107] Hill has made a strong case for a close connection between an hereditary shrievalty and the constableship of the castle,[108] which she probably held in her own right.[109] William de Roumare, her son by her second marriage to Roger Fitzgerold, was created earl of Lincoln c.1141 and her younger son, Ranulf Gernons, inherited the earldom of Chester from his father, Ranulf de Meschin, Lucy's third husband. Her sons both played active roles in the history of the castle during the civil war[110] and we know that the family constableship had led to some building under their auspices. A charter issued by King Stephen makes it clear that Countess Lucy had fortified a tower within the castle which, on fulfilment of certain obligations on both sides, her son Ranulf was allowed to keep along with the constableship of both county and castle.[111] It is most significant that the confirmation of Ranulf's right to hold the tower permanently appears to be firmly linked with his tenure of the constableship of castle and county. The Observatory Tower motte with its first phase tower, possibly of timber, seems most likely to be the tower referred to in the charter as Lucy's fortification, while the twelfth-century masonry of the spine wall, which Reynolds attributed to a second phase,[112] represents a rebuilding by Ranulf. We know that Henry III ordered repairs to the 'Lucy Tower' in 1224-25[113] and, while there is thirteenth-century work on the Observatory Tower, none is discernible on the tower now called the Lucy Tower.

Reynolds conceded that the tower Ranulf Gernons was to keep was the Observatory Tower, and he also speculated that its motte might have been built by Ranulf in response to Stephen's charter.[114] Nevertheless, he persisted in Willson's view that the tower Lucy had fortified was the shell keep on the original castle motte, apparently on the sole evidence of its name.[115] The earliest mention of this name occurs in a report of 1327 on the general state of decay of the castle. This commented on all three of the castle's towers, saying that the Lucy Tower, the West Tower and 'arountour' (a round tower) had all fallen.[116] The last was certainly Cobb Hall[117] and the report treated the gates separately, so the 'West Tower' cannot refer to the west gate tower. Unless a tower has totally vanished without trace, the present Lucy Tower seems the best candidate to be described as the West Tower, leaving the 1327 reference to the 'Lucy Tower' to mean the Observatory Tower, at the eastern end of the castle. In 1782 the antiquary King did not give names to either of the motte towers, but in 1724 an angle tower in the city walls near Brayford Pool was mistakenly called the 'Lucy Tower' by Stukeley, so there was already some confusion over names at that date.[118] Prior to its Victorian embellishment, the Observatory Tower may not have presented a very striking prospect. It may simply be that in the first half of the nineteenth century the name fostered in folk memory, which recalled one of the more colourful characters from the castle's history, came to be mistakenly applied to the shell tower, the more impressive of the castle's two donjons.

Conclusion

Despite its rather sorry history during the later Middle Ages, Lincoln Castle reveals rare and illuminating aspects of early military architecture. In the early stone walls, shell tower, west gate and barbican, Cobb Hall and the development of the east gatehouse there are many points of interest to the student. Added to these, the question of the dual mottes and the glimpsed revelations about motte construction under the Observatory Tower make the site one of the most interesting in the country. However, opportunities for modem archaeological investigation have been few. Much of the bailey is occupied by the nineteenth-century gaol and courthouse and, because of its modern role, the fabric of the castle has suffered from a century and a half of indiscriminate refacing. There is no doubt that a thorough survey is overdue and would repay the cost and effort involved.

Notes

1. E. A. Freeman, *The Norman Conquest*, vol.2 (Oxford, 1870), pp.137-38.
2. *The History of the King's Works*, edited by H. M. Colvin, 6 vols (1963-73), i, pp.21-23 and Fig.5.
3. C. Drage, 'Urban castles', in *Urban Archaeology in Britain*, edited by J. Schofield and R. Leech, CBA Research Report No.61 (1987), p.117 and Fig.52.
4. N. J. G. Pounds, *The Medieval Castle in England and Wales. A Social and Political History* (Cambridge, 1990), p.309, n.11.
5. P. Marshall and J. Samuels, 'Recent excavations at Newark Castle, Nottinghamshire', *Transactions of the Thoroton Society of Nottinghamshire*, 98 (1994), pp.49-57; P. Marshall and J. Samuels, *Guardian of the Trent* (Newark, 1997), pp.10-12.
6. Pounds, *The Medieval Castle*, pp.56-57.
7. J. Schofield and A. Vince, *Medieval Towns* (1994), p.19.
8. J. W. F. Hill, *Medieval Lincoln* (Cambridge, 1948), p.54.
9. *Ibid.*, pp.35-36.
10. *Ibid.*, p.72.
11. R. Allen Brown, *Castles from the Air* (Cambridge, 1989), p.147.
12. D. Stocker and A. Vince, 'The early Norman Castle at Lincoln and a re-evaluation of the original west tower of Lincoln Cathedral', *Medieval Archaeology* 41 (1997), pp.223-33. See also above, pp.9-22.
13. This disregard of pre-existing settlement was typical of royal military foundations, the main consideration being the acquisition of the best position. *Domesday Book* also records the destruction of property due to castle building at Cambridge, Norwich, Shrewsbury, Stamford, Warwick, Wallingford, York, Ely, Huntingdon and Worcester, *History of the King's Works*, i, p.24: see D. Parsons's essay in this volume.
14. Stocker and Vince, 'The early Norman Castle', Fig.9.
15. G. Beresford, *Goltho: The Development of an Early Medieval Manor c.850-1150*, English Heritage Archaeological Report No.4 (1987); B. K. Davison, 'Excavations at Sulgrave. Northamptonshire, 1960-1976', *Archaeological Journal*, 134 (1977), pp.105-14. See also S. J. Speight, 'Violence and socio-political order in post-conquest Yorkshire', in *Violence and Society in the Early Medieval West*, edited by G. Halsall (Woodbridge, 1998), pp.168-70.
16. A fortification, certainly, but with a strong private residential element.
17. This is based on the development of an interpretation of the cathedral west front first put forward by R. D. H. Gem, 'Lincoln Minster: *ecclesia pulchra, ecclesia fortis*', *Medieval Art and Architecture at Lincoln Cathedral*, The British Archaeological Association Conference Transactions for the year 1982 (1986), pp.9-28.
18. T. A. Hislop, *Norwich Castle Keep* (1994), p.7.
19. P. Marshall and T. Foulds, 'The Royal Castle', in *A Centenary History of Nottingham*, edited by J. Beckett (Manchester, 1997).
20. R. Allen Brown, 'Royal Castle Building in England, 1154-1216', *English Historical Review*, 70 (1955), pp.353-98, esp. p.391.
21. *Ibid.*, p.393
22. *History of the King's Works*, ii, p.704.
23. *Ibid.*, p.705.
24. *Ibid.*, p.705.
25. *Ibid.*, pp.757-60.
26. See D. Renn's paper in this volume.
27. *History of the King's Works*, i, p.119.
28. *History of the King's Works*, ii, p.705.
29. The others were Canterbury, Chester, Chichester, Colchester, Exeter, Gloucester. Leicester, Rochester, Winchester, Worcester and York. For comparative plans of their positions within these towns, see Pounds, *The Medieval Castle*, p.208, Fig.8.5.
30. Stocker and Vince have suggested that the line of the northern bank was diverted to avoid the churchyards of St Clement and St Paul which, in view of the special status apparently given to the Bail in general, might well be the case. It would display an unusual sensitivity, however, for there are plenty of examples of Norman castles impinging on graveyards as, for example, at Newark: Marshall and Samuels, *Guardian of the Trent*, pp.7-8 and 10. The shape of the enclosure is not unusual.
31. Allen Brown, 'Royal Castle Building in England', p.59; D. R. Cook, 'The Norman military revolution in England', *Anglo-Norman Studies*, 2 (1978), pp.94-102; M. Bennet, 'Peace and warfare', *Anglo-Norman Studies*, 11 (1988), pp.37-57; Pounds, *The Medieval Castle*, pp.7-8.
32. M. W. Barley and F. Straw, 'Nottingham', in *Historic Towns. Maps and Plans of Towns and Cities in the British Isles, with Historical Commentaries from Earliest Times to 1800*, edited by M. D. Lobel, vol.1 (Oxford, 1969).
33. C. Drage, *Nottingham Castle: A Place Full Royal* (Nottingham. 1989), Fig.4A.
34. Marshall and Foulds, 'The Royal Castle', p.44.
35. Leslie E. Webster and John Cherry, eds, 'Medieval Britain in 1979' *Medieval Archaeology*, 24 (1980), pp.218-64, esp. pp.228-29.
36. S. E. Rigold, *Porchester Castle, Hampshire* (1965), p.5.
37. M. Bouard, *Le Château de Caen* (1979), p.10.
38. P. Toussaint, *Gisors, le Château* (1993), p.5.
39. S. Morillo, *Warfare under the Anglo-Norman Kings 1066-1135* (1994), p.96.
40. C. H. Hunter-Blair and H. L. Honeyman, *Norham Castle* (1966), pp.9-12.
41. E. J. Willson, 'Lincoln Castle, notices of its History and the existing remains; illustrated by a plan from actual survey', *Memoirs Illustrative of the History and Antiquities of the County and City of Lincoln communicated to the Annual Meeting of the Archaeological Institute of Great Britain and Ireland held at Lincoln, July 1848* (1850), p.290. A full account of the discovery is given in the *Gentleman's Magazine* (1836), pt i, p.583.
42. D. A. Stocker, 'Lincoln Castle', *Archaeology in Lincoln 1982-1983*, Annual Report of the Lincoln Archaeological Trust, 11 (Lincoln, 1983), pp.18-27, esp. pp.21-23.
43. The phrase 'nailing the valley' is used in Germany of the distinctive local towers called *bergfrieden*; M. W. Thompson, *The Rise of the Castle* (1991), p.23.
44. Sir C. Peers, *Richmond Castle* (1981), p.17.
45. R. Allen Brown, *Rochester Castle* (1969), p.6.
46. R. Allen Brown, *English Castles* (1976), p.63.
47. *The Registrum Antiquissimum of the Cathedral Church of Lincoln*, edited by C. W. Foster and K. Major, 10 vols (Lincoln Record Society, 1931-73), i, p.267; Hill, *Medieval Lincoln*, p.82; *History of the King's Works*, ii, p.704.
48. Willson, 'Lincoln Castle, notices of its History', p.285.
49. Stocker and Vince, 'The early Norman Castle', p.224.
50. Marshall and Samuels, 'Recent excavations at Newark Castle', p.51; Marshall and Samuels, *Guardian of the Trent*, p.18.
51. Willson, 'Lincoln Castle, notices of its History', pp.285-86.
52. R. P. Wilcox has written the definitive work on this subject *Timber and Iron Reinforcement in Early Buildings*, Society of Antiquaries Occasional Paper, ns, II (1981).
53. *Ibid.*, pp.23-27.
54. *Ibid.*, pp.1-35.
55. J. P. Bushe-Fox, 'Some notes on Roman coast defences' *Journal of Roman Studies*, 22 (1932), pp.60-72, esp. p.62, quoted in Wilcox *Timber and Iron Reinforcement*, p.23.
56. Wilcox *Timber and Iron Reinforcement*, p.31.
57. *Ibid.*, p.28.
58. *Ibid.*, p.12.
59. P. Marshall, *A survey of the Twelfth-century gatehouse at Newark Castle, Nottinghamshire* (forthcoming).
60. For alternative interpretations, see Donel's and Jones's and Thompson's papers in this volume
61. See also Donel's and Jones's paper in this volume.
62. Stocker, 'Lincoln Castle', pp.23-24.
63. The chapel over the gate passage at Prudhoe is a thirteenth-century insertion: A. Saunders, *Prudhoe Castle* (1993), p.9.
64. Stocker, 'Lincoln Castle', p.25.
65. S. R. Blaylock, *Exeter Castle Gatehouse Architectural Survey, 1985* (Exeter, 1987), p.7.
66. *Ibid.*, p.10.
67. Stocker, 'Lincoln Castle', pp.24-25 and Fig.9.
68. Pipe Rolls, 18 Henry III, rot.4.
69. Stocker, 'Lincoln Castle', pp.25-26.
70. *Ibid.*, p.26.
71. *Ibid.*
72. Stocker and Vince, 'The early Norman Castle', pp.226-27.
73. Pounds, *The Medieval Castle*, p.209.
74. *History of the King's Works*, ii, p.705
75. *History of the King's Works*, i, p.118.
76. Pipe Rolls, 9 Henry III, rot.13; *Rotuti Litterarum Clausarum*, II, pp.29, 31.
77. *History of the King's Works*, ii, p.634.
78. *Ibid.*, p.705.

79. For a reconstruction drawing of this see H. Elliott and D. A. Stocker, *Lincoln Castle* (Lincoln, FLARE and Lincolnshire County Council, 1984), p.23.

80. *History of the King's Works*, ii, p.705.

81. E. King, 'Observations on ancient castles', *Archaeologia*, vi (1782), pp.261-65.

82. Willson, 'Lincoln Castle, notices of its History', p.289.

83. Elliott and Stocker, *Lincoln Castle*, p.24.

84. *Stamford Mercury and Chronicle*, October 1883, quoted in Elliott and Stocker, *Lincoln Castle*, p.24.

85. P. Toussaint, *Gisors, le Château*, p.6.

86. Willson, 'Lincoln Castle, notices of its History', pp.287-88.

87. King thought that the story of the earl of Chester's escape from Lincoln castle just as King Stephen was entering the town was made credible by the existence of this postern. King, 'Observations on ancient castles', p.262.

88. *Ibid.*, pp.263-64.

89. Willson, 'Lincoln Castle, notices of its History', p.288.

90. N. Reynolds, 'Investigations in the Observatory Tower, Lincoln Castle', *Medieval Archaeology*, 19 (1975), pp.201-05.

91. S. E. Rigold, 'Totnes Castle: recent excavations by the Ancient Monuments Department, Ministry of Works', *Transactions of the Devonshire Association*, 86 (1954), pp.228-56.

92. M. W. Thompson, 'Recent excavations in the keep of Farnham castle Surrey', *Medieval Archaeology*, 4 (1960), pp.81-94.

93. E. M. Jope and R. I. Threlfall, 'The twelfth-century castle at Ascot Doilly, Oxfordshire: its history and excavation', *Antiquaries Journal*, 39 (1959), 219-73.

94. Reynolds, 'Investigations in the Observatory Tower', p.204.

95. *Ibid.*, p.205.

96. For the role of donjons respecting lordship see P. Marshall, 'The ceremonial function of the donjon', *Château Gaillard*, 20 (2002), pp.141-51; P. Marshall, 'The great tower as residence', in *The Seigneurial Residence in Europe AD c.800-1600*, edited by G. Meirion-Jones, E. Impey and M. Jones, BAR International Series No.1088 (Oxford, 2003), pp.27-44.

97. Allen Brown, *English Castles*, p.69.

98. P. Dixon and P. Marshall, 'The great tower at Hedingham Castle: a reassessment', in *Anglo-Norman Castles*, edited by R. Liddiard (Woodbridge, 2003), pp.297-306.

99. C-L. Salch, *Dictionnaire des Châteaux et des Fortifications du Moyen Age en France* (Strasbourg, 1979), p.1053.

100. A. Chatelain, *Donjons Romans des Pays d'Ouest* (Paris, 1973), p.215, pls XVII and XLVII.

101. *Ibid.*, p.209, pl.XVI.

102. *Ibid.*, p.142, pls VIII and XXVIII.

103. *Ibid.*, p.178, pls XII and XXXVII.

104. Whether or not one accepts Reynolds' interpretation of the Observatory Tower motte and tower as contemporary structures or prefers Thompson's view that the motte was built first and the tower added later hardly affects the possibility that the tower, at least, was built by Countess Lucy.

105. J. W. F. Hill, 'The Castle and City of Lincoln', *Archaeological Journal*, 103 (1946), p.158. This interpretation was followed by Allen Brown and Colvin, *History of the King's Works*, ii, p.704.

106. Reynolds' dating is accepted in this paper, though challenged by M. W. Thompson in his paper in this volume. Although Thompson attributes the building of the motte to another person, the principle of its representing the right of occupation or the *dominium* of that individual remains essentially the same.

107. Hill, *Medieval Lincoln*, pp.92-96.

108. *Ibid.*, p.89.

109. *Ibid.*, p.96.

110. For a brief account see *ibid.*, pp.177-81.

111. *Registrum Antiquissimum*, i, pp.287-88. See also Willson, 'Lincoln Castle, notices of its History', p.280. The charter has variously been dated to 1140 by *History of the King's Works*, ii, p.704; 1149 by Hill, *Medieval Lincoln*, p.181; 1151 by Reynolds, 'Investigations in the Observatory Tower', p.205.

112. Reynolds, 'Investigations in the Observatory Tower', p.205 and Fig.78.

113. *History of the King's Works*, ii, p.705.

114. Reynolds, 'Investigations in the Observatory Tower', p.205.

115. *Ibid.*

116. *Ibid.*

117. The word cob also means round: Elliott and Stocker, *Lincoln Castle*, p.21.

118. *Itinerarium Curiosum* (1724), p.84, quoted in Willson, 'Lincoln Castle, notices of its History', p.288, who refutes the name as a mistake.

Lincoln Castle and its Occupants in the Reign of King Stephen

Paul Dalton

One of the most famous and protracted conflicts in the troubled reign of Stephen was that between the king and Ranulf II earl of Chester for control of Lincoln castle. The main events of this conflict are well known.[1] It began sometime before Christmas in 1140 when Ranulf and his half-brother and ally William I de Roumare, lord of Bolingbroke, seized the castle and expelled the king's garrison. This occurred shortly before or after the king went to Lincoln and made a pact with Ranulf, increased Ranulf and William's honours and went away in peace. Stephen was then urged to return to Lincoln to besiege the half-brothers by the bishop and citizens of Lincoln, arrived during the Christmas festival of 1140, secured control of the city but not the castle and was unable to prevent Ranulf from escaping from the castle and seeking military assistance from his father-in-law, Robert earl of Gloucester. Ranulf returned to Lincoln with Earl Robert and an army and on 2 February 1141 joined battle with Stephen. The king was captured and taken off to Empress Matilda's court, and Ranulf appears to have been left in charge of Lincoln castle. In 1144 Stephen besieged him there again, but failed to take the fortress. Two years later he finally dislodged Ranulf from the castle after arresting him in his court and forcing him to surrender his fortresses in return for his liberty. Ranulf then besieged Lincoln castle, but was forced to break off his assault. He resumed his campaign against the king in Lincolnshire in 1149 and almost subdued the city of Lincoln, but does not appear to have recovered the castle before his death in December 1153.

This paper will attempt to throw new light on the dispute over Lincoln castle, and will argue that the issues involved in it were more complicated than has hitherto been realised. The paper will demonstrate that although Ranulf and William's claims to the castle, and Stephen's policy towards the Beaumont family, the Scots and William d'Aubigny *pincerna*, who were all rivals of the half-brothers, had important effects on the dispute, several other factors are likely to have influenced and complicated events. These include the existence of the two mottes, the presence of which may indicate that Lincoln castle was subject to dual lordship; the possible interests in the fortress and the local ambitions and authority of the bishop of Lincoln, that probably rivalled those of Ranulf and William; the wider territorial and administrative aspirations of Ranulf and William in Lincolnshire, the Midlands and the North; the position of William as earl of Lincoln and local justice; the nature of the pacts or *conventiones* that King Stephen made with Ranulf and possibly with William before, in and after 1140 that further defined the terms of their political relationship and possibly incorporated conditions governing the control of Lincoln castle; and the likelihood that Stephen was attempting to employ, and perhaps to exploit, the French castle customs of rendability and pledging – or something similar to them – to recover and retain control of fortresses. A consideration of these factors shows that the more closely we look at events at Lincoln between 1140 and 1153, the greater the number of possibilities becomes. But in illuminating these possibilities the Lincoln evidence helps to illuminate the complexity and subtlety of the politics of Stephen's reign, and shows that the importance of the history of Lincoln castle in the anarchy transcends local affairs. It casts new light on baronial aims, ambitions and rivalries, Stephen's castle policy and conception of his own authority, the baronial response to his rulership and to the problems associated with the weakening of royal power, and the character and political ability of the king and some of his most important political opponents. It warns us that there may have been much more to the political conflict and castle warfare which was such a widespread and characteristic feature of the anarchy than we may have realised, and it helps to explain the subsequent determination of Henry II to retain more fortresses in the hands of the king and royal custodians.

To understand the dispute over Lincoln castle it is important to establish what the status of the fortress was before 1140, and who the occupants were. The castle was founded in 1068 by William the Conqueror, had walls by 1115, and incorporated two towers by 1146 at the latest, one of which had been built, rebuilt or fortified (*firmavit*) by Countess Lucy of Bolingbroke (died *c*.1136-38), the mother of Ranulf of Chester and William de Roumare.[2] Two mottes survive in the castle today, one crowned by a twelfth-century structure known since at least the late eighteenth century as the 'Lucy' tower, the other supporting an edifice known as the Observatory tower.[3] A tower 'de Luce' is mentioned in the fortress in 1225, but which of the two towers this refers to is uncertain.[4] Excavations beneath the Observatory tower carried out in the early 1970s indicated that this may have been the later of the two towers and consequently the one built or fortified by Lucy. However, Michael Thompson has suggested a new and radically different scenario for the early history of the castle.[5]

Thompson suggests that in 1068 the castle was a motte and bailey fortress with the motte on the site of the present 'Lucy' tower, and walls enclosing the bailey that ran north-east from this motte to the site of the present Cobb Hall tower, from there to the site of the Roman West Gate that was then the main entrance, and thence back to the motte; that when construction of the Cathedral began in the early 1070s the West Gate was buried and an annex occupied by the bishop was added to the eastern side of the castle with a gate that faced the west end of the Cathedral; and that the motte in the south-east corner of the castle beneath the present Observatory tower could have been an original feature of this annex. Thompson also suggests that the tower which a charter granted by King Stephen to Ranulf of Chester (probably in 1146) states was *firmavit* by Countess Lucy was the present 'Lucy' tower on the site of the original 1068 motte, and was constructed perhaps *c*.1125 in the king's part of the castle. Thompson proposes that Bishop Alexander may have been effectively moved out of the castle by the king into a new residence in the Roman East Gate of the Bail with its tower between 1130 and 1133, and that the structure then on top of the Observatory tower motte, that had possibly been Alexander's residence, could have been rebuilt as a consequence of Stephen's charter for Ranulf.[6]

A different, but not entirely incompatible, interpretation of the early development of the present castle has been suggested by David Stocker and Alan Vince. Like Thompson, they believe that the first motte was in the south-west corner of the old Roman enclosure of the upper city, and date its establishment to the period from 1068/*c*.1075 to *c*.1100. But they also suggest that the present castle enclosure was under construction in the period from *c*.1100 to *c*.1125, that a new east gate for the castle, associated ranges and a new motte were built between *c*.1125 and *c*.1140, that the 1130s were a significant stage in the building work and that the de la Haye family were responsible for it. They argue that the developments in the 1130s were associated with the withdrawal from the Bail of Bishop Alexander of Lincoln, who had previously 'played the dominant role in the government of the castle and in the provision of the Castle Guard, providing the castle with twenty knights'. This withdrawal is reflected by the permission granted by Henry I to Alexander between 1123 and 1133 for one-third of the knights of the bishopric of Lincoln to perform their military service at the bishop's castle of Newark rather than at Lincoln; and it was made first to the East Gate of the Bail, which was granted to Alexander by King Henry in the period 1130 x 1133, and then to a new palace just to the south of the Bail, the land for which Alexander received from Stephen in 1137. The establishment of this new palace can be viewed as the first stage in the creation of the Cathedral Close, and took place at about the same time as the completion of the present castle enclosure, a development which 'finally divorced the ecclesiastical and secular powers and so rendered the Bail – which had originally included both powers – redundant in practical terms'. In addition, Stocker and Vince suggest that in the 1140s Bishop Alexander converted the west end of the Cathedral from a heavily fortified block tower, which 'must have seemed, indeed, to be the "keep" of Lincoln Castle', into a more conventional great-church west end. They also suggest that Countess Lucy may have built a tower on the motte in the south-west corner of the castle, or a tower on a new motte in the south-east corner (though this could be the work of her son, Earl Ranulf) facing towards the western edge of the Cathedral precinct.[7] Elements of this interpretation are consistent with the rivalry which existed for a time between Ranulf and Alexander bishop of Lincoln for power within Lincoln and Lincolnshire, which will be discussed below.

The interest of Countess Lucy in the castle may have sprung from the fact that she was a kinswoman, just possibly the daughter, of Turold, who was sheriff of Lincolnshire at some point in the Conqueror's reign and may have enjoyed the custody of Lincoln castle.[8] Alternatively, it may have been due to her first marriage to Ivo Taillebois, who was sheriff of Lincolnshire in 1086, or to her tremendous local authority in Lincolnshire where she held extensive estates assessed later at sixty knights' fees, which were divided between her two sons.[9] The existence of this interest by 1116 is suggested by a charter issued by Henry I notifying Lucy's third husband, Ranulf le Meschin, Osbert the sheriff and Picot son of Colswein that he had granted permission to Bishop Robert of Lincoln to make an exit or door in the wall of the castle.[10]

The situation at Lincoln was very unusual. Dual mottes exist at only one other castle in England, Lewes, and their presence at Lincoln considerably complicates the history of the fortress in Stephen's reign.[11] The exact status in 1140 of the two mottes or towers that King Stephen's charter for Ranulf shows to have been in existence by 1146, and that had possibly been built by 1138 on the sites of the present 'Lucy' and Observatory towers, is unclear. Given the fact that in England neither William Rufus nor Henry I are known to have 'conceded hereditary castellanies, much less private castles, without some attempt at control', it is likely that the fortress had remained under some form of royal supervision before 1135, despite the position of the bishop of Lincoln there.[12] Henry I's charter granting Bishop Robert permission to make an exit in the castle wall is certainly indicative of such control. It is clear that in 1140, not long after the suggested withdrawal of the bishop from the castle, at least part of the castle was in the charge of a royal garrison. One of the chroniclers uses the words 'arcem' and 'turrim' to describe the fortification occupied by the king's men at that date, suggesting that they were not in possession of the entire castle; but such an interpretation may be too dogmatic.[13] As Thompson points out, more excavation is needed before we can be certain about the dates and occupancy of the two mottes.[14]

We do not know for certain the names of the royal constables of Lincoln castle before 1135, though it is possible that some of the sheriffs of Lincolnshire served in this capacity.[15] None of the sources that describe the seizure of the castle in 1140 name the royal constable. It may have been Robert de la Haye, who had acquired extensive Lincolnshire estates through marriage to Muriel, daughter of the Domesday Lincolnshire tenant in chief Colswein, a man who may have been related to Countess Lucy.[16] Robert, who was probably still alive in September 1134, was possibly the same man as the Robert de la Haye who attested as steward several charters of Henry I in 1131 and who acted as a royal justice in Normandy.[17] Described as 'the constable', Robert attested with his son Richard a charter granting land in the Bail.[18] Between 1155 and 1162 Richard himself received from Henry II a restoration of his constabulary of Lincolnshire, the custody of Lincoln castle and all the lands of his father in Lincolnshire.[19] In August 1189 Richard's eldest daughter, Nicholaa, who inherited his English estates, was confirmed in the constableship of Lincoln castle as her father and grandfather had held it by King Richard I.[20] There is no direct evidence, however, that Robert de la Haye was ever constable of Lincoln, and even if he was it could be that he died in or shortly after 1134, and that the castle then passed to Reginald the constable of Lincoln. Reginald is addressed together with Hugh son of Eudo the sheriff of Lincolnshire and the burgesses of Lincoln in a writ of Bishop Roger of Salisbury that may have been issued between December 1135 and June 1139.[21]

Whoever the royal constable of Lincoln castle was in 1140, he was ousted when the earl of Chester and his half brother, William de Roumare, seized the castle. H. A. Cronne and R. H. C. Davis did much to illuminate the reasons for this seizure. Cronne pointed out that it is possible that either Ranulf or William 'might have inherited through their mother colourable claims to the shrievalty of Lincolnshire and with it the constableship of the castle, for the two offices were sometimes held together, and feudal ambition aimed at making them hereditary'.[22] He also noted how Ranulf's father, Ranulf le Meschin, lost the lordship of Carlisle, and was deprived by Henry I of the dowry and inheritance of his wife and the wardship of his stepson William de Roumare's lands. This was possibly part of the price for allowing le Meschin to inherit the earldom of Chester c.1120. As a result of this and other offences of Henry I against Countess Lucy and her sons, Ranulf II inherited 'a sense of grievance in respect of the treatment his parents had received at the hands of the crown, and a debt of £1,000 which his father still owed for the [earldom of Chester]'.[23] Cronne and Davis linked the seizure of Lincoln castle in 1140 to Ranulf's ambitions to recover control of the lordship of Carlisle. Together with the earldom of Huntingdon and the town of Doncaster, Carlisle was granted by Stephen to the Scots in February or March 1136, and effectively confirmed by him to them in April 1139 in a treaty that granted the earldom of Northumbria to Henry of Scotland and may have led to William de Roumare being deprived of the earldom of Cambridge.[24] According to John of Hexham, the seizure of Lincoln castle followed an attempt by Ranulf to capture Henry, son of King David of Scots, who went to the English court in 1140, and who was saved from falling into Ranulf's hands by King Stephen.[25] Cronne added other items to the list of grievances that are supposed to have inspired Ranulf and William's hostility to Stephen. These included the marriage that Stephen arranged between Henry of Scotland and Ada, daughter of William II de Warenne, who was the half-sister of the Beaumont twins, Robert and Waleran. They also included the great favour Stephen bestowed upon the Beaumonts, adding to their considerable power in the Midlands, where they were rivals and potential enemies of Earl Ranulf.[26] Cronne also argued that the creation of William d'Aubigny *pincerna* as earl of Lincoln about 1139 may have 'filled up the cup of Ranulf's resentment', since William de Roumare 'had a claim upon Stephen's gratitude for his services as justiciar of Normandy; and the extent of his Lincolnshire fiefs . . . made a strong case for the priority of his claims to the earldom . . . while his rival had no lands in the shire at all'.[27]

There is almost certainly some substance to Cronne's and Davis's interpretations, but they do not provide the whole story.[28] It should be noted that in the treaty he made with King David in 1149, Ranulf was quite prepared to surrender his claims to Carlisle in return for a recognition of his claims to the lordship of Lancaster.[29] His claims to Lincoln castle, and those of his half-brother William, must have been encouraged by the weakening of royal control and competition for allegiance in Stephen's reign that led several barons to demand or to try to establish, and the king and the empress occasionally to grant, custodianship or possession (sometimes hereditary) of royal and private castles.[30] It is significant, as Cronne realised, that one of these barons was William de Roumare's brother-in-law, Baldwin de Redvers, who in an episode that parallels in many ways what happened at Lincoln in 1140 seized the royal castle of Exeter in 1136 and attempted to dominate the city there.[31] 'On hearing this the king was enraged at the rash presumption of Baldwin, especially because it was clearer than daylight that his rebellion against him was unjust, since the king had a reasonable claim to the custody of the castle of Exeter, which had always been a royal possession.'[32]

Another factor that was probably involved in Ranulf and William's seizure of Lincoln castle was competition between the half-brothers and Bishop Alexander of Lincoln for local authority in Lincoln and Lincolnshire. The half-brothers and the bishop were probably already rivals for authority in Lincoln before the reign of Stephen; and, if the suggestion that the bishop withdrew from the castle in the 1130s is correct, this may have strengthened the resolve of the half-brothers to assert their claims to control the fortress. Further encouragement or provocation may have been provided by Alexander's position as a local justice in Lincolnshire and his possession of castles at Sleaford (Lincs.), Newark (Notts.) and Banbury (Oxfords.), and by his receipt of a series of royal grants in the late 1120s and early 1130s conveying an extensive body of property and rights.[33] As we have seen, Henry I granted Alexander control of the Roman East Gate of the Bail of Lincoln. In addition, he made several grants allowing Alexander to develop his interests at Newark, where he had built or fortified the castle, including the right to build a bridge over the Trent, to divert the royal highway, to make a causeway and ditch for his fish-pond, to hold a fair at the castle, and to transfer there a third of the knights' service of his knights belonging to the bishopric of Lincoln, who had been accustomed to serve at Lincoln castle.[34] By the end of 1139 King Stephen added the fee of Adam de Hothfield and the transfer of its castle-guard service from Dover to Newark or elsewhere, a site for a new bishop's palace at Lincoln, a house and messuage there, the church of the king's manor of Torksey, release from the annual payment of ten pounds for the farm of Well wapentake, the service of two knights formerly dependent on the honour of Lancaster, and possibly the king's manor of Eagle (Lincs.), a four-day fair at Sleaford, and Alice de Condet's castle of Thorngate in the suburbs of Lincoln together with other lands of hers and the wardship of her son.[35]

Some of Alexander's powers and the grants he received from the crown were in direct conflict with the interests of Ranulf and William. Ranulf later secured grants from King Stephen of Torksey, the honour of Lancaster and a restoration to Alice de Condet (who may have been Ranulf's sister) of all her land including Thorngate after the destruction of the castle there. For his part, William appears to have been granted judicial powers in Lincoln by Stephen either before 1142 or in 1145-46.[36] Alexander's fortress town at Newark must have been particularly irksome to the half-brothers, in view of its

domination of major road and water routes to and around Lincoln which they also sought to control.[37] The rivalry between the half-brothers and Alexander may also have been intensified shortly before or in 1140 because of Stephen's temporary confiscation of the temporalities of the bishopric of Lincoln for a period between 24 June and September 1139 after his arrest of Alexander. In this period Stephen gave and conceded property belonging to the bishop to 'William earl of Lincoln'.[38] Although the recipient may have been William d'Aubigny pincerna, and although Stephen promised to give an exchange to the earl when the bishop made peace with him or was replaced, this grant established another potential conflict of interests between Alexander and William de Roumare who probably succeeded d'Aubigny as earl of Lincoln during 1140, and who had almost certainly coveted the earldom earlier.[39] The conflict between Alexander and the half-brothers is clear after the seizure of Lincoln castle in 1140, when Alexander appears to have put aside the fact that the king had recently arrested him and deprived him of his castles, joined the citizens in complaining to Stephen about the conduct of the earls and said Mass for the royal army immediately prior to the battle of Lincoln.[40]

The conflict of interests between the half-brothers and Bishop Alexander suggests that the seizure of Lincoln castle in 1140 should be viewed within the context of Ranulf and William's wider ambitions within Lincolnshire, the Midlands and the North. The half-brothers sought to use their family lands as a springboard from which to expand their power in these regions, where they were seeking to establish what appears in some respects to have been almost a private regality.[41] The control of the city of Lincoln with its castle, city defences, mint, royal and ecclesiastical administrative institutions, valuable annual farm, vibrant commercial centre and position as an important focus of communications was crucial to this political scheme.[42] Ranulf appears to have made the city something of an administrative and political base of operations when he controlled it between 1140 and 1146.[43]

These observations take us part of the way toward a fuller understanding of events at Lincoln in 1140. To progress further it is necessary to compare and contrast the various chronicle accounts, assess the reliability of the churchmen who wrote them, determine the possible sequence or sequences of events, and use the narrative record in conjunction with information contained within royal and baronial charters.

Several of the chroniclers portray Ranulf and William's seizure of Lincoln castle in 1140 as an act of wrongful or rebellious aggression. Among them is Orderic Vitalis, who provides the most detailed account. Orderic states that the half-brothers 'rebelled against King Stephen and, by a trick, captured the castle which he held at Lincoln for the protection of the city'.[44] The half-brothers waited until the household troops of the garrison were widely dispersed and then sent their wives into the castle under the pretext of a friendly visit to the wife of the castellan, after which Ranulf arrived unarmed with three knights to escort his wife home, gained entry to the castle, expelled the king's guards and was joined by Roumare with an armed force. After this Bishop Alexander and the citizens of Lincoln sent word to the king of what had happened. Stephen,

was very angry at the news and astounded that his close friends, on whom he had heaped lands and honours, should have committed such a crime. After Christmas he assembled an army, hurried to Lincoln, and one night without warning, aided by the citizens, captured about seventeen knights who were quartered in the town. The two earls were in the castle with their wives and close friends, and were alarmed and uncertain what course to take when they found themselves suddenly surrounded.[45]

Orderic's contemporary, Henry of Huntingdon, confirms certain elements in this account, stating that 'during Christmas, King Stephen laid siege to the city of Lincoln, the defences of which Ranulf, earl of Chester, had taken by deceit', and that this seizure had been achieved by trickery.[46] Describing events at the subsequent battle of Lincoln, Huntingdon puts a speech into Baldwin Fitz Gilbert's mouth that defends the justice of the king's cause, portrays Stephen's opponents as false to their oaths, and describes Ranulf as 'a man of reckless daring, ready for conspiracy, unreliable in performance, impetuous in battle, careless of danger, with designs beyond his powers, panting for the impossible'.[47] Huntingdon also puts a speech into Ranulf's mouth in which he refers to Stephen as a 'treacherous king, who has broken the peace after a truce had been allowed'.[48]

Another contemporary account that appears to place the blame on Ranulf and William is the *Gesta Stephani*. This has a lacuna where the description of the seizure of Lincoln castle might have been and gives only a partial record of what happened in 1140. This states that

> . . . [Ranulf] would take great care to put right all that he had done amiss. Wherefore the king was advised to receive him as his man and renew the compact and make peace again, to watch quietly to see if he fulfilled his promises, and so to go elsewhere to perform other tasks. Then when a very long time had passed and the earl obeyed the king no more loyally than usual and staying at the castle of Lincoln with his wife and sons issued harsh orders to the townsmen and the people of the neighbourhood, the townsmen privately and secretly sent messages to the king, urging him . . . to come as quickly as possible with reinforcements to besiege the earl. The king, arriving suddenly and unexpectedly, was admitted by the townsmen and found the castle almost empty, except for the earl's wife and brother and a few of their adherents, whom the earl had left there when the king entered the town, just managing to escape by himself.[49]

Later, in 1146, according to the *Gesta*, Ranulf repented for the 'cruelty and treachery he had shown to [Stephen] when he stretched forth his hands against his king and lord at the capture of Lincoln'.[50]

The accounts of the Anglo-Saxon chronicler and the northern chronicler, John of Hexham, provide only a few details, but these also paint Ranulf in a bad light. The former refers to the beginning of a great war between Stephen and Ranulf, 'not because [Stephen] did not give [Ranulf] all that he could ask him (as he did everybody else) but always the more he gave them the worse they were to him. The earl held Lincoln against the king, and deprived him of all that he ought to have had, and the king went there and besieged him and his brother, William [de] Roumare, in the castle'.[51] The latter links the seizure of Lincoln to Stephen's dealings with the Scots:

> Earl Henry with his wife proceeded to the king of England. Ranulf earl of Chester rose in hostility against him because of Carlisle and Cumberland, which he demanded to be given back to him by right of inheritance; and upon [Earl Henry's] return wished to entrap him with an armed band. But the king [Stephen], urged by the queen's prayers, protected him from the threatened danger, and restored him to his father and to his country; and [Ranulf's] displeasure was transferred to plotting against the king's safety. Earl Ranulf seized all the fortifications of Lincoln.[52]

Some of the chroniclers are more favourable to Ranulf and William. William of Malmesbury, writing soon after the events he describes, informs us that

> King Stephen had gone away in peace from Lincolnshire before Christmas, and had added to the honours of the earl of Chester and his brother . . . Meanwhile the citizens of Lincoln, wishing

to lay the king under a great obligation, informed him by messengers when he was staying at London that the two brothers had settled unsuspiciously in the city's castle. As they expected nothing less than the king's arrival, they could easily be surrounded . . . He, unwilling to miss any chance of increasing his power, hastened thither joyfully. And so the brothers were surrounded and besieged during the Christmas festival itself. This seemed unfair to many because . . . [Stephen] had left them before the festival without any suspicion of ill-will, and had not, in the traditional way, renounced his friendship with them, which is termed defiance.[53]

Malmesbury considered that Ranulf was 'in no way at fault'.[54]

Finally, one account appears to be more neutral in its tone. The author of Book III of the *Liber Eliensis*, the chronicle of the abbey of Ely, completed between 1169 and 1174, states that in 1140 'the king demanded back from Ranulf, earl of Chester, Lincoln with the castle, because he [Stephen] had handed over the custody to him, and he [Ranulf] not only refused to give it back to him, but brought there with him very many earls and barons in a column prepared to undergo battle'.[55]

The weight of the evidence appears to be in favour of Stephen's conduct and against that of Ranulf and William. But there are difficulties with the accounts of some of the chroniclers who condemn the half-brothers that need to be borne in mind. Marjorie Chibnall has pointed out that although Orderic's account probably contains genuine information, it was written in an abbey that had experienced the weak government in Normandy of Duke Robert Curthose, when some of the barons had expelled ducal garrisons from ducal fortresses, constructed new castles, treated these strongholds as family patrimony and used them to ravage and exploit the countryside. Chibnall has argued that Orderic believed strongly that the king had a right 'to control even the castles of his vassals in times of danger', and has suggested that a desire on the part of the royal garrison at Lincoln to excuse themselves for being caught unawares may have distorted the story of what happened at Lincoln before it reached Orderic. Chibnall has also suggested that the story may be further corrupted if Orderic got it from or via *jongleurs* or the household knights of William de Roumare who was a benefactor of Saint-Evroult, and that it reflects common literary themes that were part of the 'fictional element that crept into history at every level'.[56]

Henry of Huntingdon's account should also be treated with caution because Henry had been brought up in the household of Bishop Robert Bloet of Lincoln, was an archdeacon of Lincoln diocese and a canon of Lincoln Cathedral, and produced his history at the direction of (and dedicated it to) Bishop Alexander of Lincoln. Henry produced it, moreover, in a way in which, according to Diana Greenway, ' "Observation" in the sense of first-hand reporting, was limited and controlled by the conventions of rhetoric, which required that all literary material – including history – should be selected and ordered according to a pre-determined interpretation, or, in rhetorical terms, an argument', and 'historical persons and their doings are used as moral *exempla*'.[57] Huntingdon's hostility to Ranulf is suggested by the speech he put into the mouth of Baldwin Fitz Gilbert at the battle of Lincoln, although it has to be said that speeches of this kind must be treated with caution and, as Greenway points out, the arguments in those made at Lincoln 'seem evenly balanced, and leaders on both sides are wittily denigrated and ridiculed'.[58]

The account provided by the author of the *Gesta Stephani* is also unlikely to be free from bias because when he wrote about Stephen's siege of Lincoln he was still a supporter of the king and hostile to Earl Ranulf.[59] We should even be wary of taking the story of the Anglo-Saxon chronicler at face value, given that he regarded baronial construction and control of castles to be one of the worst symptoms of the troubles of Stephen's reign.[60]

Just as the chroniclers who were hostile to Ranulf and William may have been more biased against them than is sometimes supposed, so those who cast their deeds in a more favourable light may have been less biased towards them than has been appreciated. Although William of Malmesbury, who dedicated his history to Ranulf's father-in-law, Robert earl of Gloucester, appears to have had more sympathy in the civil war for the cause of the empress (or more exactly the cause of Robert of Gloucester) than for that of the king and may distort the truth in favour of Ranulf, neither the strength of his Angevin partisanship, nor his affinity with Ranulf, should be overestimated, and it is possible that what he tells us is accurate.[61] As for the author of the *Liber Eliensis*, although he may be presenting some memory of Ranulf's version of events, an attempt by the earl to misrepresent the position to justify his actions, there is no direct evidence for this. It is significant that the author was not altogether hostile to Stephen.[62]

One of the problems of interpreting the various chronicle accounts is establishing the correct sequence of events at Lincoln in 1140. The problem is an important one because different sequences suggest markedly different possible interpretations regarding the legitimacy of the actions of the king and the half-brothers. It is also a difficult one because of the discrepancies in the accounts and the possibility that the chroniclers confused or repeated events.[63] William of Malmesbury indicates that Stephen made two visits to Lincoln, one before Christmas 1140, and one during Christmas. This raises the question of whether the first visit happened before Ranulf's seizure of the castle or was a response to it. In an article published in 1937 Cronne put forward an argument for the latter scenario, which has been accepted by Davis and, quite recently, by Jim Bradbury. Cronne stated that the favourable moment for the seizure occurred before Stephen's first visit, when he was occupied with serious rebellions, rather than after it, when he had time to deal with a new rebellion; and that if Ranulf and William had seized the castle after Stephen's first visit then their subsequent conduct is hard to understand, because they did not behave like rebels. Cronne also suggested that it seems as though Stephen felt justified in attacking the earls because Ranulf had broken the spirit if not the letter of an agreement they had made during the king's first visit to Lincoln. Although acknowledging that the terms of this agreement are unknown, Cronne speculated that they may have embraced the castle but not the city, that the attempt of Ranulf and William to dominate the city could have constituted the breach, and that this would account for the anger of the citizens who had secured the right to hold the city from the king in chief in the reign of Henry I.[64] By 1970, however, when he published his book on the reign of Stephen, Cronne's view appears to have changed, though he did not explain why: 'It seems clear that late in 1140 Stephen made a serious effort at conciliation. He met Rannulf and William de Roumare in Lincolnshire and "increased the honours" of the former and probably gave the earldom of Lincoln to the latter . . . There followed the seizure of Lincoln castle by Rannulf and William . . .'.[65]

Cronne's 1937 sequence of events may well be right. If the author of the *Gesta Stephani* had the seizure of Lincoln castle in mind when he refers to Ranulf taking care to put right all that he had done amiss, and if his description of Stephen then being advised to receive Ranulf as his man and renew a compact with him before going elsewhere to perform other tasks is a reference to the king's first visit to Lincoln in 1140 when he increased Ranulf and William's honours, then his account would certainly support this sequence. But Cronne's 1970 sequence, although perhaps less likely than the one advanced in 1937, could be right. This is suggested

by the king's grant of honours to Ranulf and William, which Orderic states happened before the seizure and William of Malmesbury says occurred during the king's first visit to Lincoln in 1140. It is possible, of course, that the chroniclers were describing different grants, and that those Orderic had in mind had been made before Stephen's first visit to Lincoln. But if they were describing the same grants, then it follows that the earls' seizure of the castle occurred after rather than before this visit. If this sequence of events is correct, and if Cronne's suggestion that Stephen granted some form of rights in Lincoln castle to Ranulf during his first visit to Lincoln is right, then the seizure of the fortress by the half-brothers was perhaps less arbitrary and unjustified than some of the chroniclers would have us believe.

Whether or not this possible sequence of events is correct, and it may well be wrong, Cronne's suggestion about the grant of rights in the castle to Ranulf and William before the Christmas siege has an important bearing on understanding the events at Lincoln. The suggestion is probably correct. The accounts of Orderic, William of Malmesbury and the *Gesta Stephani* support Cronne's point about the non-rebellious conduct of Ranulf and William after their seizure of the castle. This indicates that the half-brothers considered their occupation of the castle to be justified, and that they believed they had some form of rights and powers in the castle and possibly the city which had been granted to them by the king. This grant may have been among the additional honours that William of Malmesbury states Stephen gave to the half-brothers during his first visit to Lincoln, and was possibly part of the pact that the author of the *Gesta Stephani* says that the king renewed with Ranulf shortly before the siege.

This suggestion is strengthened by the events of 1146, when Ranulf 'was restored to favour' by Stephen, 'after the pact of their old friendship had been renewed between them'.[66] We are better informed about the 1146 pact because we have an abbreviated copy of a charter which has been dated to this year and appears to set out its terms. The charter is referred to by the fourteenth-century chancery clerk who copied it as a *Concordia inter regem Stephanum et Rannulfum comitem Cestr(ie)* in the margin of his parchment.[67] In the charter Stephen gave and conceded to Ranulf the castle and city of Lincoln until he could make Ranulf have his Norman lands and all his castles, and promised that Ranulf was to build, rebuild or strengthen (*firmare*) one of his towers of Lincoln castle until the king was free to give him the fortress of Tickhill, and that thereafter the king was to retain the tower and the city of Lincoln and Ranulf was to retain the tower that his mother had built, rebuilt or strengthened (*firmavit*) together with the constableship of Lincoln castle and Lincolnshire in hereditary right. It is not impossible that this 1146 *concordia* was a composite document compiled by the chancery clerk from several charters granted to Ranulf representing different aspects of complicated negotiations, and its form is unlikely in any case to have followed exactly that of the 1140 pact which it renewed because of the Angevin seizure of Ranulf's Norman lands and a degree of political realignment in England in the intervening period. Nevertheless, its terms add weight to the evidence that the pact of 1140 also included a grant or concession by Stephen to Ranulf of some form of rights and powers in Lincoln castle.

Stephen increased not only Ranulf's honours during his first visit to Lincoln in 1140 but also those of William de Roumare, and it may be that this also amounted to a pact conveying rights in Lincoln castle.[68] It is possible that the pact, which may have incorporated a truce, and the rights were connected with the creation of William as earl of Lincoln, which occurred by 1142 at the latest, and which, given his conduct in 1141, probably happened before Christmas 1140.[69] It was, of course, Ranulf rather than William who seems to have adopted the more prominent role in Lincolnshire and addressed at least one of his charters to his sheriff and officials of the county, and there is no mention of William in the pact that Ranulf made with the king in 1146 concerning control of Lincoln castle. All of this suggests that Stephen may have granted William the earldom without the county.[70] However, it would be unsafe to rule out the possibility that William's promotion to the earldom may have strengthened his claim to the castle, because some of the new earldoms created in Stephen's reign, and a few created before 1135, do appear to have incorporated control over the shrievalty of the comital county, and in some counties there was a close link between the shrievalty and the constableship of the castle of the county town; offices that barons sought to make hereditary.[71] It is interesting that there is no conclusive evidence for the existence of a sheriff of Lincolnshire between c.1139 and 1154,[72] suggesting that the office may have been integral to the earldom. It is also possible, in light of the fact that some of Stephen's earls were expected or took it upon themselves to defend their counties, that the earldom incorporated, or was interpreted by William as incorporating, the public supervision of castles. William's claim to Lincoln castle may have been further reinforced by his position as local justice, which appears to have carried with it some form of authority over the city of Lincoln, and which he possibly held by 1140.[73] Moreover, it may be, as Thompson has suggested, that the creation of an earl of Lincoln in Stephen's reign was connected with the movement of the bishop of Lincoln out of a residence within Lincoln castle.[74]

There is a possibility, therefore, that during his first visit to Lincoln in 1140 Stephen made a pact with Ranulf and possibly his half-brother in which he granted them some form of rights and powers in the fortress and possibly the city before departing in peace, a pact that Ranulf appears later to have accused Stephen of breaking. But what exactly could these rights and powers have been? The *concordia* of 1146 shows the possible variety, complexity and transitory nature of the authority that could be granted in a castle that incorporated more than one motte or tower and in the city within which it was situated. This authority might involve complete control of the entire castle and city, or private possession or mere custody of one or more of the towers, or rights to munition or fortify particular towers, or the constableship of (we can only presume) the entire castle and county. Moreover, with the possible exception of munitioning, each of these rights could presumably be granted either temporarily or in hereditary right. We do not know how many of these rights and powers Stephen granted to Ranulf in 1140, how many Ranulf sought to exercise without royal permission, or how many he already possessed before his seizure of the castle.

The fact that the dispute over Lincoln castle involved a pact or *conventio*, and the possibility that this pact included an agreement concerning rights in the castle and a truce which Ranulf claimed was broken by the king, complicates it considerably; not least because such political pacts or *conventiones*, which appear to have been common in Stephen's reign and often concerned castles, could take the form of complex agreements that might define, or qualify, in a variety of ways the relationship, promises and obligations, sometimes those integral to homage and fealty, between two parties – frequently lord and man.[75] The complexity and variety is clear from the few Stephanic *conventiones* the terms of which we know in detail, and that it was even greater than it appears in these agreements is strongly suggested by the much better documented continental political *conventiones*. These agreements were common throughout large parts of Lombardy, Provence, Languedoc and Catalonia, and to a lesser extent the Loire valley and Aragon, between the tenth and twelfth centuries.[76] Many concern the same or similar issues and obligations dealt with by the political pacts of Stephen's reign, including castles, and are remarkable for their sophistication and diversity. Reference to a few of the many possible variations in form must suffice to illustrate the point. Some were for fixed periods of time. Some were supposed to terminate if there was a change in the position of the lord's man. Others were imprecise as to duration, leaving the man insecure in his rights, and vulnerable to be deprived of them. Some of those concerning castles could involve the surrender of fortresses in return for other strongholds, lands and rights, or could oblige lords not to enter the castles of their men, except following some form of abuse for which they could not make reparation. Others could exempt men from their oaths of fealty to their lords for certain of their castles, or could guarantee the neutrality or military support of castles. The variety in the terms of such *conventiones* was partly a function of the variety of castle customs. 'Fortress-law supplied models', according to Charles Coulson, 'capable of adaptation to requirements and norms of conduct of wide application'.[77] Castle rights might occasionally, but briefly, be renounced to pacify strong suspicions. Rights of entry could be conditional rather than absolute, and insisted upon for a variety of reasons. Those summoned to render might try and avoid doing so by demanding the lord's provision of pledges that he would not hand the castle over to the renderer's enemies. Rendability could involve either the entry of the lord in person or the intrusion of his garrison or the enforced admittance of his constable, and it could stem from a previous grant by lord to man of a licence to fortify.[78]

There is reasonable evidence that castle customs similar to those common in France were known and practised in England in Stephen's reign, and that they – or something similar to them – further complicated the dispute over Lincoln castle. Part of it appears in the description of the dispute in the *Liber Eliensis*, that provides the most specific statement we have concerning the rights in Lincoln that Stephen probably granted to Ranulf in their *conventio* of 1140. Contrary to Cronne's suggestion that Ranulf's attempt to control the city may have been a breach of his pact with the king, the *Liber* records that Stephen conveyed to Ranulf custody over not only the castle but the city as well. The redeemable nature of this custody resembles the French castle custom of rendability, under which a lord might justifiably claim temporary but indefinite use, possession and control of a fortress during a time of necessity, without undermining the tenant's right to possession.[79]

There is certainly evidence for the existence of such a custom, or something similar to it, in the Anglo-Norman dominions after 1066 and, more specifically, in England during the reign of Stephen. The custom can certainly be found in Normandy in 1091 in a document known as the *Consuetudines et Iusticie*.[80] Whether William the Conqueror or his successors had the right to apply the custom of rendability universally in Normandy, and whether such a custom was simply transferred by them to England, is open to question.[81] Henry I may have tried to implement or exploit rendability to secure control of a number of castles.[82] Stephen possibly used French castle customs on occasions to provide some kind of formal or added legitimisation for fortress confiscations that he appears to have considered were justified by the suspected treachery of certain barons in a time of crisis. This is suggested by his seizure in 1139 of the castles of the bishops of Salisbury, Lincoln and Ely, who were suspected by Stephen's intimate counsellors of plotting to support Empress Matilda's claim to the throne and against the majesty of Stephen's crown.[83] On the basis of these suspicions the counsellors urged the king that it would be judicious and expedient for the king's peace to lay hands on the bishops, who were suspected enemies of this peace and public order, and demand the surrender of their castles.[84] At the time of the seizure the pretext for it was the disturbance of the peace of the king's court by the bishops' men when they were drawn into a brawl there, which required a guarantee of their future trustworthiness.[85] But at the subsequent council of Winchester, where the legitimacy of Stephen's actions was debated, one of the arguments put forward in the king's defence was that the bishop of Salisbury 'had not allowed Roger de Mortimer, with the king's troops whom he was leading, to stay even one night at Malmesbury, when he was in the greatest dread of the people of Bristol'.[86] It is possible that the bishop was being accused of failing to allow his lord – or in this case the troops of his lord – the right to resort to a castle with a field force, which was one of the elements of continental rendability.[87] Another argument, advanced by Archbishop Hugh of Rouen, was that:

> Even granted that it is right for [the bishops] to have the castles, yet certainly, as it is a time of uncertainty, all the chief men, in accordance with the custom of other peoples, ought to hand over the keys of their fortifications to the disposal of the king, whose duty it is to fight for the peace of all. So the bishops' whole case will fall to the ground. For either it is unjust, according to canon law, for them to have castles, or, if this is permitted by the king as an act of grace, they ought to yield to the emergencies of the time by delivering up the keys.[88]

John of Worcester states that after the bishops were arrested, '[a]fter discussion in a council [at Winchester] it was decided that all towns, castles, and fortified places throughout England where secular business was conducted should submit to the jurisdiction of the king and his barons'.[89] This decision is also mentioned in the *Gesta Stephani*, which states that it was enacted that 'any receptacles of war and disturbance in the hands of any of the bishops should be handed over to the king as his own property'.[90]

Stephen's attempt to impose or exploit rendability or something similar is also suggested by his quarrel with a certain Turgis, to whom he granted the castle of Saffron Walden after confiscating it from Geoffrey de Mandeville in 1143. 'The cause and source of this quarrel was the castle of Walden and all the neighbouring district, which the king had given [Turgis] to guard rather than to possess: when the king wished to have entry into the castle as usual, because it belonged to him legally and had, he thought, been won by his efforts, Turgis, fearing that what he held might be entrusted to another, flatly refused.'[91]

There are elements in Stephen's policy towards castles that are indicative not so much of rendability but of another commonplace French practice relating to castles that Coulson regards as subtly related to it: the pledging of fortresses to purge a lord's reasonable suspicions about the conduct of his man. Whereas a rendable fortress was 'deliverable on demand with no reason given, no prevarication allowable, no ill-will or misconduct, real or imagined, having been alleged', 'with pledging it [ill-feeling] was of the essence and normally had to be reasonable and just before the demand to hand over could be made. Pledging diagnosed incipient breakdown of lord-vassal relations'.[92] This may have been the case with the bishops in 1139, who were suspected of treachery and had the temporalities of their sees temporarily confiscated along with their castles.[93] Elements of pledging can perhaps also be discerned in Stephen's confiscation of the castles of Robert of Bampton in 1136, Eustace Fitz John in 1138, Geoffrey de Mandeville in 1143, and Ranulf of Chester in 1146.[94] In each case the barons were suspected or accused of treason or other misdeeds, arrested or tried in the king's court, and compelled to surrender castles. It could be that the similarities to pledging are purely coincidental, especially in the cases of Bampton and Fitz John who lost their castles before Archbishop Hugh of Rouen's speech at the council of Winchester in 1139. The fact that there are no direct references to notice of suspicion being given, or dates being set for the surrender of fortresses, that might occur under pledging, is significant. But it may be that the absence of such references is due to the subtleties of pledging being ignored by the chroniclers, or by the king.[95]

Other lords appear to have used elements of castle customs familiar in France during the anarchy. Coulson has argued that Ranulf of Chester himself and his rival Robert earl of Leicester did so in their famous *conventio* made between 1149

and 1153.[96] The fact that these customs were employed to define and regulate their rights in different parts of the same castle is especially interesting in light of the dispute between Ranulf and the king over the jurisdictionally or proprietorially partible fortress of Lincoln. Henry of Anjou also appears to have been using components of rendability in 1149 when he promised to restore the manor of Bishop's Cannings to Bishop Jocelin of Salisbury except for the castle of Devizes, '*quod ego adhuc propter necessitatem meam in manu mea retineo in bona sufferentia episcopi donec me deus exemplificet quod ego ei reddere possim*'; and in 1153 when he made a *conventionem et pacem* with Jocelin in which Henry was to hold Devizes castle for three years, during which time '*si . . . jus suum recuperaverit, tunc per consilium domini Cant(uariensis) archiepiscopi, H(enrici) Wynton(iensis), R(oberti) Bathon(iensis), H(ilarii) Cicestr(ensis) episcoporum reddet idem castrum. Q(uod) si jus suum infra predictum terminum non recuperaverit, tunc per consilium eorum in fine ipsius termini castrum idem restituet Sar(esberiensi) ecclesie et episcopo*'.[97] Rendability may also feature in the dealings of several other lords during the civil war.[98]

There is good evidence, therefore, that French castle customs or something similar to them were used by Stephen and other lords to compel, or to help compel, the surrender of castles during the anarchy, including perhaps Lincoln castle in 1140 and 1146. This raises the question of whether this was legitimate. In certain parts of Europe to dispute or refuse a summons to render a castle was regarded as a felony and breach of fealty or as a repudiation of homage.[99] In Norman and Angevin England, Richard Eales believes that

> there remained always something of a legal vacuum so far as castles were concerned. Whatever notions of right and obligation there were, specific to castles, they were not elaborated or written down in standard forms. Into this vacuum . . . kings especially might draw such elements of French custom as might serve their interests at any time . . . But the evidence as a whole indicates that such borrowings never took root in English law, any more than they are all traceable back to the Norman customs of 1091 . . . Rulers were not obliged to pursue a universal claim to castle licensing or rendability as a matter of principle, and the evidence suggests they did not . . . The inheritance of Norman England – of rights derived from long possession of castles rather than from any formal system of royal authorization – was not easily cancelled or eroded.[100]

Coulson has argued that French castle customs applied to the seigniorial superior rather than specifically to the king, and although 'persuasive in special circumstances, failed to take formal hold [in England]' where 'the cooperation of castle-lords was rarely formulated as rendability, whether as nominally royal . . . or as seignorial, so far as the evidence goes', and where 'only a theoretical royal cognisance of major *castellatio* . . . appears', and '[t]he Anglo-Norman magnates, not the kings, were undoubtedly its exponents by the customs established by the scramble for England and umbilically reinforced since then'.[101]

In practice, according to Eales, customs of castle licensing and rendability 'often served as a kind of legalistic thicket through which political operators manoeuvred to gain their ends, while paying lip service to the rules'.[102] This may have been true of Stephen who, according to Coulson, regarded his obligations under rendability much less scrupulously than the earls of Chester and Leicester in their *conventio* '[d]emanding castles in pledge was standard form, and was acceptable if "reasonable", but it was not reasonable to make this demand with the intention of depriving their owners. Temporary use only was the superior's right.'[103] Stephen's actions in seizing the castles of the bishops clearly stimulated a debate in which many people expressed different opinions.[104] Archbishop Hugh of Rouen's opinion supported Stephen, but his statement concerning rendability, as Eales has stated, 'is subject to different interpretations, as clerical ideas of the public good may not have been synonymous with secular custom, and Hugh qualified his remarks with the perhaps significant phrase "in accordance with the custom of other peoples".'[105] Even Stephen's brother, the bishop of Winchester, opposed the seizures, reminded the king that the bishops' castles had been built at their expense and on their land, and accused him of having committed a lamentable crime in being led astray by his counsellors, ordering hands to be laid on the bishops in the peace of the royal court, and robbing the Church of its property.[106]

Further opposition to Stephen's actions can be seen in the rebellion of the barons whose castles he seized, some of whom clearly felt wronged. In 1138 Eustace Fitz John 'left the English king because he had been seized by him in court, contrary to ancestral custom, and had been forced to give back the castles which King Henry had entrusted to him. For this reason he was offended, and betook himself to [Stephen's] enemies, to avenge the wrong inflicted upon him'.[107] In 1139 Bishop Nigel of Ely was eager to 'avenge . . . the wrongs [Stephen] had done to his uncle [Bishop Roger of Salisbury] . . . and also help King Henry's children . . . to obtain the kingdom more quickly'.[108] In 1141 Ranulf of Chester condemned Stephen at Lincoln as a faithless king who had broken a peace to which he was pledged. The condemnation may have been stimulated partly by the use of castle customs, or Stephen's strict enforcement or abuse of them. If Stephen insisted on rendability at Lincoln in 1140, he may have been within his rights, or have seen himself as so. But such a request for the return of the castle so soon after it had probably been conveyed to Ranulf in a pact of peace could have been regarded by Ranulf as unreasonable, especially if the custody that the author of the *Liber Eliensis* states that Stephen had given him had been granted in perpetuity.[109]

There are other signs of sharp practice in Stephen's dealings with Ranulf. According to William of Malmesbury, Stephen's siege of Lincoln castle in 1140 seemed unfair to many because the king had left Ranulf and William 'without any suspicion of ill-will, and had not, in the traditional way, renounced his friendship with them, which is termed defiance'.[110] For William of Malmesbury more honourable procedure had been followed by Robert of Gloucester in 1138 when he sent messengers to formally announce his abandonment of friendship and faith and his renunciation of homage with the king, thus defying him, after consulting with many ecclesiastics about the oath he had taken to Matilda.[111] John Gillingham has argued that in asserting that this was done in traditional fashion William of Malmesbury intended, in the interests of his patron, to deceive his readers and 'found himself inventing a new political language, partly to justify Robert of Gloucester's conduct . . . but partly also as a way of describing a new reality, a new perception of revolt, declared in a new way'.[112] Gillingham chose to 'leave aside the question of whether *diffidatio* was, as Round believed, an "essential feature of continental feudalism" '.[113] Whether it was essential or not is uncertain, but that it, or something like it, was known and practised in parts of Frankia before and after Stephen's reign is both clear and significant.[114] It suggests that its appearance in England in the anarchy may have been due not to the concoction of an individual monk, but to the use made of continental practices by several English barons.[115] Not only Robert of Gloucester used *diffidatio*. Robert de Brus and Bernard de Balliol broke their ties with King David of Scots in a manner very suggestive of *diffidatio* shortly before the battle of the Standard in 1138. Moreover, in the famous Chester-Leicester *conventio* the earls promised that they would not for any cause or chance lay snares for each other unless they had 'defied' each other fifteen days before.[116] The period of fifteen days recalls another *conventio* between Henry II and Louis VII at Montlouis in 1174 that embodied the terms of peace following the rebellion of Henry the Young King: 'Our lord the king and all his liegemen and barons are to

receive possession of all their lands and castles which they held fifteen days before his sons withdrew from him; and in like manner his liegemen and barons who withdrew from him and followed his sons are to receive possession of their lands which they held fifteen days before they withdrew from him'.[117] Just as advanced notice was regarded by some as an essential prerequisite of *diffidatio*, so it appears to have occurred in the recovery of castles under pledging. Thus, if Stephen was employing pledging rather than rendability in regard to Lincoln castle in 1140, his lack of notice before besieging the fortress could have been considered doubly offensive.

The possibility that Stephen sometimes invoked conventions or customs governing relations between lords and men without including the notification component that was considered by some of his contemporaries to have been essential to them, is suggested again by his dealings with Ranulf in 1145/1146. Prior to his arrest at court Ranulf had been restored to the king's favour 'after the pact of their old friendship had been renewed between them', but was regarded with suspicion by the king and his advisers because he had not returned royal revenues, land and castles and had not offered hostages or guarantors as security for his loyalty.[118] After coming to the king's court to seek help against the Welsh, Ranulf was asked to restore the king's property and provide greater security by giving a guarantee and offering hostages.[119] His response was that he 'had not even been given any notice of the matter or deliberated over it with his advisers', which indicates that he may have been aware that the king was trying to insist on pledging but not adhering strictly to correct procedure.[120] As in 1140, this may not have been the king's only offence. In 1146 Stephen appears to have been acting under the influence of advisers at court who were envious of Ranulf's power. It was they who are said to have made the king change his mind about helping Ranulf in Wales, demand guarantees and hostages from the earl, and arrest him when he tried to avoid doing so.[121] It was 'counsellors' or advisers who urged Stephen to take over the castle of Robert of Bampton in 1136, orchestrated the arrest the bishops in 1139, and secured the arrest of Geoffrey de Mandeville in 1143.[122] The impression is of a king acting in the interests of, and being led astray by, a faction of court favourites to the detriment of other barons.[123] The offence this caused to Ranulf and others who suffered as a result of it was probably heightened by the methods Stephen was encouraged by his favourites to use, which flouted the king's peace. Stephen's relations with Bishop Nigel of Ely in 1144 or 1145 provide an interesting parallel with those he had with Ranulf. Here was another magnate who had come into conflict with the king over possession of castles. A charter issued by Stephen at this time granted that Nigel was to hold his men, lands and rights in peace and freely '*quoniam pacem de me habet et concordiam mecum fecit*'.[124] The bishop had an agreement with the king, and he had his promise of peace. This may well describe what Ranulf had too, and what Stephen took from him. According to the *Gesta Stephani*, 'it was with good cause that the earl, as long as he lived, exerted all his efforts to attack the king's party . . . because the king, when the earl had entered his court with confidence in a safe conduct, gave orders for his arrest and imprisonment'; a view supported by William of Malmesbury who saw the manner of Stephen's arrest of barons in court 'on mere suspicion of siding against him' as 'unbefitting a king'.[125]

Bishop Nigel of Ely's conflict with Stephen over castles had begun with the king's arrest of the bishops in 1139. This introduces another parallel with Earl Ranulf's dispute with Stephen in 1146 which, although not exact, is close enough to throw light on it, and which is probably closer to the circumstances of the anarchy than appears at first sight: the trial of Bishop William de St Calais of Durham in 1088. The trial is recorded in a tractate known as *De iniusta vexacione Willelmi episcopi primi*, accepted by many historians as an authentic contemporary description, but regarded by H. S. Offler as a concoction of the monastic community of Durham in the second quarter of the twelfth century for the purpose of defending the conduct and reputation of Bishop William.[126] Offler pointed to anomalies and anachronisms in the text as signs of later composition, but his views have not found general acceptance.[127] However, if the tract is viewed within the context of Stephen's arrest of the bishops and other barons while under safe conduct at court, there is much to suggest that it may have been composed during or shortly after the anarchy, and that it reflects and illuminates the politics of that period.[128] Bishop William was another magnate who was accused by the king and his advisers of various misdeeds, went to the royal court under a safe-conduct guaranteed by a *conventio*, was put on trial there before the king and his barons, prevented from deliberating with some of the men he considered as advisers and compelled to surrender his castle on an agreed date in the future in order to secure his liberty. His case is complicated, of course, by his ecclesiastical status, frequent reference to the procedures of canon law, and making of a *conventio* with three of the king's magnates rather than with the king himself. But it still reveals much about the intricacies of the relationship between lords and those of their men who were suspected of treachery in times of crisis, and whose relationship with the lord was qualified or further defined by *conventiones* and intensified by the possession of fortresses.[129] It shows how *conventiones* could be bound up with notions of fealty, and could regulate or be connected with the appearance of men in their lord's court, promises of safe-conduct, the terms on which the lord's jurisdiction might be accepted, refused or appealed against, and the conditions on which castles might be retained, surrendered and fortified.[130] Crucially for our present purpose, it suggests that some or all of these things could be matters of debate or dispute. With regard to Bishop William's castle of Durham, for example, Archbishop Lanfranc told William Rufus in open court that '[i]f the bishop goes on refusing his castle to you, you may well arrest him, for by first breaking the agreement he has now given up the free conduct which he has so far enjoyed, and he tries to prove against your barons that they have not acted loyally'.[131] Many there present agreed with Lanfranc. But one of the king's barons who had made the *conventio* with the bishop on the king's behalf, did not. Count Alan, lord of Richmond, reminded the king of the terms of the *conventio* under which he was pledged either to return the bishop in safety to his castle of Durham or to provide him with harbour and ships to go overseas, and asked the king not to compel him to break his faith.[132] When the king tried to impose further conditions on the bishop in order to ensure the return of his ships, contrary to the terms of the *conventio*, another baron, Reginald Paynel, reminded the king that these terms should be kept, but was told by Rufus to be silent and that the king would 'not suffer the loss of [his] ships for anyone's surety'.[133]

The *De iniusta* shows how, especially in times of crisis, conventions of aristocratic political behaviour could come into conflict with the demands of realpolitik, especially where castles were concerned. It is biased in favour of Bishop William, but this adds to rather than diminishes its value because it offers a rare alternative perspective on conflicts between kings and barons to the one normally provided by chroniclers who were more commonly royalist than not. The royalist perspective must, of course, be taken into account. It is important to stress that Stephen's policy towards barons like the earl of Chester, whose loyalty was clearly suspect, who were attempting massively to increase their power in the localities (sometimes at the expense of the crown), who had significant attachments to Stephen's Angevin opponents and who were prepared to offer armed resistance, was regarded by many of his intimate counsellors, several of the chroniclers and perhaps by the king himself, as just, because in a time of crisis it was pragmatic and necessary. Further justification may have been derived from a belief, expressed by Stephen after the battle of Lincoln, that those who fought against the king were guilty of a monstrous crime in acting contrary to the oaths of fealty and acts of homage they had performed to their ruler and lord.[134] But an appreciation of that other perspective revealed to us by the *De iniusta*, and perhaps by William of Malmesbury, is no less important for an understanding of Stephen's conflicts with his barons, including the one over Lincoln castle that raged in the 1140s.

The complexity and variety of *conventiones* and castle customs, the questions they raise about legitimacy, and the opportunities they provided for manipulation, exploitation, disagreement and misunderstanding, increases greatly the number of possible scenarios for the dispute over Lincoln castle, both in 1140 and 1146. To take just one example: both *conventiones* and castle customs might define the duration of an agreement, an obligation or a right in terms of 'necessity'.[135] It may be that in his pact with Ranulf in 1140 or in the pact that the 1140 agreement renewed, Stephen promised to grant Ranulf and William custody of Lincoln castle or some portion of it in the future, but had insisted that in the short term because of the king's necessity the fortress was to remain in the hands of the royal garrison. It is possible that the king failed to hand the earls the castle at the appointed time, or that Ranulf and his half-brother grew impatient of waiting – especially if the earlier pact was made in the first two years of the reign when Stephen alienated rights in castles to several barons.[136] Such agreements concerning castle occupancy occur elsewhere in Anglo-Norman and Angevin history,[137] and there are certainly cases from early and late in the anarchy of Stephen apparently alienating control over some castles while insisting that they be occupied by royal garrisons or officials. Such appears to have been the case before 1141 at Tickhill, which was under the control of the count of Eu *cum forinsecis terris*, but occupied in part by the king's constable, William de Clerfei, who kept the *motam*; and in 1153 at Warwick, which was in charge of the earl but garrisoned by the king's troops.[138]

After 1140 Lincoln castle was besieged by Stephen in 1144, but remained in Ranulf's hands until his arrest in 1146.[139] Whether he or his half-brother retained the constableship themselves or granted it out to their retainers is uncertain. It is significant, however, that Ralph de la Haye, one of the sons of Robert de la Haye who may have held the constableship in the reign of Henry I, was very prominent in the entourage of Ranulf at Lincoln between 1142 and 1146;[140] and that he attested Stephen's charter issued at Stamford in 1145/1146 granting William de Roumare the Lincolnshire manor of Kirton and conceding to him the castle and bridge of Gainsborough, that was also witnessed by Ranulf.[141]

Stephen wore his crown at Lincoln after Ranulf's expulsion from the castle, in defiance of certain superstitions.[142] It is not known to whom he entrusted the castle after his departure, but it is interesting that Ralph de la Haye attested one of his charters issued at Lincoln between 1146 and 1153, and another two that may have been granted in the same period.[143] Whoever the constable was, he was soon besieged by Ranulf, but managed to hold out.[144] The earl campaigned against the king in Lincolnshire again in 1149, and almost subdued the city of Lincoln.[145] The hostilities were probably exacerbated by Stephen's decision in or very shortly after October 1149 to make Gilbert II de Gant earl of Lincoln in opposition to William de Roumare.[146] It is possible that the grant of the earldom to Gilbert included the shrievalty of Lincolnshire and embodied rights in Lincoln castle. Of this, however, there is no proof, and it is significant that none of the large number of Gilbert's charters which have survived give any direct indication that he ever controlled the fortress.[147]

The war in Lincolnshire may have continued into 1151, but the indications are that it was unsuccessful for Earl Ranulf. There is no direct evidence that he besieged Lincoln after 1149, which may have been due to his increasing involvement from this time in the politics of the succession dispute.[148] Ranulf issued a number of charters at Lincoln in the later years of Stephen's reign, but their precise dates are uncertain. Geoffrey Barraclough dated them to 1153 or c.1153 on the basis of a belief that Ranulf probably did not have access to Lincoln between his arrest in 1146 and 1153, but this may not be correct.[149] William de Roumare issued a charter at Lincoln which Kathleen Major dated to between December 1148 and c.1151.[150] The likelihood is, however, that Lincoln castle was in the hands of forces loyal to King Stephen from 1146 until 1153.

When Duke Henry of Normandy landed in England to fight for the crown in January 1153 he was probably aware of the trouble there had been at Lincoln, and anxious not to provoke any more. Lincoln castle is conspicuous by its absence from the sweeping charter granted by Henry to win Earl Ranulf's support between January and April 1153.[151] Theobald archbishop of Canterbury, who was hard at work trying to establish peace between Stephen and Henry in that year, was probably also concerned to extinguish the fire of contention that had raged at Lincoln. He attested, and probably encouraged the grant of the charter issued by Henry at the siege of Crowmarsh probably in July or August 1153 in which the duke confirmed a recompense granted by Earl Ranulf to the church of Lincoln for the damage he had caused it.[152] The charter was reissued in a more extended, rigorous and specific form, as a *conventionem* in fact, at Henry's siege of Stamford on 31 August 1153, and may, as Barraclough suggested, reflect pressure from a duke who was perhaps anxious to pave the way towards the surrender of Lincoln.[153]

Lincoln castle was one of those fortresses that Duke Henry considered important to the security of the treaty of Winchester he agreed with Stephen in November 1153 that effectively put an end to the civil war. It was one of several major castles that were entrusted to custodians who swore and guaranteed by placing hostages in the hands of the archbishop of Canterbury that they would hand the fortresses over to Henry after Stephen's death.[154] The man named as custodian of Lincoln castle in the treaty was Jordan de Bussy, who may have been the same man as Jordan de Blosseville who attested charters of William II and William III de Warenne, and the Jordan de Blosseville who was sheriff of Lincolnshire in the financial year 1154-55.[155] Jordan was almost certainly as good as his word. Between 1155 and 1162 Henry II restored to Richard de la Haye in heredity the constableship of the castle that his predecessor was supposed to have held in the reign of Henry I. But this was done by means of a royal charter that made it clear that the king regarded Lincoln castle as his, and no more was apparently heard until the turbulent first quarter of the thirteenth century of the tower that Lucy had built or fortified, or the claims to the fortress which her sons had advanced.[156]

In conclusion, we will probably never know the full truth about the dispute between the earls of Chester and Lincoln and King Stephen for control of Lincoln castle in the 1140s. There are simply too many conjectural possibilities. It is possible that Ranulf and William may have claimed, and Stephen may have granted, different rights at different times in one or both of the two towers, or over the entire Lincoln castle complex. It may also be that the half-brothers and the king interpreted their rights in the castle and the two mottes in different and conflicting ways, or that they misunderstood (perhaps deliberately) each other's positions. Whatever the case, the aims, motives, claims and justifications of those involved in the dispute are likely to have been much more complicated than has hitherto been realised. Herein lies the wider significance of the dispute. It not only suggests that the same or similar complications may have influenced the many other castle controversies that were such an important characteristic of the political conflict of Stephen's reign, but also shows just how important control of castles was to those who sought to acquire and exercise power in the English

countryside in the twelfth century, and how dangerous a loss of control could be to royal authority. This point, as the dispute over Lincoln castle demonstrates, was realised by Stephen, who used a variety of methods to retain and recover castles, and it was realised by Henry II whose greater authority allowed him to adopt a more direct approach to the problem. Henry's determination to establish wider royal control of fortresses probably owed a great deal to the castle disputes of the anarchy, of which the one at Lincoln was perhaps the most furious and memorable.[157]

Acknowledgements

My thanks are due to Dr Marjorie Chibnall and Professor Edmund King whose advice on aspects of the subject of this paper has been invaluable, and to Liverpool Hope University College for financial assistance towards the costs of research.

Notes

1. The main chronicle accounts are *The Ecclesiastical History of Orderic Vitalis*, edited by M. Chibnall, 6 vols (Oxford, 1969-80), vi, pp.538-46 (hereafter *OV*); *Gesta Stephani*, edited by K. R. Potter and R. H. C. Davis (Oxford, 1976), pp.110-14, 184, 192-202, 220 (hereafter *GS*); *William of Malmesbury Historia Novella The Contemporary History*, edited by E. King, translated by K. R. Potter (Oxford, 1998), pp.80-86 (hereafter *HN*); *Henry, Archdeacon of Huntingdon Historia Anglorum The History of the English People*, edited by D. Greenway (Oxford, 1996), pp.724-50 (hereafter *HA*); John of Hexham, continuation of the *Historia Regum* attributed to Symeon of Durham, in *Symeonis Monachi Opera Omnia*, edited by T. Arnold, 2 vols (Rolls Series, 1882-85), ii, p.306 (hereafter *SMOO*); *The Anglo-Saxon Chronicle*, edited by D. Whitelock with D. C. Douglas and S. I. Tucker (1961), p.201 (hereafter *ASC*); *Liber Eliensis*, edited by E. O. Blake (Camden Society, third series, 1962), pp.320-21 (hereafter *LE*).
2. J. W. F. Hill, *Medieval Lincoln* (Cambridge, 1948), pp.44, 82; *Regesta Regum Anglo-Normannorum*, edited by H. W. C. Davis *et al.*, 4 vols (Oxford, 1913-69), iii, no.178 (hereafter *RRA*). For a description of the castle, see D. F. Renn, *Norman Castles in Britain* (second edition, London and New York, 1973), p.226. A date of 1129 to 1136 has been suggested for the fortification of a tower by Lucy: D. Stocker and A. Vince, 'The early Norman castle at Lincoln and a re-evaluation of the original west tower of Lincoln Cathedral', *Medieval Archaeology* 41 (1997), p.226.
3. Hill, *Medieval Lincoln*, p.84.
4. *Ibid.*, p.91.
5. For the excavations, see N. Reynolds, 'Investigations in the Observatory Tower, Lincoln Castle', *Medieval Archaeology*, 19 (1975), pp.201-05. The excavator argued that a twelfth-century tower had been built on this site and attributed it tentatively to Ranulf rather than Lucy on the grounds that Stephen had granted the earl the right to strengthen or build one of the towers at Lincoln. Coulson accepted the evidence for a twelfth-century tower here, but suggested that its base could have been erected by Lucy and added to by Ranulf: C. Coulson, 'The castles of the Anarchy', in *The Anarchy of King Stephen's Reign*, edited by E. King (Oxford, 1994), p.89.
6. M. Thompson, 'The early topography of Lincoln castle', *infra*, pp.23-29. I am very grateful to Dr Thompson for his kindness in allowing me to read his paper in advance of publication.
7. Stocker and Vince, 'The early Norman castle', pp.223-33, quotations at pp.227, 231.
8. For Lucy's parentage, see Hill, *Medieval Lincoln*, pp.92-93, 96, 98; G. E. Cokayne, *The Complete Peerage of England, Scotland, Ireland . . .*, revised edition by V. Gibbs *et al.*, 13 vols (London, 1910-59), vii, 743-46.
9. Hill, *Medieval Lincoln*, p.93; J. A. Green, *English Sheriffs to 1154* (1990), p.54. For Lucy's lands, see H. A. Cronne, 'Ranulf de Gernons, earl of Chester, 1129-1153', *Transactions of the Royal Historical Society*, fourth series, 20 (1937), p.106; G. White, 'King Stephen, Duke Henry and Ranulf de Gernons, earl of Chester', *English Historical Review*, 91 (1976), pp.555-65; P. Dalton, 'Aiming at the impossible: Ranulf II earl of Chester and Lincolnshire in the reign of King Stephen', in *The Earldom of Chester and its Charters: A Tribute to Geoffrey Barraclough*, edited by A. T. Thacker, *Journal of the Chester Archaeological Society*, 71 (1991), p.110.

10. *RRA*, ii, no.1118; *The Registrum Antiquissimum of the Cathedral Church of Lincoln*, edited by C. W. Foster and K. Major, 10 vols (Lincoln Record Society, 1931-73), i, pp.20-21, no.21 (hereafter *RA*).

11. Hill, *Medieval Lincoln*, p.84.

12. For the policy of Rufus and Henry I, see M. Chibnall, 'Robert of Belleme and the castle of Tickhill', in *Droit privé et institutions régionales: études historiques offertes à Jean Yver* (Paris, 1976), quotation at p.154.

13. The chronicler is Orderic: *OV*, vi, p.538; and I owe the interpretation to Dr Chibnall.

14. Thompson, 'Early topography', p.27.

15. The constableship and shrievalty were later associated at times in the reigns of Richard I and John: Hill, *Medieval Lincoln*, pp.88-89.

16. For Colswein, the de la Hayes and their lands, see *The Red Book of the Exchequer*, edited by H. Hall, 3 vols (Rolls Series, 1896), i, pp.390-91; Hill, *Medieval Lincoln*, pp.48-50, 87-88; J. C. Holt, 'The carta of Richard de la Haye, 1166 a note on "continuity" in Anglo-Norman feudalism', *English Historical Review*, 84 (1969), pp.289-97; R. W. Goulding, 'Notes on the lords of the manor of Burwell', *Associated Architectural Societies' Reports and Papers*, 24 (1897), pp.62-63; H. M. Colvin, *The White Canons in England* (Oxford, 1951), pp.70-73; C. W. Foster, *A History of the Villages of Aisthorpe and Thorpe in the Fallows* (Lincoln, 1927), pp.93-94, 96. For the possible relationship of Colswein and Lucy, see R. H. C. Davis, 'Goltho: the manorial history', in G. Beresford, *Goltho: The Development of an Early Medieval Manor c.850-1150*, English Heritage Archaeological Report No.4 (1987), p.129.

17. Hill, *Medieval Lincoln*, p.88; J. A. Green, *The Government of England under Henry I* (Cambridge, 1986), p.258.

18. Hill, *Medieval Lincoln*, p.87.

19. *Ancient Charters Royal and Private Prior to A.D. 1200*, edited by J. H. Round (Pipe Roll Society, 1888), no.36.

20. Nicholaa held the castle with her husband, Gerard de Camville, sheriff of Lincolnshire, became sheriff herself, and still held the fortress in 1226: Hill, *Medieval Lincoln*, pp.88-89.

21. *RA*, vii, no.2050. Dr Major appears to have based her dating of this charter upon a belief that the constableship was hereditary in the family of de la Haye, and on an assumption that the de la Hayes were dispossessed in the anarchy and that Reginald was an interloper intruded into the castle at that time.

22. Cronne, 'Ranulf de Gernons', p.105. See also H. A. Cronne, *The Reign of Stephen 1135-54: Anarchy in England* (1970), pp.175-76. Hill and, more recently, Coulson have also been alert to the probability that hereditary or at least family claims lay behind Ranulf's actions: Hill, *Medieval Lincoln*, pp.93-98; Coulson, 'Castles of the Anarchy', p.88.

23. Cronne, 'Ranulf de Gernons', p.105, quotation at p.107.

24. *Ibid.*, p.111; Cronne, *Reign of Stephen*, pp.31-32, 42, 176-77; R. H. C. Davis, *King Stephen 1135-1154* (third edition, 1990), pp.46-48, 135.

25. *SMOO*, ii, p.306.

26. Cronne, 'Ranulf de Gernons', p.112; Cronne, *Reign of Stephen*, p.177. For the full scale of Stephen's grants to the Beaumonts, see D. Crouch, *The Beaumont Twins: The Roots and Branches of Power in the Twelfth Century* (Cambridge, 1986), pp.29-31, 34, 38-49; E. King, 'Waleran, count of Meulan, earl of Worcester (1104-1166)', in *Tradition and Change: Essays in Honour of Marjorie Chibnall . . .*, edited by D. Greenway *et al.* (Cambridge, 1985), pp.165-81.

27. Cronne, 'Ranulf de Gernons', pp.112-13. See also Cronne, *Reign of Stephen*, pp.142-43, 177.

28. Ranulf's hostility to Henry of Scotland had surfaced earlier in the reign in 1136: *SMOO*, ii, p.287; Richard of Hexham, *De Gestis Regis Stephani et de Bello Standardii*, in *Chronicles of the Reigns of Stephen, Henry II, and Richard I*, edited by R. Howlett, 4 vols (Rolls Series, 1884-89), p.146.

29. *SMOO*, ii, p.323.

30. See *GS*, pp.46-48, 200; *RRA*, iii, nos 68, 178, 274-76, 314, 387, 391, 393-94, 430, 437, 482, 494, 582, 634, 959; N. J. G. Pounds, *The Medieval Castle in England and Wales* (Cambridge, 1990), p.27.

31. *GS*, pp.32-42; Cronne, 'Ranulf de Gernons', pp.114-15.

32. *GS*, p.32.

33. *RRA*, iii, p.xxv; *RA*, i, p.196.

34. *RRA*, ii, nos 1660-61, 1770, 1773, 1791; *RA*, i, nos 26, 46, 49, 51, 55, and see nos 53-54, 54a, 69, 70; Hill, *Medieval Lincoln*, p.86.

35. *RRA*, iii, nos 463-65, 468-70, 475-76, 482. It is possible that Sleaford fair and the Eagle and Condet properties were granted after 1139.

36. *RRA*, iii, nos 178, 472; *RA*, i, p.289. It is significant that in a charter granted at Lincoln, probably in 1146, Stephen enforced the earlier grant to Bishop Alexander of the knights' fees belonging to the honour of Lancaster, commanding that they were to be held just as on the day when he first went to the siege of Lincoln: *RRA*, iii, no.471.

37. The highway which the bishop had obtained the right to divert at Newark was the Fosse Way, which went to Lincoln. The bridge he obtained the right to build there crossed the Trent which was a major route from the Midlands to Lincoln via the Foss Dyke, and on the banks of which were situated the settlements of Torksey and Gainsborough. William de Roumare built or fortified a castle at Gainsborough and secured from Stephen control of the bridge there: Hill, *Medieval Lincoln*, Fig.24 (p.406); Dalton, 'Ranulf II and Lincolnshire', pp.117-18, 133.

38. *RRA*, iii, no.493 and note. For Stephen's arrest of the bishops of Salisbury and Lincoln in June 1139, see E. J. Kealey, *Roger of Salisbury Viceroy of England* (Berkeley and London, 1972), pp.173-200.

39. Davis, *King Stephen*, p.134.

40. *OV*, vi, p.538; *HA*, p.732.

41. Dalton, 'Ranulf II and Lincolnshire', pp.109-34.

42. As was recognised by Round: J. H. Round, 'King Stephen and the earl of Chester', *English Historical Review*, 10 (1895), pp.87, 90-91. For the farm and communications, see Hill, *Medieval Lincoln*, pp.184-85, 406 (Fig.24).

43. It was probably then that Ranulf issued charters in Lincoln attested by powerful Lincolnshire lords and knights, including Ralph de la Haye, Simon Fitz William lord of Bullington, William Fitz Hacon de Saleby a former sheriff of Lincolnshire, Baldwin Fitz Gilbert de Clare lord of Bourne, Hugh Bardulf lord of Riseholme, Gilbert de Neville, William de Coleville and William Malebisse: *The Charters of the Anglo-Norman Earls of Chester, c.1071-1237*, edited by G. Barraclough (Record Society of Lancashire and Cheshire, 1988), nos 66, 69, 71, 77 and notes (hereafter *CEC*). For de la Haye, see above note 16. For Fitz William, see C. J. Wales, 'The knight in twelfth-century Lincolnshire' (unpublished University of Cambridge, Ph.D. thesis, 1983), pp.1-108. For Fitz Hacon, see Foster, *Aisthorpe*, pp.6, 9, 33-37, 70; *Transcripts of Charters relating to the Gilbertine Houses . . .*, edited by F. M. Stenton, Lincoln Record Society, 18 (Horncastle, 1922), pp.xi-xii; W. Farrer, *Honors and Knights' Fees*, 3 vols (London and Manchester, 1923-25), ii, pp.151, 198; Green, *Sheriffs*, p.55. For Bardulf, see C. Clay, 'Hugh Bardolf the justice and his family', *Lincolnshire History and Archaeology*, 1 (1966), pp.5-28.

44. *OV*, vi, p.538.

45. *Ibid.*, pp.538-40.

46. *HA*, pp.724, 748.

47. *Ibid.*, p.734.

48. *Ibid.*, p.726. Entry by guile is also recorded by *William of Newburgh: The History of English Affairs: Book I*, edited by P. G. Walsh and M. J. Kennedy (Warminster, 1988), pp.60-62.

49. *GS*, p.110.

50. *Ibid.*, p.184.

51. *ASC*, p.201.

52. *SMOO*, ii, p.306. Translation based upon that in Alan O. Anderson, *Scottish Annals from English Chroniclers A.D. 500 to 1286* (1908; reprinted Stamford, 1991), p.216.

53. *HN*, pp.80-82.

54. *Ibid.*, p.82.

55. *LE*, pp.320-21.

56. M. Chibnall, 'Orderic Vitalis on castles', in *Studies in Medieval History presented to R. Allen Brown*, edited by C. Harper-Bill *et al.* (Woodbridge, 1989), pp.43-56, quotations from pp.53, 56. I am grateful to Dr Chibnall for the suggestion, made via personal correspondence, about Roumare's household knights.

57. *HA*, pp.xxix-xxx, xlviii, lvii; A. Gransden, *Historical Writing in England c.550 to c.1307* (1974), pp.193-94. The quotation is from D. Greenway, 'Authority, convention and observation in Henry of Huntingdon's *Historia Anglorvm*', *Anglo-Norman Studies*, 18 (1996), p.114. Henry of Huntingdon was not entirely favourable to Alexander, writing a section after Alexander's death in which he criticised the bishop for spending beyond his means.

58. Greenway, 'Authority, convention and observation', p.113.

59. *GS*, pp.xviii-xxi. Bradbury has recently suggested that the *Gesta* may be the work of two authors with different views rather than the work of a single author who changed his mind: J. Bradbury, *Stephen and Matilda: The Civil War of 1139-53* (Stroud, 1996), pp.141-42.

60. *ASC*, p.199.

61. Malmesbury has been condemned by some historians as a conscious deceiver. However, the implications of his description of Robert of Gloucester's conduct in London in 1141 are revealing: 'It is well established that, if the other members of his party had trusted his restraint and wisdom, they would not afterwards have endured such a turn of ill-fortune.': *HN*, p.96. Consider also his statement that at the siege of Winchester later that year, 'Ranulf earl of Chester's arrival

was late and ineffective': *ibid*, p.102. See also the remarks of Davis in his *King Stephen*, p.145, and of Edmund King in his 'Introduction', in *Anarchy of Stephen's Reign*, p.6, and in his 'Introduction' to *HN*, pp.xxxiii-lxvii.

62. *LE*, pp.314-20; Gransden, *Historical Writing*, pp.271, 280-88.

63. The possibility of confusion or repetition is pointed out by Bradbury, *Stephen and Matilda*, p.88.

64. Cronne, 'Ranulf de Gernons', pp.115-17, and see Davis: *King Stephen*, p.47, 48 and note 11; Bradbury, *Stephen and Matilda*, pp.88-89.

65. Cronne, *Reign of Stephen*, p.177, and see pp.42-43, 104.

66. *GS*, p.184.

67. *RRA*, iii, no.178. For an assessment of the quality of the text, see *RA*, i, pp.287-89.

68. In the same year that Ranulf renewed his pact with Stephen (1145/1146), William received substantial grants from the king: *RRA*, iii, no.494.

69. Davis, *King Stephen*, p.134.

70. *CEC*, no.77; Dalton, 'Ranulf II and Lincolnshire', pp.111-13. For the grant of earldoms without shrievalties, see G. White, 'Continuity in government', in *Anarchy of Stephen's Reign*, pp.125, 127-28.

71. For earldoms and shrievalties, see D. Crouch, 'Geoffrey de Clinton and Roger, earl of Warwick: new men and magnates in the reign of Henry I', *Bulletin of the Institute of Historical Research*, 55 (1982), p.122; Crouch, *Beaumont Twins*, pp.39-40; J. A. Green, 'Financing Stephen's war', *Anglo-Norman Studies*, 14 (1992), pp.92-98, 100, 102-03, 109; White, 'Continuity in government', pp.127, 129-30. For shrievalties and constableships, see *RRA*, iii, nos 68, 275; Hill, *Medieval Lincoln*, pp.88-90, 96-98; Green, 'Financing Stephen's war', pp.96-97, 100, 109; J. H. Round, 'The early sheriffs of Norfolk', *English Historical Review*, 35 (1920), pp.495-96.

72. Green, *Sheriffs*, p.55. William Fitz Hacon, who was sheriff of Lincolnshire in 1133 and a tenant of the honours of Chester and Roumare, attests a charter of Earl William between *c*.1141 and 1154, another *c*.1142, and three charters of Earl Ranulf: one issued at Lincoln *c*.1143-44, and also attested by Earl William; one issued at Lincoln between 1144 and 1146; and one issued at Lincoln *c*.1153: Farrer, *Honors*, ii, pp.151, 198; *RA*, vi, no.1869; *Facsimiles of Early Charters from Northamptonshire Collections*, edited by F. M. Stenton (Northants. Record Society, 1930), p.3; *CEC*, nos 69, 77, 111.

73. *RRA*, iii, no.472. The editors date the charter either to 1140 or to 1146-1147.

74. Thompson, 'Early topography', p.25.

75. E. King, 'Dispute settlement in Anglo-Norman England', *Anglo-Norman Studies*, 14 (1992), pp.115-30, esp.119-26; P. Dalton, '*In neutro latere*: the armed neutrality of Ranulf II earl of Chester in King Stephen's reign', *Anglo-Norman Studies*, 14 (1992), pp.44-49, 54-56; D. Crouch, 'A Norman "conventio" and bonds of lordship in the Middle Ages', in *Law and Government in Medieval England and Normandy: Essays in Honour of Sir James Holt*, edited by G. Garnett and J. Hudson (Cambridge, 1994), pp.299-324; M. Chibnall, 'The charters of empress Matilda', in *Law and Government*, p.283.

76. P. Bonnassie, 'Feudal conventions in eleventh-century Catalonia', in his *From Slavery to Feudalism in South-Western Europe* (Cambridge, 1991), pp.170-94; King, 'Dispute settlement', pp.115 and note 4, 116 note 7, 117 note 13; J. Martindale, 'Conventum inter Guillelmum Aquitanorum comes et Hugonem Chiliarchum', *English Historical Review*, 84 (1969), pp.528-48. *Conventiones* also occur in Normandy in the eleventh century: Crouch, 'Norman "conventio"', p.307.

77. C. Coulson, 'The French matrix of the castle-provisions of the Chester-Leicester conventio', *Anglo-Norman Studies*, 17 (1995), p.83.

78. *Ibid*., pp.78-80, 83; I. W. Rowlands 'King John, Stephen Langton and Rochester castle, 1213-15', in *Studies . . . presented to R. Allen Brown*, p.278; R. Eales, 'Royal power and castles in Norman England', in *The Ideals and Practice of Medieval Knighthood III: Papers from the Fourth Strawberry Hill Conference 1988*, edited by C. Harper-Bill and R. Harvey (Woodbridge, 1990), p.70.

79. For rendability and other French castle customs, see C. Coulson, 'Rendability and castellation in medieval France', *Château Gaillard*, 6 (1973), pp.59-67; C. Coulson, 'Castellation in the county of Champagne in the thirteenth century', *Château Gaillard*, 9-10 (1982), pp.347-64; C. Coulson, 'Fortress-policy in Capetian tradition and Angevin practice: aspects of the conquest of Normandy by Philip I', *Anglo-Norman Studies*, 6 (1984), pp.13-38; C. Coulson, 'The impact of Bouvines upon the fortress-policy of Philip Augustus', in *Studies . . . presented to R. Allen Brown*, pp.71-80.

80. C. H. Haskins, *Norman Institutions* (Cambridge, Ma., 1918), pp.277-84. See Coulson, 'Rendability and castellation', p.59; Coulson, 'Fortress-policy', pp.15, 37; Coulson, 'Castles of the Anarchy', pp.72-73; Eales, 'Royal power and castles', pp.70-72.

81. It is likely that the *Consuetudines* should be interpreted as an exceptional response to the civil war in Normandy, rather than as an accurate reflection of the normal castle-powers of Duke William: Eales, 'Royal power and castles', pp.72, 76-77.

82. See *RRA*, ii, no.598. Coulson notes that Robert of Torigni states that Henry I had 'used the fortresses of many of his barons as though they were his own', and that this represents normal rendability: C. Coulson, 'Fortress-policy', p.16.

83. See Rowlands 'Rochester castle', pp.277-78; Eales, 'Royal power and castles', pp.74-75; Pounds, *The Medieval Castle*, p.29; Coulson, 'Castles of the Anarchy', p.74. For the seizure and the suspicion, see *OV*, vi, pp.530-34; *GS*, pp.72-80; *HN*, pp.44-48.

84. *GS*, p.74.

85. *HN*, pp.46-48.

86. *Ibid*., p.54. Bishop Roger held a castle at Malmesbury.

87. For this element, see Coulson, 'Impact of Bouvines', p.74.

88. *HN*, p.58.

89. *The Chronicle of John of Worcester, Volume III*, edited by P. McGurk (Oxford, 1998), pp.266-68.

90. *GS*, p.80.

91. *GS*, p.176.

92. For pledging in France see Coulson, 'Impact of Bouvines', pp.75-77; Coulson, 'Fortress-policy', pp.33, 36.

93. *OV*, vi, p.530; *GS*, pp.72-80; *HN*, pp.44-48; *RRA*, iii, no.493 and note.

94. *GS*, pp.28, 160-64, 184, 192-98; *SMOO*, ii, pp.290-91; Ailred of Rievaulx, *Relatio de Standardo*, in *Chronicles of the Reigns*, iii, p.191; *HA*, p.748; P. Dalton, 'Eustace Fitz John and the politics of Anglo-Norman England: the rise and survival of a twelfth-century royal servant', *Speculum*, 71 (1996), pp.367-70. Robert of Bampton was required to surrender not just his castle but 'all he possessed': *GS*, p.28.

95. Coulson discusses the arrest of the bishops, Mandeville and Chester in the context of rendability and (apparently) pledging: 'Castles of the Anarchy', pp.74-75.

96. *Ibid*., pp.73-74; Coulson, 'French matrix', pp.65-86.

97. *RRA*, iii, nos 795-96.

98. See the relations between Robert of Gloucester and Robert Fitz Hubert; Ranulf of Chester and Alan lord of Richmond; and Empress Matilda and Bishop Henry of Winchester: *GS*, pp.104-06, 116, 118; *HN*, pp.76, 100-02.

99. In southern France and Catalonia, for example: Coulson, 'French matrix', p.77 note 45; Coulson, 'Rendability and castellation', pp.62-63; Bonnassie, 'Feudal conventions', p.182.

100. Eales, 'Royal power and castles', pp.76-77.

101. Coulson, 'French matrix', pp.74-75, 82.

102. Eales, 'Royal power and castles', p.70.

103. Coulson, 'Castles of the Anarchy', p.74. See also Rowlands, 'Rochester castle', p.278.

104. *HN*, p.48.

105. Eales, 'Royal power and castles', p.75.

106. *HN*, pp.50-52.

107. Ailred, *Relatio*, p.191; Anderson, *Scottish Annals*, pp.199-200.

108. *GS*, p.98.

109. Grants of castles in perpetual custody were not unknown in England before Stephen's reign, may sometimes have escaped the attention of chroniclers, and 'created the possibility of the blurring of the distinction between *custodia* and *dominium*': Rowlands, 'Rochester castle', p.278.

110. *HN*, p.82.

111. *HN*, pp.40-42.

112. J. Gillingham, '1066 and the introduction of chivalry into England', in *Law and Government*, p.49.

113. *Ibid*., p.49 note 69.

114. See M. Bloch, *Feudal Society* (1962), p.227; Martindale, 'Conventum', pp.535, 547-48; J.-P. Poly and E. Bournazel, *The Feudal Transformation 900-1200* (New York, 1991), pp.73, 76-77. The practice of *exfestucatio* appears similar in some ways to that of *diffidatio*, though it has not always been interpreted in this way. For examples, see *The Murder of Charles the Good*, translated by J. B. Ross (Toronto, 1988), pp.171 and note 7, 269-70, 278; M. Bloch, 'Les formes de la rupture de l'hommage dans l'ancien droit féodal', in his *Mélanges Historiques* 2 vols (Paris, 1963), i, pp.189-209; Poly and Bournazel, *Feudal Transformation*, pp.62-63. For useful comments, see J. Le Goff, *Time, Work, & Culture in the Middle Ages* (Chicago, 1980), pp.246-48, 259-60. For the later use of defiance in England by Henry III, see Sir F. Pollock and F. W. Maitland, *The History of English Law before the Time of Edward I*, 2 vols (second edition, Cambridge, 1968), i, p.303.

115. The suggestion of importation was made by Edmund King, in a paper given to the Liverpool Centre for Medieval Studies at the University of Liverpool in December 1995. M. Strickland, *War and Chivalry: The Conduct and Perception of War in England and Normandy, 1066-1217* (Cambridge, 1996), p.40 note 47 points out that defiance is mentioned in the *De iniusta vexacione*, which describes the trial of the bishop of Durham at Salisbury in 1088; but it is possible that this tractate dates from the second quarter of the twelfth century. Strickland has other examples from Orderic, referring to a renunciation of fealty in Normandy in 1119, and from Geoffrey Gaimar, writing *c*.1140. Strickland points out that it is highly unlikely whether kings 'felt any obligation to defy erstwhile vassals before attacking them', and presents evidence that challenges 'the idea that rebellion might be placed on some form of legal footing by the act of *diffidatio*': *ibid.*, pp.40-41, 232-34.

116. Gillingham notes the cases of Brus and Chester-Leicester, and the fact that the chroniclers who inform us about Brus did not use the word *diffidatio*: Gillingham, '1066', p.49 note 70. However, the breaking of chains of fealty or returning of homage or fealty by these lords looks very similar to *diffidatio*.

117. Quoted by W. L. Warren, *Henry II* (1973), pp.136-38, and see p.138 note 1. See also M. Strickland, 'Against the Lord's anointed: aspects of warfare and baronial rebellion in England and Normandy, 1075-1265', in *Law and Government*, p.65.

118. *GS*, p.184. See also *Annales Cestrienses*, edited by R. C. Christie (Record Society of Lancashire and Cheshire, 1887), p.20.

119. *GS*, pp.192-96.

120. *Ibid.*, p.196.

121. *Ibid.*, pp.184, 194-96; *ASC*, p.201.

122. *GS*, pp.28, 72-78, 160-64; *HN*, pp.44-48; *OV*, p.532.

123. See the comments of William of Malmesbury: *HN*, pp.38, 52.

124. *RRA*, iii, no.267. I am grateful to Professor King for drawing this document to my attention.

125. *GS*, p.236; *HN*, p.44. Davis believed that the section of the *Gesta* in which this passage occurs was written after the author had changed his allegiance to the Angevin party. But, see above note 59 for an alternative possibility. The Anglo-Saxon chronicler states that Stephen arrested Ranulf 'through bad counsel': *ASC*, p.201. See also the comments in *HA*, p.748; *Newburgh, History of English Affairs*, p.72.

126. *SMOO*, i, pp.170-95, translated in *English Historical Documents 1042-1189*, edited by D. C. Douglas and G. W. Greenaway (1968), pp.609-24, and *English Lawsuits from William I to Richard I*, edited by R. C. Van Caenegem, 2 vols (Selden Society, 1990-91), i, no.134 (hereafter *EL*); H. S. Offler, 'The tractate *De iniusta vexacione Willelmi episcopi primi*', *English Historical Review*, 66 (1951), pp.321-41. A new edition of the tractate by Offler was published recently: *De iniusta vexacione Willelmi episcopi primi per Willelmum regem filium Willelmi magni regis*, edited by H. S. Offler, revised by A. J. Piper and A. I. Doyle, in *Chronology, Conquest and Conflict in Medieval England: Camden Miscellany XXXIV* (Camden Fifth Series, 10, 1997), pp.49-104 (hereafter *DIV*).

127. See M. Philpott, 'The *De iniusta vexacione Willelmi episcopi primi* and canon law in Anglo-Norman Durham', in *Anglo-Norman Durham 1093-1193* edited by D. Rollason, M. Harvey and M. Prestwich (Woodbridge, 1994), pp.125-37, esp.127 and note 14; H. S. Offler, 'Introduction', in *DIV*, pp.60-65.

128. I hope to develop this argument elsewhere.

129. One of the three magnates is stated to have been acting for the king, and the implication is that this was true of them all: *SMOO*, i, p.178. For some of the connotations of this dispute for lord-man relations, see C. L. Dier, 'The proper relationship between lord and vassal: toward a rationale for Anglo-Norman litigation', *The Haskins Society Journal*, 6 (1995), pp.1-12.

130. In his *conventio* with the three magnates the bishop promised that if he was conducted safely back to his castle from the royal court, and the castle had been strengthened or expanded by his men during his absence, then he would cause the additional armament to be removed. Seven of his men promised that if the bishop rejected a right judgement, and chose to go into exile, they would surrender the castle of Durham to the king. When faced later with the king's demand for the surrender of Durham castle, the bishop told Rufus that 'There was never an agreement between us that I would surrender my castle to you unless I refused a canonical judgement and unless (if there arose a contradiction of judgment) I refused to go for that contradiction to that place where I ought justly to receive the final sentence on this

contradiction': *SMOO*, i, pp.177-78, 186 (translation from *EL*, i, pp.95, 100).

131. *SMOO*, i, p.186 (translation from *EL*, i, p.100).

132. *Ibid.*, p.187; *EL*, i, p.100.

133. *Ibid.*, p.190 (translation from *EL*, i, p.102).

134. For Ranulf's Angevin attachments and suspect loyalty, see Dalton, '*In neutro latere*', pp.44, 50-51, 54-56. For Stephen's reaction to rebellion, see *GS*, pp.112-14. For commentary, see Cronne, *Reign of Stephen*, p.106; Strickland, 'Against the Lord's anointed', p.57.

135. For the link between necessity and rendability, see Coulson, 'Fortress-policy', p.4 note 31.

136. For these alienations, see *RRA*, iii, no.387; *HN*, p.40; Davis, *King Stephen*, pp.19-20; Crouch, *Beaumont Twins*, pp.29-30.

137. See Rowlands, 'Rochester castle', pp.267-79.

138. The situation at Tickhill was reported by the knights of the honour to the king in 1200: *Pleas Before the King or his Justices 1198-1202*, edited by D. M. Stenton, 4 vols (Selden Society, 1953-67), i, no.3135 and for comments, see p.68. There are problems with this report because the knights named the count as Henry rather than John son of Henry, to whom Stephen had actually entrusted the honour, and stated that after Stephen's capture Henry of Anjou seized the castle, which seems unlikely in 1141. In Henry I's reign the castle and honour of Tickhill were held separately, and the castle was considered to be royal: Chibnall, 'Robert of Belleme', pp.151-56. For Warwick, see *GS*, p.234.

139. For the siege in 1144, see *HA*, p.744; *Newburgh, History of English Affairs*, p.72.

140. Ralph attests three charters for Ranulf which Barraclough dated between 1142 and 1146. In two his name appears first in the list of witnesses. In one it appears second after that of William de Roumare. He also attests a charter of Ranulf for Robert earl of Leicester issued in the fields between Leicester and Mountsorrel between 1145 and 1147, and another charter issued by Ranulf at Lincoln possibly in 1153: *CEC*, nos 66, 71, 77, 82, 93.

141. *RRA*, iii, no.494.

142. *HA*, p.748.

143. *RRA*, iii, nos 482, 487, 624. Earl Simon de Senlis attested no.482, and also no.736 which was granted by Stephen at Lincoln in 1146 when he wore his crown.

144. *HA*, pp.748-50; *GS*, pp.198-200; *The Chronicle of Pierre de Langtoft . . .*, edited by T. Wright, 2 vols (Rolls Series, 1866-68), i, pp.494-95.

145. *GS*, p.220.

146. M. R. Abbot, 'The Gant family in England, 1066-1191' (unpublished University of Cambridge, Ph.D. thesis, 1973), no.59; Dalton, 'Ranulf II and Lincolnshire', pp.124-26.

147. Abbot, 'Gant family', Appendix. It is interesting that the former sheriff of Lincolnshire, William Fitz Hacon, and the son of a former possible constable of Lincoln castle, Ralph de la Haye, attested charters of Gilbert late in Stephen's reign: Green, *Sheriffs*, p.55; Abbot, 'Gant family', Appendix, nos 59, 79, 123. One of these charters (no.79) was also attested by Robert de Tateshale the son and heir of Hugh son of Eudo. Hugh was the sheriff of Lincolnshire at some point between 1135 and 1139: *RA*, vii, pp.85-86. The de la Hayes and the Hacons were Gant tenants: Foster, *Aisthorpe*, pp.6, 22-23; Abbot, 'Gant family', p.129; Green, *Sheriffs*, p.55.

148. *CEC*, nos 64, 84-86 and notes.

149. *CEC*, p.72, nos 93, 107, 111 and notes.

150. *RA*, vi, no.1856.

151. *RRA*, iii, no.180.

152. *Ibid.*, no.491. For an earlier recompense charter issued by Ranulf, see *CEC*, no.104.

153. *RRA*, iii, no.492; *CEC*, no.106 and note.

154. *RRA*, iii, no.272.

155. Green, *Sheriffs*, p.55; Green, 'Financing Stephen's war', p.98 note 49. He may also be the same man as the one who attests a charter of King Stephen for the priory of Colchester issued between 1135 and 1154: *RRA*, iii, no.212.

156. Hill, *Medieval Lincoln*, p.91.

157. For Henry's policy towards castles, see R. Allen Brown, 'Royal castle-building in England, 1154-1216', *English Historical Review*, 70 (1955), pp.353-98; R. Allen Brown, 'A list of castles, 1154-1216', *English Historical Review*, 74 (1959), pp.249-80; *The History of the King's Works*, edited by H. M. Colvin, 6 vols (1963-73), i, pp.64-81; ii, pp.553-894, 1023; Coulson, 'Fortress-policy', pp.13, 22-23.

Cobb Hall Tower

Derek Renn

Introduction

Lincoln Castle has a very unusual plan. Michael Thompson suggests an original equilaterally triangular bailey, north of the larger *motte*, with a subsequent semicircular addition (with the smaller *motte*) to the south-east, facing the cathedral and overlooking the city.[1] The castle has three long, fairly straight, sides each formed by a substantial earth bank carrying a stone curtain wall. Near one end of each of these sides was an entrance: one is a plain doorway and the other two are plain square gatehouses.[2] The sharp junctions of the sides facing either open country or the high ground of the upper part of the city were all left exposed at first, but one corner was later covered by a tower, carefully sited to command much of the north and east sides of the castle. This tower (called Cob's [*sic*] Hall at the beginning of the nineteenth century) is the only active defensive feature of the perimeter which survives.

From outside the castle, Cobb Hall looks like an ordinary medieval round tower. But it extends backwards into the castle courtyard, tapering slightly so that its plan is that of an elongated horse-shoe, or of a toy magnet. The external ashlar is tight-jointed but there are many breaks in the coursing. In particular, the top third of the tower is in a different stone and of a different block size from the rest, and the architect and antiquary Edward Willson who measured and surveyed the castle in detail in May 1829[3] described it as modern. The sketch of the castle on the town plan inset in Speed's county map of 1610 shows the tower as standing one storey above the curtain walls. In 1815, a recent half-pyramidal tiled roof (with a triangular gable above the entrance) was taken off, and the eroded wall top was levelled and leaded over to form the platform for the prison gallows (the 'New Drop'). The first execution here took place in 1817 and in March 1829 – only a few weeks before Willson's survey – the first burial took place of a hanged man within the Lucy Tower of Lincoln Castle. Willson says that Cobb Hall was formerly used for lodging vagrants, deserters and casual prisoners.[4] Did it become the condemned cell about 1829? Willson obviously had frequent access to Cobb Hall, and mentions the removal of partitions, so it may have been left empty. The 'New Drop' was closed in 1859.[5]

Description

Cobb Hall is entered from within the castle by a narrow doorway (heightened in 1825) with chamfered jambs and a two-centred head under a hoodmould. The interior is vaulted in asymmetric bays, with small bosses and chamfered ribs usually carried down as shafts without capitals other than as a continuation of the chamfered string-course. The vaults are plastered and the walls are of coursed rubble.

The first bay has a quadripartite vault widening to the north-east, with flanking quadripartite vaulted rectangular bays, which are lit by tall narrow square-headed windows with chamfered reveals, one on each side of the door. The south-west wall ribs stand on moulded corbels. The flanking bay on the north-west side has an arcade of two pointed chamfered arches and contains a straight staircase which rises to the present wallwalk. Neither arcade nor stair are shown on Willson's 1829 plans, and they may have been inserted during his repair work in 1835-45, either for convenience or to restore an earlier feature, although there is no evidence of a central boss or of a former vault-rib where the vault is traversed by the stair-passage.

The next axial bay has four sides, each of a different length, with a passage on each side which opened through a square-headed doorway into thin air, above the level of the earth bank at the junction of the tower and curtain wall. The upper side walls of each passage are recessed so as to have an irregular six-sided plan, like the side view of a clenched fist, with a slit through the outer wall above the doorway. These passages seem to be modifications from arrowloop recesses like those about to be described. The outermost bay of the tower is two-thirds of a circle in plan, with five ribs to the vault. Between each pair of ribs is an arrowloop recess of fairly uniform five-sided plan, each side being somewhat larger than those of the flanking passages. The right-hand recess is undercut to the right, perhaps to correct the field of view. Each arrowslit has a lintel at the level of the springing of the vault of the recess and runs down to floor level (Figs 1 and 3).

An off-centre trapdoor in the central bay leads to a steep wooden stair which passes through a sloping hole in the lower vault, which is irregularly sexpartite with similar ribs and boss to that of the floor above. However, the ribs here spring from the stringcourse and are not carried down the piers. This vault is roughly two-thirds of a circle in plan, like that of the bay above it, but here the four recesses are less uniform. One is a blind recess, one side following the outer face of the curtain wall,[6] which suggests that the tower was applied to a plain corner, unless a previous tower was completely removed and the angle made good. Another recess is a fairly regular pentagon in plan, similar to those of the outermost bay immediately above. Those on either side of it are six-sided and fist-like, again rather like those flanking the upper central bay. At both levels, the recesses are fitted up for restraining prisoners, with iron rings fastened to the side walls and vertical bars in the slits themselves. The arrowslits have an external chamfer on their vertical sides and run from the floor to the level of the pointed vault of the recess (Figs 2 and 3).

From outside the castle, the rounded face of Cobb Hall is set back above the foundation courses by four chamfered offsets. The uppermost horizontal chamfer is stepped up with a vertical chamfer on either side. The right-hand chamfer reaches the sill of the square-headed north doorway, whereas the left-hand one runs a metre or so below the east doorway (Figs 4 to 7). This may be reinforcement of the junction with the earlier curtain wall, to prevent the tower from settling or pulling away from the wall.[7] The three lower arrowslits are cut through the top chamfer coursing at the foot and are offset from the six arrowslits above (Figs 5 and 6). Here the outermost pair are smaller but higher than the other four, being above the doorways. The exterior coursing suggests that the doorways were alterations, at least in their latest form, before they were blocked up.

Dating

A very ancient prototype still remains within five minutes' walk of Cobb Hall, in the car-park of the Eastgate Hotel. In 1133 King Henry I gave Bishop Alexander the east gate of the city and the tower over it as a lodging.[8] The Roman east gate (Fig.8) had a passage flanked by two apsidal towers straddling the line of the legionary fort wall. The base of the northern tower is approximately the same size and shape as Cobb Hall externally, but has thinner walls (compare Figs 8 and 9). Some internal walling was inserted into the Roman tower in the second half of the twelfth or the early thirteenth century. The Roman tower was still used in the fifteenth century, well after the castle had passed out of use as a fortress.[9]

Most authorities place the building of Cobb Hall in the thirteenth century but there is no conclusive evidence for this date.[10] As a royal castle from its foundation in 1068, Lincoln Castle's major building works should appear in the royal accounts, which are continuous from 1154.[11] But these accounts seldom specify the exact nature of the 'works' paid for, and so we must turn to more general historical evidence and architectural parallels. If we accept that Cobb Hall was not part of the original castle of 1068, it might have been added soon after the fire of 1113 or after one of the nine recorded attacks on the castle (1140, 1141, 1144, 1146, 1149, 1191, 1216, 1217, 1265),[12] any one of which would have drawn attention to the weak defences of this part of the castle. Let us look at the four most likely scenarios:

A.   The castle had a stone wall (*murus*) by 1115 and Henry of Huntingdon (writing 1129x33) refers to the castle's very strong towers (in the plural).[13] Ranulf, earl of Chester seized the castle in 1140 and as part of his settlement with king Stephen in 1146 was permitted to *firmare* a tower, which might have resulted in a new building.[14] However, the shape of Cobb Hall and its architectural detail (particularly the vaulting) would be remarkable for a building in the first half of the twelfth century. Arrowloops are unknown elsewhere in England or Normandy before the 1170s.[15]

B.   The castle gaol was repaired in 1188, the first royal expense recorded on the castle. Just across the way are the tapering bays and experimental vaulting in St Hugh's choir in the cathedral (*c*.1192-1200).[16] In 1191, the castle was besieged and briefly captured by William Longchamp, chancellor of King Richard I, from Gerard de Camville, a supporter of count John.[17] Over £110 was spent on repairs and on *firmandi balliam* in 1190-94. Another £35 was spent in 1199-1200, much of it on repairing the *nove turris* and the

gaol. Further small sums were spent on the gaol in 1205 and 1212.[18]

Longchamp had spent nearly £3,000 in 1189 on the Tower of London, including the Bell Tower. This is octagonal at its solid base and vaulted first floor, tapering to round at second floor level. The high pointed vault is of irregular plan, supported by five unchamfered ribs which rise from the floor without capitals. Two of the arrowloop recesses are slewed round in a way reminiscent of the smaller ones of Cobb Hall. The apsidal Wardrobe Tower may also be due to Longchamp.[19]

Angle towers were being added to the curtain walls of several other royal castles at this time. At Dover, the semi-octagonal Avranches Tower of the 1180s has a solid base and a unique style of multiple but very narrow arrowloops on two levels, the lower tier opening off a narrow passage.[20] The Tour du Moulin at Chinon, probably built before 1189, has a solid square base which is chamfered upwards through octagonal to round. It has two hexagonal vaulted storeys with three and four arrowloop recesses respectively.[21] At Gisors, the half-round Tour du Diable is considered to be Angevin work (*i.e.* before 1193). It has four floors with an irregular ribbed vault between the second and third floors. There are up to seven arrowloop recesses to each floor, two being of experimental types.[22] The round towers of Château Gaillard (1196-1204) are dilapidated but the arrowloops in the open-backed angular latrine tower are simple embrasures at three levels. This can also be seen in Coulton's Gate at Dover (which chamfer from square to semi-octagon upwards both inside and out) which is considered to be part of the work of 1208-12.[23]

The recorded expenditure at Lincoln Castle in the 1190s is fairly small, but might be enough for the building of a new tower. Cobb Hall can be related typologically to the Bell Tower. However, no description of the siege of Lincoln by the baronial and French forces in 1216-17 makes any mention of such a tower, neither when Faulkes de Bréauté's force of crossbowmen fired from the castle ramparts nor when they sallied out eastward into the city, nor when the relieving royalists came in from the north and west of the city.[24]

C.   The Tour de la reine Mathilde is regarded as part of the major strengthening of Caen castle made by Philip

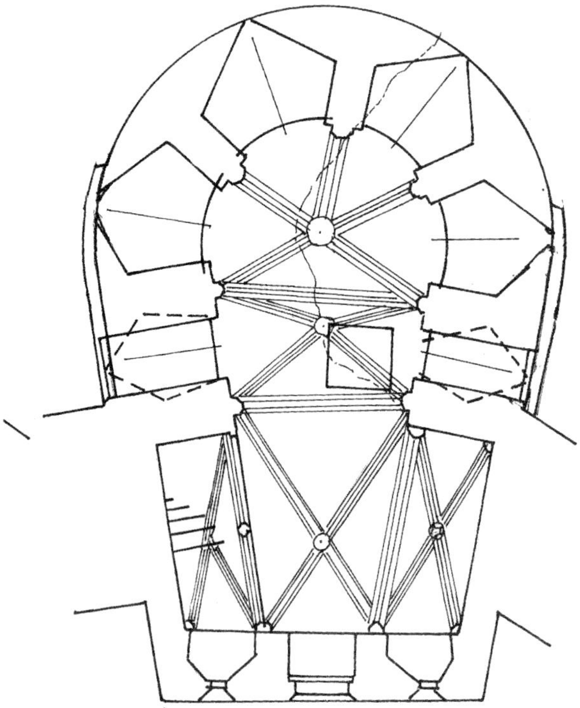

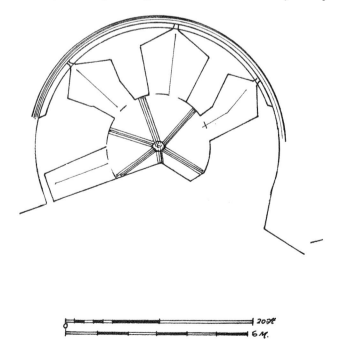

Fig.1. Cobb Hall: plan of upper vaulted floor, scale as Fig.2.

Fig.2. Cobb Hall: plan of lower vaulted floor.

Fig.3. Cobb Hall: cross-section looking south-east.

Augustus (1165-1223) after the surrender of the town in 1204.[25] It is a three-quarter round tower covering the south-east angle of the curtain wall, of two vaulted stories below a parapet with regular arrowslits, some altered for handguns. The vaulted rooms are of one quadripartite bay with a semihexagonal one facing the field. The latter bay has three diamond-plan embrasures at the lower level and one at the upper level, altered for handguns. The lower storey is entered from the castle either by steps up from an underground vaulted tunnel which ran under the tower as a sallyport, or by a passage

to a spiral stair in the wall thickness which links the two vaulted stories. This is a somewhat smaller version of Cobb Hall, but with two similar floors above a solid(?) basement. Given the symbolic importance of Caen as the capital of Normandy, one might expect its castle to be updated quickly, but the first campaign might have been the inner rectangle with corner towers and the Tour de la reine Mathilde might be as late as the 1220s (or even the 1430s according to Jean Mesqui, personal communication). One might be a conscious imitation of the other.

Fig.7

Fig.4

Fig.5

Fig.6

Fig.4. Cobb Hall: elevation of east door and slit over.
Fig.5. Cobb Hall: copy of Willson's sketch from the north, shewing the 'New Drop'.
Fig.6. Cobb Hall: lower north-facing slit.
Fig.7 Cobb Hall: elevation of north door and slit over.

The 1217 siege of Lincoln resulted in repairs, new works and other expenses in 1218-20 for which the earl of Salisbury was eventually paid £374 and the hereditary castellan, Nicola de la Haye, £130.[26] Comparison of these amounts with the £20 spent on the gate, the Lucy tower and barbican in 1224 points to major work somewhere else in Lincoln Castle. An entirely new tower could have been built for much less than £500 at that time. Major grants for a town wall begin in 1225 although the citizens were reimbursed for money spent before 1217 and a new south Bailgate was mentioned 1217x1220.[27] The apparently combined flanking doorway and arrowloop at Cobb Hall can be compared with that recorded in the south tower of the 1224 barbican of the east gate of Lincoln Castle (Fig.11).[28] The external chamfer of arrowslits is rare, but occurs in the inner gatehouse of Montgomery Castle (1224-35).[29]

Round foretowers were added to other royal castles in the 1220s. That protecting the damaged *donjon* of Rochester Castle was begun in 1221-22. It is pierced by two levels of simple embrasures with arrowloops and traces of doorways at the junction with the curtain wall on each side. The *donjon* angle itself, rebuilt very solidly in 1226-31, has two (possibly three originally) diamond-plan arrowloop recesses opening off a wall passage at first-floor level, and a single diamond-plan one opening off an oblong recess on the floor above, a smaller and shallower version of those at Cobb Hall.[30] These three (or four) arrowloops have lost their dressings, but (with those of the Tour de la reine Mathilde at Caen mentioned above) are the closest known parallels in plan to those at Cobb Hall. They would not have given complete coverage against attack, but this was provided by the outer tower on the curtain wall.

The new tower in the ditch at Dover Castle of 1226-27 is a plain cylinder with a simple doorway at ground level to each flank and one backward-facing arrowloop.[31] It was built to be a sallyport opening from the underground passage running under the newly-blocked gatehouse which had been partly destroyed ten years earlier. New entrances, with their own underground passages, were built elsewhere. The outer part of what is now called Peverell's Gate, a semicircular wall-tower with two tiers of arrowloops, is attributed to King John's time, probably after 1208. Its extension into the castle as a gatehouse is attributed to the 1220s.[32]

The basement of a solid round tower dated to 1222 survives at Winchester Castle, threaded by a passage which led down from the earlier *donjon* before dividing and leading onto two sides of the castle ditch.[33]

Two of the towers added to Windsor Castle between 1223 and 1240 have features like Cobb Hall. They are apsidal and contain single-chamfered rib-vaults rising from corbels, but each is twice the size of Cobb Hall and their arrowloops are of a common pattern and regularly set. That now called King Edward III's Tower bestrides the earlier curtain wall; starting from the central doorway (in the upper ward), there are two quadripartite bays before a sexpartitite one to the apse (Fig.10). The Curfew Tower is similar but its only quadripartite bay protrudes very little into the lower ward, the entrance being flanked by two windows like Cobb Hall.[34] Near each tower is an entrance to an underground passage which ends in a sallyport in the ditch. This sallyport feature seems to be a common theme running through castle building in the 1220s The apsidal *donjon* at Helmsley Castle, attributed to Robert de Roos (1186-1227), straddles the curtain wall. The tower

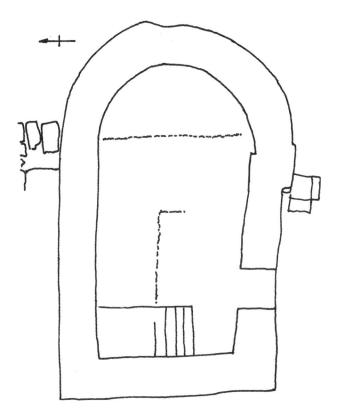

Fig.8. Roman East Gate of Lincoln city [after Thompson and Whitwell (note 9), Fig.10].

was vaulted at two levels and there are two lancets in the back wall, but the vaulting arrangement differs from that at Cobb Hall and the apse and its sallyport may be an addition.[35]

D.   Later possibilities are for its building either after the siege of the castle in 1265, or its being the *aroundtour* which had fallen shortly before 1327 and was then rebuilt. Either date is unlikely, since by then the castle had passed to the earls of Lincoln and was simply being kept up as a county court and prison.[36] It is possible that Cobb Hall was that prison, albeit rather small: as we have seen, Cobb Hall certainly was a lock-up five hundred years later.

I suggest that the balance of evidence favours scenario C and that Cobb Hall was built soon after 1217, primarily as a defensive foretower with sallyports, the latter feature being poorly designed because of a need to compromise between different uses. The lack of such a tower must have been appreciated during the major sieges of Lincoln, Dover, Rochester, Winchester and Windsor castles between 1215 and 1217, and each of these five royal castles was greatly improved immediately afterwards. At Dover and at Winchester the improvements included adding a round foretower in the ditch with sallyports, and at Rochester a repair in the shape of a mainly solid round angle to the old *donjon* was further protected by an outer hollow round tower. But at Lincoln (and more than once at Windsor) the round tower which was added extended into the castle to provide domestic accommodation. The 'Fair of Lincoln' did not end the war of 1215-17, but was a significant event. Thereafter the importance of Lincoln Castle was acknowledged by updating its defences to the same standard as royal work elsewhere. The citizens, too, were

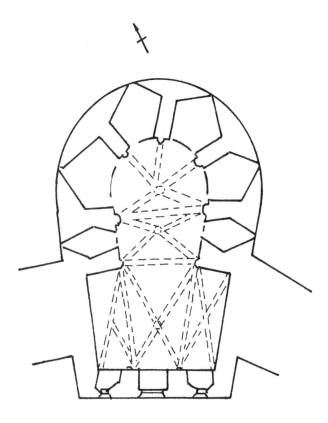

Fig.9. Plan of main floor of Cobb Hall for comparison with Fig.8.

encouraged to improve the city defences of Lincoln.

How did Cobb Hall work, and why the elaboration?

I have titled this paper 'Cobb Hall Tower' to emphasize that it was designed as a defensive structure as well as for domestic use. We may imagine a party of soldiers filing into the tower either to man the arrowloops or for a sally. Such a party would have necessarily been small because of the limited space.

An arrowloop consists of the *slit* proper (the opening in the outer face of the wall) and the *embrasure* (with converging faces in the thickness of the wall). It may also have a *casemate*, a recess in the inner face of the wall often higher and wider than the embrasure. At Cobb Hall, the arrowloops are unusual, in that there is no casemate and the embrasure almost always first widens before narrowing to the slit. The external splay of the Cobb Hall slits is also unusual: such a splay may marginally increase both the field of view and the places to which an arrow might be shot (the 'beaten zone') but it also frames the slit as a target for a *besieging* archer.

An arrow bends on being loosed, as the bowstring's energy is initially applied to the rear end of the arrow. So the arrow veers from side to side before flying true, and is likely to strike the side of an arrowslit if released close by. Longbowmen normally have to stand some distance behind the slit to avoid this 'archer's paradox', unless they use completely rigid arrows or are skilled at 'aiming-off'. Crossbowmen do not have this problem, since their bolts (missiles) are rigid, but they often have a more restricted 'beaten zone' than the longbowmen because of the larger lateral space requirement of the crossbow.[37]

Although the lateral field of view from the widest embrasures in Cobb Hall approaches 90°, that field could not be covered by arrows. The permanent garrison of a castle were no more likely to use longbows than crossbows. Either form of bow might not be available, or the defender might be a refugee unskilled in archery. Experimental measurement suggests that a crossbowman *within* the embrasure could cover approximately the same 'beaten zone' (30° arc) as a longbowman standing in the room *behind* the embrasure. Given the number of arrowloops in Cobb Hall, a 'beaten zone' covering the entire field outside the castle walls to east and south might just about be obtained. But in order to do this, the walls had had to be hollowed-out greatly, and the vaults lack symmetry and have cracked.

The field of view is much wider than the' beaten zone', so that a sentry inside Cobb Hall would have been able to watch the whole of the upper town, provided that he moved frequently from one arrowloop to another, which would keep him awake. However, a patrolling sentry on the wallwalk above would have had an even better view. There may well have been a third storey, as Speed's sketch suggests, perhaps only accessible from the wallwalk.

Sallying out from Cobb Hall would be hazardous. The doorways are some way above the top of the bank – let alone the bottom of the ditch – so that entrance and exit would have been slow and difficult, needing a ladder. Perhaps in peacetime there were semi-permanent wooden stairs, up and down which people could have processed dramatically or as part of their normal duties. The two doorways at ground level on the outer face of the Lucy Tower shellwall would have been as useful as sallyports as they would have been as posterns, which is not saying much, given their difficulty of approach up the *motte*. If this idea was revived at Cobb Hall, it was even less successfully done there.

The side passages were converted **from** and would have been reconvertible **into** arrowloops. In 1829, the right-hand passage was closed by a door about two feet from its end. The door was made from two planks four inches thick and was fastened by a four-inch drawbar.[38] An alternative explanation is that the passages gave access to (timber-framed) latrines, necessities for prisoners or sentries. Whether the lower blind recess was an abandoned sallyport, an arrowloop or a latrine passage, is uncertain. Such a dual or even a triple use

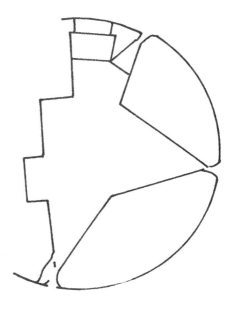

Fig.11. Plan of south tower of east gate of Lincoln Castle.

may have been planned from the outset.

The stout vaulting would have both given protection **from** and also support **for** heavy artillery. The counterpoise trébuchet, which appeared in England in 1217, slung its projectile in a high arc to crash down on roofs.[39] Only the narrowness of the doorway and windows protects Cobb Hall from attack from within the castle; alterations may have swept away evidence for an earlier drawbar or portcullis.

Prison apart, what was Cobb Hall's role in peacetime? It could have been a chapel, something not found elsewhere in the castle. The surviving storeys have neither a respectable latrine nor a fireplace so it could hardly have been suitable quarters for the constable of the castle or for an eminent visitor. The one 'plus' feature of the wide embrasures is in providing reflected as well as direct light to the interior: morning sunlight comes through the slits and, from noon onwards, through the windows inside the castle. The two remaining floors appear to have been self-contained and separate from any former higher floors, just like the Tour du Diable at Gisors or the Tour de la reine Mathilde at Caen. There may have been a grander third floor and even a penthouse suite. But what remains of Cobb Hall is a structure of architectural quality apart from its purely military function, a room of some grandeur responding to contemporary improvements at the cathedral and bishop's palace nearby. The design was repeated in the south and west parade-fronts added to Windsor castle by King Henry III. Cobb Hall may have been a private room for occasional (perhaps ceremonial) use, a modest local equivalent of the contemporary Wakefield Tower in the Tower of London.[40]

Cobb Hall Tower was a remarkably effective improvement to Lincoln Castle, both in military and domestic architectural terms. It owes its survival to its ability to serve various purposes over the last eight centuries.

Notes

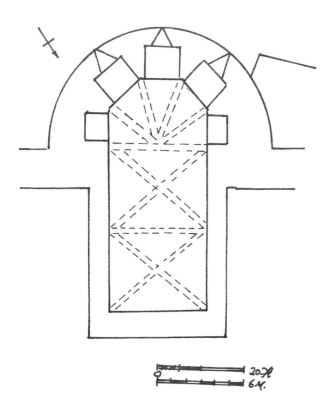

Fig.10. Plan of ground floor of King Edward III's Tower, Windsor Castle.

1. Michael Thompson, 'The early topography of Lincoln Castle', above pp.23-29. The north side of the castle slanted across the Roman grid, so that the outer edge of the Norman ditch avoided the Saxon church later known as St Paul-in-the-Bail, and the inner edge of that ditch ran outside the Roman west gate. That gate and the wall of the *colonia* formed a ready-made foundation for the west bank and wall of the castle. For a later hypothesis, see D. Stocker and A. Vince, 'The early

Norman Castle at Lincoln and a re-evaluation of the original west tower of Lincoln Cathedral', *Medieval Archaeology* 41 (1997), pp.223-33.

2. M. Jones and Lisa Donel, 'Lincoln Castle before and after 1068', above pp.41-52. There is a fourth doorway in the south curtain wall between the two *mottes*. There is no bank on this side. At the conference, Dr Donel mentioned that the base of a small chamber had been found in the bank inside the north curtain wall, possibly the cistern mentioned by Clark (note 10 below). She also described a flat platform at the south-west angle of the castle; this, together with the thin wall recorded here by Willson, may be evidence for a former tower, possibly the round tower rebuilt in the fourteenth century (page 47).

3. Society of Antiquaries of London, Ms.786, portfolio G. Titled 'LINCOLN CASTLE. Surveys, plans drawings, notes architectural and historical – down to recent times – The Gaol – precincts', (hereafter referred to as *Willson portfolio)*; drawings and notes on Cobb Hall appear on pages 56 to 65 and 97. For Willson see, H. M. Colvin, *A Biographical Dictionary of English Architects 1660-1840* (1954), pp.678-79.

4. An 1812 plan loose in the *Willson portfolio* shews a lock-up outside the castle, just opposite Cobb Hall. At the conference it was pointed out that such a lock-up meant that the prison gate need only be opened at fixed times.

5. *Willson portfolio* pp.64-65.

6. *Willson portfolio* p.62 notes a vertical joint and an arch on the exterior here. A loose plan in the portfolio shews three similar narrow externally-chamfered slits facing south-west. This might be an incorrect first draft, or just possibly there were originally three windows, the central one being above the original doorway.

7. Within, the upper vault has a large crack and one of the lower arch ribs has settled. The castle manager assured the conference that recent movement had been compensatory and not progressive.

8. *Regesta Regum Anglo-Normannorum*, edited by H. W. C. Davis *et al.*, 4 vols (Oxford, 1913-69), ii, no.1784. The opening permitted to the bishop in 1115 (*ibid.*, no.1118) might be that in the north wall of the castle adjacent to Cobb Hall, which also might have been the blocked doorway that was reopened in 1217 (note 24 below). The bishop of Winchester jokingly claimed the bishop of Lincoln's house as his prize for finding the blocked doorway: *L'Histoire de Guillaume le Maréchal*, edited by P. Meyer [Société de l'histoire de France, 1891-1901] lines 16521-30 cited by D. A. Carpenter, *The Minority of Henry III* (Berkeley and Los Angeles, 1993), p.40.

9. F. H. Thompson and J. B. Whitwell, 'The gates of Roman Lincoln', *Archaeologia*, 104 (1973), pp.129-207, esp. pp.150-56. Although the Roman west gate was still standing when rediscovered in 1836, it must have been unusable by c.1068 for the Norman gate to have been built alongside it.

10. J. W. F. Hill, *Medieval Lincoln* (Cambridge, 1948), p.86; R. A. Brown, H. M. Colvin and A. J. Taylor, *The History of the King's Works*, volume II, *The Middle Ages* (1963), p.705; Sir Nikolaus Pevsner and John Harris, *Buildings of England: Lincolnshire* (Harmondsworth, 1964), p.150; G. T. Clark, 'Lincoln Castle', *Archaeological Journal*, 33 (1876) reprinted in *Medieval Military Architecture* (1885), 1, at p.197 attributed it to Thomas of Lancaster, earl of Lincoln 1312-22, without explanation.

11. It was suggested at the conference that the earls of Chester and the de la Haye family may have carried out 'works' on what they regarded as their own property and the costs went unrecorded in the royal accounts.

12. See Paul Dalton, 'Lincoln Castle and its occupants in the Reign of King Stephen' above pp.66-78.

13. See note 8 and *Henry, Archdeacon of Huntingdon* Historia Anglorum *The History of the English People*, edited by D. Greenway (Oxford, 1996), pp.408-09.

14. *The Registrum Antiquissimum of the Cathedral Church of Lincoln*, edited by C. W. Foster and K. Major, 10 vols (Lincoln Record Society, 1931-73), i, pp.287-88; *Regesta Regum Anglo-Normannorum*, edited by H. W. C. Davis *et al.*, 4 vols (Oxford, 1913-69), iv, no.178; N. Reynolds, 'Investigations in the Observatory Tower, Lincoln Castle', *Medieval Archaeology*, 19 (1975), pp.201-05, reported a rectangular stone shaft on rubble filling with pottery of c.1175 underlying the later tower. See C. Coulson, 'The castles of the Anarchy', in *The Anarchy of King Stephen's Reign*, edited by E. King (Oxford, 1994), pp.88-89; Stocker and Vince, 'The early Norman Castle', and P. Dalton, 'Lincoln Castle and its occupants in the Reign of King Stephen' above p.66

15. The earliest surviving seem to be those at Dover (D. F. Renn, 'The Avranches Traverse at Dover Castle', *Archaeologia Cantiana*, 84 (1969), pp.79-92), at Châteauneuf-sur-Epte (*ex inf.* J. Mesqui), and

probably those of Dover-type 2 at Gisors (J. Mesqui and P. Toussaint, 'Le château de Gisors aux XIIe et XIIIe siècles', *Archéologie Médiévale*, 20 (Caen, 1990), plates 6-8), and Framlingham (D. F. Renn, 'Defending Framlingham Castle', *Proceedings of the Suffolk Institute of Archaeology*, 33 (1974), pp.58-67). Possible arrowloops formerly at Windsor castle may belong to the works of 1172-78: D. F. Renn, 'Castle fortification in England and adjoining countries from 1150 to 1250' in *Le Château Médiéval et la Guerre dans l'Europe du Nord-Ouest - Mutations et Adaptations*, Revue du Nord, hors série, Collection Art et Archéologie no.5 (1998), pp.53-59.

16. John Baily, 'St Hugh's Church at Lincoln', *Architectural History*, 34 (1991), pp.1-35.

17. Pipe Roll 34 Henry II, p.67. J. W. F. Hill, 'Lincoln Castle: the Constables and the Guard', *Associated Architectural Societies' Reports and Papers*, 40 pt 1 (1930), pp.1-14.

18. Pipe Roll 2 Richard I, p.76; 3 Richard I, p.1; 5 Richard I, p.31; 9 Richard I, p.94; 1 John, p.130; 2 John, pp.64, 80; 6 John, p.63, 13 John, p.69. Roger of Wendover, *Flores Historiarum*, I, Chronicles and Memorials, Rolls series, 84 (1886), hereafter *Wendover*, p.305 mentions *lapides et caementum cum suis baculis ferreo* at Lincoln Castle in 1200. The *nove turris* may be the Observatory Tower (note 14 above).

19. R. Allen Brown and P. E. Curnow, *The Tower of London, Greater London*, (1984), pp.16, 44-46. The Wardrobe Tower is an enigma. It is sited just to the south of the bend in the Roman city wall, the bend itself backed by a rectangular turret (Geoffrey Parnell *et al.*, 'The excavation of the Roman city wall at the Tower of London and Tower Hill, 1954-76', *Transactions of the London and Middlesex Archaeological Society*, 33 (1982), at p.105). Because of its position and some Roman tiles in its structure, the Wardrobe Tower is usually taken to be a late Roman bastion, although it is one of only two hollow bastions of the eastern group and the next but one hollow bastion (11a) was medieval, (J. Maloney, 'The discovery of bastion 4A in the City of London and its implications', *Transactions of the London and Middlesex Archaeological Society*, 31 (1980), pp.68-76). The Wardrobe Tower aligns with the south side of the White Tower and was linked to it. An early photograph shows it three storeys high with a striking resemblance to the White Tower in its details (Parnell *et al.*, 'The excavation of the Roman city wall', at pp.118-21). Brown and Curnow (*The Tower of London*, p.71) say that the Wardrobe Tower 'is generally attributed to Longchamp in the 1190s, though it may just possibly date from Henry II's time...'

20. See note 15 above.

21. Eugene Pepin, *Chinon*, (Petites Monographies des Grands Édifices de la France, Laurens, Paris *c.*1927), pp.73-76. The Tour des Chiens there is apsidal plus two square bays but is attributed to Philip Augustus (*i.e.* after 1204). See Scenario C, p.81 and the Tour de la reine Mathilde at Caen (note 25).

22. Mesqui and Toussaint, 'Le château de Gisors', p.276, plates 9 and 10, Fig.13.

23. R. Allen Brown, *Dover Castle, Kent* (1966), p.11.

24. F. W. Brooks and F. Oakley, 'The Campaign and Battle of Lincoln, 1217', *Associated Architectural and Archaeological Societies' Reports and Papers*, 36 (1921-22), pp.295-312; Carpenter, *The Minority of Henry III*, pp.36-40; Hill, *Medieval Lincoln*, p.202; *Wendover*, II, pp.211-23.

25. *Congrès Archéologique de la France* 75: Caen 1909, I, pp.109-11; M. de Bouard, *Le Château de Caen* (special number of *Archéologie Médiévale*), 1979.

26. Brown, Colvin and Taylor, *The History of the King's Works*, II, p.705, Pipe Roll 2 Henry III p.94; 3 Henry III, p.78; 4 Henry III, pp.14, 89; 5 Henry III, pp.144, 186, *Rotuli Litterarum Clausarum* (hereafter *RLC*), I, pp.356, 367b, 382, 383, 466b; II, pp.5, 144b. Immediately before the 1218 payments in respect of Lincoln castle is one to *Magistro Alberto ingeniator regis*. He was probably the master of the same name serving with the artificers at Chinon in 1204 (*RLC*, I, p.12) but from 1206-26 given lands and money in and around Lincolnshire (*Chronicles of the abbey of Ramsey*, I, p.232, Pipe Roll 9 John, pp.13, 111; *RLC*, I, pp.76, 95b, 290, 361; *Book of Fees* pp.158, 187, 359; *Red Book of the Exchequer*, II, p.800). Possibly an engineer rather than a mason, he might be the man working at Corfe Castle in 1214-15 among the miners and sappers, with other masters on the same rate of pay. At Winchester Castle in 1222 Master Albert was top of the payroll, where he might have been working on the new tower. Brown, Colvin and Taylor, *The History of the King's Works*, I, p.39 note 11 and *Building Accounts of King Henry III* edited by H. M. Colvin, (Oxford, 1971), pp.94, 102, 106.

27. *RLC*, II, pp.28b, 31; Calendar of Patent Rolls 1216-25, p.518. C. P. C. Johnson and A. G. Vince, 'The South Bail Gates of Lincoln', *Lincolnshire History and Archaeology*, 27 (1992), pp.12-16.

28. Pipe Roll 9 Henry III r.13 cited by Brown, Colvin and Taylor, *The History of the King's Works*, II, p.705; *RLC*, II, pp.29, 31, 135b. The barbican (pulled down in 1790) is often dated to the fourteenth century, perhaps because the slits are shown in Grose (Camden's *Britannia*, second edition (1806), II, p.365) with oillets at the lower end like early gunports. But even if the drawings are scrupulously accurate, oillets can be found in early thirteenth century arrowslits (for example, Chepstow, by 1210: J. K. Knight, *Chepstow Castle* (Cardiff, 1986), p.7). Further, Willson's plan (*portfolio*, p.107) makes it clear that the loops were not platefronted, (*i.e.* an embrasure narrowed sharply immediately behind the outer face of the wall) which is the normal design for gunloops.

29. Brown, Colvin and Taylor, *The History of the King's Works*, II, pp.739-42; J. D. K. Lloyd and J. K. Knight, *Montgomery Castle* (1973).

30. D. F. Renn, 'Refortification at Rochester in the 1220s – a public/private partnership?', *Archaeologia Cantiana*, 124 (2004), p.352, Fig.3.

31. Colvin, *Building Accounts*, pp.66, 84. For the tunnelling work of 1212, and the later Constable's Gate, see Brown, Colvin and Taylor, *The History of the King's Works*, II, pp.634ff. and p.637 n.11.

32. Colvin, *Building Accounts*, pp.30, 84 and plate 3; Allen Brown, *Dover Castle*, pp.17-20. The 'beak' inserted between the Norfolk gatehouse towers there is similar to that above the Lincoln castle east gate.

33. Colvin, *Building Accounts*, pp.90, 136, 158; M. Biddle, 'Excavations at Winchester, 1969: eighth interim report', *The Antiquaries Journal*, 50 (1970), plate XL and Fig.2 facing p.292.

34. Sir William St John Hope, *Windsor Castle*, (1913), plan portfolio; Brown, Colvin and Taylor, *The History of the King's Works*, I, pp.865-67. Another parallel is the early thirteenth-century Tour des Chiens at Chinon (note 21 above). There is also a resemblance in plan between the Tour du Bissy at Chinon and King Henry III's Tower at Windsor.

35. Sir Charles Peers, *Helmsley Castle, Yorkshire*, (1932) and William Dugdale, *Monasticon Anglicanum* V, p.280; de Roos was a leading rebel against John; another was Llywelyn ap Iorwerth, who built long apsidal towers at Carndochan, Castell y Bere and Ewloe probably between 1215 and 1240: R. Avent, *Cestyll Tywysogion Gwynedd / Castles of the Princes of Gwynedd*, (Cardiff, 1983). Unlike that at Helmsley, these towers did not straddle the curtain wall.

36. *Calendar of Inquisitions Miscellaneous*, I, p.313; *Annales Monastici*, II, p.368; Brown, Colvin and Taylor, *The History of the King's Works*, II, p.705.

37. P. N. Jones and D. F. Renn, 'The military effectiveness of arrow loops – Some experiments at White Castle', *Château Gaillard*, 9-10 (1982), pp.445-56. For a further comparison and contrast of the two weapons and their missiles, see Renn (note 15 above). Further experiments were carried out in 1995 by N. Faucherre and P. N. Jones at Loches (*Bull. Société des Amis du Pays Lochois*, 11, pp.83-86) and in 1995-96 by P. Durand at Coudray-Salbart, Castelnaud and Budos (*Bulletin Monumental*, 156, pp.257-74).

38. *Willson portfolio*, p.56.

39. D. J. Cathcart King, 'The Trébuchet and other siege-engines', *Château Gaillard*, 9-10 (1982), pp.457-71; Jim Bradbury, *The Medieval Siege* (Woodbridge, 1992), pp.259-71. *Willson portfolio* p.65 mentions that one passage was full of stone balls 'roughly chopped to a round figure'. These might be trébuchet shot, like those found at Kenilworth and Pevensey castles; some of the latter were similarly unfinished.

40. Brown and Curnow, *The Tower of London*, pp.17-20, 53-59.